What's the Buzz with Teenagers?

Pre-teens and teenagers are faced with a continually changing and complex social world that not only involves face-to-face action, but also online and social media interaction. *What's the Buzz with Teenagers?* offers a highly practical programme designed to explicitly teach young people to get along and maintain healthy relationships with their friends, family and the broader community.

Embracing current thinking on 'self-awareness and behaviour transformation' in adolescents, it uses highly interactive role plays, film-making, thinking exercises, quizzes, group discussions and confidence-building games to improve social skills and promote inclusion in a fun, effective and appealing way. Easy to implement in upper primary and middle schools, in healthcare settings and beyond, *What's the Buzz with Teenagers?*:

- is a deeply structured resource to teach young people in the 12- to 15-year-old developmental range;

- offers a connecting approach to bring young people together to learn without the pressure of 'getting social interaction right' all the time;

- aims to normalise the anxieties, sensitivities and loneliness that many young people experience during adolescence by sharing thoughts and exploring this common ground;

- explicitly teaches how to 'read' the emotional needs of others, show empathy and build relationships; and

- uses a developmental model that ensures relevance and inclusion to young people with a broad range of backgrounds, abilities and challenges.

The programme provides lessons that educators and health professionals can adapt to suit their individual circumstances and time frames, and creates a framework for a warm, engaging and interactive space in which learning is optimised.

The book is complemented by the website www.whatsthebuzz.net.au, which offers online downloadable resources and a further six lessons.

Also available are *What's the Buzz?: A Social Skills Enrichment Programme for Primary Students* and *What's the Buzz? For Early Learners: A Complete Social Skills Foundation Course.*

Mark Le Messurier is a teacher, counsellor, author and public speaker.

Madhavi Nawana Parker is an author, keynote and public speaker who counsels young people to develop social emotional literacy, resilience and Positive Mindsets. Madhavi can be found at http://www.positivemindsaustralia.com.au.

What's the Buzz with Teenagers?

A universal social and emotional
literacy resource

*Mark Le Messurier and
Madhavi Nawana Parker*

Routledge
Taylor & Francis Group

LONDON AND NEW YORK

First published 2019
by Routledge
2 Park Square, Milton Park, Abingdon, Oxon OX14 4RN

and by Routledge
52 Vanderbilt Avenue, New York, NY 10017

Routledge is an imprint of the Taylor & Francis Group, an informa business

British Library Cataloguing-in-Publication Data
A catalogue record for this book is available from the British Library

Library of Congress Cataloging-in-Publication Data
Names: Le Messurier, Mark, author. | Parker, Madhavi Nawana,
    author.
Title: What's the buzz with teenagers? : a universal social and
    emotional literacy resource / Mark Le Messurier and Madhavi
    Nawana Parker.
Description: Abingdon, Oxon ; New York, NY : Routledge, 2019.
Identifiers: LCCN 2018050279 (print) | LCCN 2019002437 (ebook) |
    ISBN 9780429054235 (eb) | ISBN 9780367149772 (hbk) |
    ISBN 9780367149789 (pbk) | ISBN 9780429054235 (ebk)
Subjects: LCSH: Interpersonal relations—Study and teaching
    (Secondary) | Social skills—Study and teaching (Secondary) |
    Teenagers—Conduct of life. | Teenagers—Family relationships. |
    Adolescent psychology.
Classification: LCC HM1106 (ebook) | LCC HM1106 .L46 2019
    (print) | DDC 305.235—dc23
LC record available at https://lccn.loc.gov/2018050279

ISBN: 978-0-367-14977-2 (hbk)
ISBN: 978-0-367-14978-9 (pbk)
ISBN: 978-0-429-05423-5 (ebk)

Typeset in Bembo and Franklin Gothic
by Swales & Willis Ltd, Exeter, Devon, UK

Printed and bound in Great Britain by
CPI Group (UK) Ltd, Croydon, CR0 4YY

Contents

An additional six lessons are available from www.whatsthebuzz.net.au/main-menu/content-whats-the-buzz-with-teenagers. They are:

Lesson 11: Maintaining relationships: Feedback and compliments

Lesson 12: Effective listening

Lesson 13: Competition, winning and losing

Lesson 14: Charity: Acts of kindness

Lesson 15: Perseverance

Lesson 16: Self-identity

Photocopiable and online resources

These resources can also be downloaded in colour from
www.whatsthebuzz.net.au/main-menu/content-whats-the-buzz-with-teenagers

Introduction

Lesson 1: The ins and outs of friendships

Lesson 2: What is a friend?

Lesson 3: Switching on positivity

Lesson 4: Wellbeing and social media

Lesson 5: Empathy

Lesson 6: Resilience

Lesson 7: Dealing with disappointment (loss and grief)

Lesson 8: Handling anxiety

Lesson 9: Responding to dominating behaviours

Lesson 10: Being hurt, trolled or abused online

A quick guide to the games

The 41 socially connecting games in this program are popular choices for teachers in mainstream classes to build group unity and social cohesion between students. They have the capacity to positively switch the emotional climate of the classroom as well as being wonderful icebreakers at the beginning of the year or term. Equally, they are perfect to use to repair any emotional fallout in class following an unpleasant incident. So, when the going gets tough, or when there seems to be one too many tough kids in your classroom, think about using one of the socially connecting games as an emotional rebalance.

Lesson 1: The ins and outs of friendships

- Friend or foe (moderately exciting)
- What do friends have in common? (passive)
- A good friend is . . . (passive)
- The ins and outs of friendship circles (passive)

Lesson 2: What is a friend?

- Friendship chain (passive)
- Nail hang (passive)
- Student interviews (passive)
- Random things about us (passive)
- Cooperative building (moderately exciting)

Lesson 3: Switching on positivity

- Shrinking blanket stand (exciting)
- The 10 glads game (passive)
- Negative thought toss (moderately exciting)

Lesson 4: Wellbeing and social media

- Widen the network (passive)
- How would you know, and what would you do? Prove it! (moderately exciting)
- Share jokes together (passive)
- "Come back!" (passive)
- Body scan (passive)

Lesson 5: Empathy

- Heads or tails? (exciting)
- Mind-reading in four guesses (moderately exciting)
- Mind-reading in 20 questions (moderately exciting)
- Dots and boxes (moderately exciting)

Lesson 6: Resilience

- Master and servant (passive)
- What's this? (passive)
- More than you think! (moderately exciting)
- Who am I? (passive for all ages)
- Killer Uno (exciting)

Lesson 7: Dealing with disappointment (loss and grief)

- Dealing with disappointment (passive)
- Let's catastrophise! (exciting)
- Disappointment 10-pin bowling (moderately exciting)
- Guard the pin (exciting)

Lesson 8: Handling anxiety

- 'Too high', 'just right' or 'too low' (passive)
- Calm, stressed and why? (passive)
- What's the mood? (passive)

Lesson 9: Responding to dominating behaviours

- Saying only 'yes' or 'no' (moderately exciting)
- Two truths, one lie (passive)

- Draw me if you can (moderately exciting)

- Have you ever had . . .? (exciting)

- Cucumber-face challenge (moderately exciting)

Lesson 10: Being hurt, trolled or abused online

- Find the troll (exciting)

- Kim's memory game (passive)

- Take the troll's device away! (exciting)

- Trolls versus the law (exciting)

A further 24 socially connecting games are available within the extra six lessons available online at www.whatsthebuzz.net.au/main-menu/content-whats-the-buzz-with-teenagers

About the authors

Mark Le Messurier

Mark works as a mentor with children and adolescents he affectionately calls the 'tough kids'; these are young people who do life tougher than most. They struggle to accurately interpret the social and emotional cues from others, can't filter out distractions, and find it tough to listen, process new information, remember, plan, persist, adapt to change and self-regulate emotion. His goal is to promote individual and family wellbeing.

Through invitation, Mark presents at conferences for universities, schools, parent groups, government, disability groups, and socially inclusive organisations throughout Australia and Australasia. Presentations relate to mentoring, positive education, emotion and behaviour, the teaching of social and emotional literacy and *What's the Buzz?*, ADD, ADHD, autism spectrum disorder, specific learning difficulties, and a deep range of topics for parents.

Mark is the author of 11 publications, and is especially proud of the *What's the Buzz?* series, co-authored with his friend Madhavi Nawana Parker, and now found in many schools and organisations across the world.

Mark is on Facebook, and can always be contacted at mark@marklemessurier. com.au (see also www.marklemessurier.com.au and www.whatsthebuzz.net.au).

Madhavi Nawana Parker

Madhavi has worked in the area of social and emotional literacy and resilience for over 20 years with young people from a diverse range of backgrounds and needs.

Madhavi is co-author with Mark Le Messurier of the *What's the Buzz?* series, and delivers the program in schools, healthcare and community settings in Australia.

Madhavi is author of *The Resilience and Wellbeing Toolbox*, a globally published resource offering practical ways to teach the skills underpinning resilience and wellbeing.

Madhavi is a public and keynote speaker on topics including *What's the Buzz?*, *The Resilience and Wellbeing Toolbox*, happiness in children and their families, mind-set, and other topics focusing on the enrichment of young people, their families and schools.

Madhavi writes regularly at *Solutions for Kids* on Facebook and Instagram, and can be contacted at solutionsforkids@outlook.com.

Acknowledgements

What's the Buzz? is driven by an understanding that all people thrive from a sense of belonging and being connected to others. When a young person struggles with their communication and actions, *What's the Buzz?* teaches skills to self-regulate emotions and feel emotionally freer to more confidently navigate the intricacies of the social world.

It also provides a social and emotional literacy framework to young people, providing gentle touchpoints on the importance of empathy, kindness, responsible handling of feelings and healthy friendships.

Thank you to everyone who has made *What's the Buzz?* what it is today. The countless educators and health professionals around the world administering it with care, consistency and dedication. The incredible parents and carers we work with, who tirelessly support their children to navigate the social world. The children themselves, who delight us by being themselves, coming along, doing their best and persevering, no matter how tough things in the social world are for them. You are champions, and knowing you has always been the driving force behind our work and books!

Thank you to Lauren Eldridge Murray for embracing Archie and his friends and bringing them to life through your beautiful drawings. Thank you Adele Murphy and Silvia Cardoso Kuncar for your enthusiasm and dedication for completing a world-first clinical trial into the efficacy of *What's the Buzz?* It's wonderful to have our own research as it makes the program even more influential.

Thank you to both our wonderful partners and children for their never-ending love, support and encouragement throughout all stages of writing.

Finally, for those of you picking up this program for the first time, leap in, add your own style, and always have faith in everything you've already learned and experienced to make this program exactly what you and your students want it to be!

Mark and Madhavi

Introduction

Practical considerations for implementation

In 2011, *What's the Buzz? A Social Skills Enrichment Programme for Primary Students* was released by Routledge for teachers, school support workers, parents, home-schoolers and a range of allied health professionals to awaken the social and emotional awareness in youngsters. This program was originally pitched at students aged from 8 to 12 years. It quickly found its way into dozens of countries, hundreds of schools, charities, government organisations and the private practices of allied health professionals.

Then, in 2015, *What's the Buzz? For Early Learners: A Complete Social Skills Foundation Course* was launched, and experienced greater success. Over 16 lessons, younger students aged 4 to 8 years are immersed in a variety of essential inter-personal skills, stimulated by the experiences of a character called Archie. In each lesson, the children help Archie solve the very same social dilemmas that occur in their everyday lives. As they do this, through activity, discussion, role play, games and quizzes, they learn how to express feelings and become more positive problem-solvers.

Welcome to a new program, *What's the Buzz with Teenagers? A Universal Social and Emotional Literacy Resource*. It is the latest addition to the series, and Archie has grown up! He's now about 14 years of age, although his age is never revealed. He faces the same everyday social and emotional challenges that young teens in middle school encounter in their lives.

What is social and emotional literacy (SEL)?

The idea of social and emotional literacy emerged through humanistic education. It sought to engage the whole person – the intellect, imagination, feelings, social capacities, and artistic and practical skills for optimal growth and development of young people. In 1997, the term was introduced by Claude Steiner. He described it as 'the ability to understand your emotions, the ability to listen to others and empa-thise with their emotions, and the ability to express emotions productively' (Steiner and Perry, 1997: 11). To be emotionally literate is to display and work with emotions in a way that improves the quality of life around you. Social and emotional literacy counts for so much; it improves relationships, creates affectionate potentials between people, makes for accepting and helpful workplaces, and can facilitate the feeling of community in classrooms and schools.

Why teach SEL?

For most, social thinking is hardwired at birth. Consequently, being able to interpret the messages behind the actions and words of others and how to appropriately respond develops naturally over time. However, for a variety of reasons, ranging from disadvantage, neglect, trauma-based responses or disability, increasing numbers of children are finding it much harder to think socially and use their social tools in environments when it really counts. The Collaborative for Academic, Social, and Emotional Learning (www.casel.org) draws our attention to five specific capabilities that should be embedded in quality SEL programs. These are the basis of *What's the Buzz?* They include the development of:

- self-awareness;

- self-management;

- social awareness;

- relationship skills; and

- responsible decision-making.

We now understand that without reasonable social success, children and adolescents are more likely to be at risk from emotional and mental health difficulties (Hay et al., 2004). The ability to create and foster friendship, accompanied by opportunities to feel accepted by others, is significant.

Who is SEL for?

Teaching SEL advantages everyone, especially those who struggle to go with the flow, read the social and emotional play, and participate in the free-flowing reciprocal nature of interpersonal interactions. An emphasis on SEL has proven to be helpful for children with higher-functioning forms of autism spectrum, those identified with language disorder, specific learning difficulties, auditory processing disorder, ADHD, reactive behaviours, anxiety, shyness, social phobia and so on (Kenworthy et al., 2014).

A judgement for educators to make is whether an individual's social/emotional struggle is a 'skill deficit' or a 'performance delay'. A 'skill deficit' means the skill has not been taught, and therefore is not present. The premise is that if we teach the skills and embed them within the group or school culture, then over time they should become a part of their performance. A 'performance delay' means there is evidence that the skills have been well taught but the student is not yet able to perform them in situations when they would be useful. Students on the autism spectrum often illustrate a 'performance delay'. Many have received and engaged in quality social and emotional skills but struggle to apply them, and will for some time. It is a work in progress, and we persist – gently, gently.

Is there evidence that teaching SEL improves student performance?

A body of highly regarded studies reveal that social and emotional capabilities are completely teachable and measurable gains can be anticipated (Jenkins and Batgidou, 2003; Payten et al., 2008). Not only are there quantifiable improvements in the social and emotional competencies, but improvements in moods, cooperation, and risky and disruptive behaviours (Tse et al., 2007). A review of 317 SEL programs by the Collaborative for Academic, Social, and Emotional Learning (www.casel.org), which involved 324,303 students, displayed conclusive gains for students, with and without social, emotional and behavioural difficulties. The bonus is that when educators choose to work within an SEL framework, we can expect at least a 10 per cent gain in academic achievement for students (Diekstra, 2008).

John Hattie, in *Visible Learning*, stated that 'social skills programs can make a positive difference to social outcomes' (Hattie, 2009: 150). His evidence, based on 84 studies and 27,064 students, indicates that the most effective programs employ coaching, direct modelling and feedback, and a focus on individual peer relationship issues. Studies continue to add a growing evidence base for social and emotional literacy training for all children and adolescents (Koning et al., 2013). And what surprises many is that these initiatives provided in the early years have a long-lasting effect well into the high school years (Kenworthy et al., 2014). Finally, working within the context of an SEL program or framework permits us to build deeper relationships with students, and offers possibilities to arrange better relationships between students themselves.

What's the Buzz? is based on the SAFE principles – what does this mean?

The program's direct method of instruction is based on an extensive body of research referred to by the acronym SAFE (Durlak et al., 2011). Such programs have a specific structure and intent that improves the transference or generalisation of skills from the learning situation to the child's point of performance. In short, this method is proved to increase efficacy. The SAFE principles embrace these components (Pace, 2013):

- *Sequenced* – show a logical step-by-step breakdown of each skill.

- *Active or kinaesthetic* – use role plays and rehearsal with feedback.

- *Focused* – dedicate time each day, each week or each fortnight towards teaching SEL skills.

- *Explicit* – teach a specific social/emotional skill each session.

What's the Buzz? breaks each skill into individual components and directly models them so children can see how they look and sound. Social thinking is also highlighted through role play, rehearsal, feedback and play-based activities in the context of a small group or as a whole-class approach. In this way, children gain the understandings, language and confidence required to transfer the newly acquired skills to other settings (Godfrey et al., 2005; Attwood, 2007).

How does *What's the Buzz?* fit into the curriculum?

Here in Australia, there's a wind of change, and it's palpable. The Australian curriculum has traditionally been packed with teaching reading, writing, mathematics, science, information and technology, and so on. Suddenly, a new capability termed 'personal and social – recognising others' emotions, supporting diversity and working together' has emerged, and is expected to be taught to all students.

This addition to the curriculum has caught a few educators off guard. They cannot understand why teaching and learning social and emotional skills have found parity with the traditional subjects. Yet the obvious truth is that these skills are at the heart of being human. Regrettably, too many leadership teams in schools remain unaware of, or indifferent towards, their responsibility to teach SEL. Others justify their obligation by dabbling, and this approach has limitations. It is unrealistic to expect a child to quickly incorporate the concepts learned in a weekly specialised session into their everyday life when a class teacher and parents have little or no idea what's going on and the child has little opportunity to practise the skills. Evidence of social learning is gradual, and generalises best within home and school environments that build a tangible social and emotional culture involving all students, staff and parents (Verduyn et al., 1990).

Is *What's the Buzz?* backed by its own clinical research?

Yes! The preliminary results for the world-first clinical trial on the efficacy of the *What's the Buzz?* social and emotional literacy program have now been collated and evaluated. The trial ran for the first six months of 2018, and 2,000 South Australians – teachers, parents and school students aged from 4 to 10 years of age – took part. Feedback was sought from teachers, parents and students through comprehensive pre and post questionnaires. Experimental and control groups were compared, and all 16 lessons from the early learners program were used.

Teachers scored students higher in self-awareness, relationship skills and responsible decision-making/positive problem-solving skills after completing a *What's the Buzz?* group compared to those students in the control group who did not participate in a *What's the Buzz?* program. Furthermore, the improvement in responsible decision-making/positive problem-solving skills was statistically significant.

At the time of writing, the results from parents and students are still being finalised, although the early indications show a strong and similar trend. *What's the Buzz?* can now officially be considered as an evidenced-based program. Contact the authors of the program or go to www.whatsthebuzz.net.au for links to this research.

What age group will this version best suit?

This version is pitched at young people aged 12 to 15 years. We now have extensive experience delivering this program successfully to upper primary and middle school students. Bear in mind that the way you present the material to students will either enhance or diminish their engagement. To illustrate this, we have plenty of educators using *What's the Buzz? For Early Learners* to young people above 9 years of age who have delayed social, emotional or intellectual capacities. To be honest, before releasing the 'early learners' version, we adapted the original 'primary' version to meet the needs of 5-year-olds.

Should I read the Archie stories from the early learners and primary programs to my teen students?

Yes, and have fun with them. By reading these, you tune your students into Archie's history and the backstories of his friends. The bonus is for your group to listen to each story, because we now know through a series of studies that when young people listen to stories, as well as participating in directed conversations and explicit discussions that analyse the behaviour and emotions of characters, they develop their empathic or 'social and emotional mind-reading' abilities (Dewar, 2015).

Is the program a fix for misbehaviour?

The program is not a tonic for immediately taming ugly or unruly behaviour. *What's the Buzz?* offers multiple opportunities for all young people to understand and practise key social and emotional skills. Interestingly, educators, facilitators, parents and caregivers often comment about positive behavioural changes of participants. What they see reflects what the research tells us. There is a softening in attitude, greater personal flexibility and behaviours become more respectful towards others (Diekstra, 2008).

Should I teach the lessons in exact order?

While we recommend you follow the contents, some scope exists to rearrange individual lessons to meet social/communication needs within your group.

Why is each lesson structured in the same way?

For a program to be used and valued, it must be easy to read, easy to absorb and easy to place into action. The predictable format builds familiarity for facilitators and students alike. Consequently, each lesson is presented with the following design:

- *Topic.*

- *Learning intention* – alerts facilitator(s) and students to the aim of the lesson and the flow of activities. They frame what success looks like and assist everyone to make judgements about the quality of learning that takes place.

- *Materials required for the lesson.*

- *The lesson.*

    1 *What's the Buzz?* – introduces students to the topic and places the set of skills to be learned in context. We begin by listening to *Archie's story*.

    2 *Show me the Buzz* – provides students with the opportunity to research and discuss a variety of social and emotional ideas, listen to the thoughts of others, debate them, create role plays and receive feedback from the group. We have learned that role play heightens understandings and the transference of skills (Nelis et al., 2009). There is always a Part 1 and Part 2 in *Show me the Buzz*. Choose one activity from either Part 1 or Part 2, depending on what appeals to you, the time you have and your group's likely preferences. There's plenty of content in *Show me the Buzz*, so the lesson can be revisited time and time again while continuing with the same topic. To reinforce the role plays, develop a BIG BOOK and capture the action by using your iPad, camera or smartphone. Add the images with captions to a handmade BIG BOOK for all to review. Alternatively, use video and develop a video diary so students can keep track of their role plays. Encourage students to review role-play footage. This is such an appealing way to strengthen the learning intention within each lesson. In effect, these options create a social story as they give the rules and guidance about making appropriate choices.

    3 *Do you know the Buzz?* – a lively group 'discussion time' where students briefly respond to a series of questions and statements highlighted by *Archie's story*. The goal is for them to exchange ideas, and in the process 'mind map' their way more empathically through the complexities. This should also provide facilitators with an insight into the depth with which students have grasped the key social principles.

4   *The Buzz* – students play social games to have fun together and build their newly learned skills.

- *After the Buzz: Social thinking ideas for parents and caregivers* – this section offers additional practical advice from the lesson. Educators will also find extra activities they can draw from here. They can be photocopied from this book or downloaded from www.whatsthebuzz.net.au/main-menu/content-whats-the-buzz-with-teenagers

- *Photocopiable and online resources* – located at the end of lessons ready to be photocopied. These can also be downloaded from www.whatsthebuzz.net.au/main-menu/content-whats-the-buzz-with-teenagers

What are the group values?

The group values alert students to what is expected and how to achieve expectations. They are phrased positively. The best way to strengthen the behaviours associated to these is by catching the children as they follow them – jump in, praise and give them a 'Thumbs up feedback card'. The group values, feedback and reminder cards are in the photocopiable resources at the end of this introduction, or can be downloaded from www.whatsthebuzz.net.au/main-menu/content-whats-the-buzz-with-teenagers

Why should I use feedback cards?

A noticeable quality of a positive educator is the skilled way they capture the desirable behaviours of young people. Nothing supports behavioural change as well as quality feedback, marking the moment a child presents a valued behaviour (Cornelius-White, 2007). Praise is priceless. It gives children the idea that they can meet our expectations and lets them know we're paying attention.

The research is conclusive: a proven way to increase the engagement and behaviour of a group or an individual is to employ a 'social token economy' that keeps them in a 'sweet spot' (Hattie, 2009). This is where an educator earmarks a set of desired behaviours required from the group – in our situation, it is the 'group values'. Then, as the children display these, they receive recognition in the form of positive verbal feedback combined with a token. Rewards may be involved, although material reward alone is not what feedback is about. There are oodles of creative ways to deliver a 'social token economy'. The best designs are where our focus is on language and an intent that guides students to success. We offer you three 'social token economy' methods to catch and maintain a cooperative group spirit.

Feedback and reminder cards

First, print and laminate about 10 'Thumbs up feedback cards' per child on bright blue card. Similarly, print and laminate two or three 'Group values feedback cards' per child on green card (these resources are in the photocopiable section at the end of this introduction). As you'll see, the 'Thumbs up feedback cards' will become a desired currency that inspires much more than collecting.

We place a small plastic container under each participant's chair so they can keep their cards safe. If anyone needs reminding to stay with the group values, they are handed a 'Group values feedback card' to prompt them. No words are required because students always know why you've handed it to them, and they place the card into their container. Then, as soon as they show the desired behaviours, immediately hand them one or two of the highly prized 'Thumbs up feedback cards'. Throughout the lesson, continuously hand students 'Thumbs up feedback cards' for participating good-naturedly. At the end of the session, regardless of age, students love to count how many 'Thumbs up feedback cards' they each have been awarded. Sometimes tell the group that today is a reward day. On these days, we use lucky dips!

Lucky draw

During the session, students are handed small coloured Post-it note-size pieces of paper. As students receive a ticket, they write their name on it. This is an easy way to acknowledge their engagement, cooperation or helpfulness. Surprise them every so often and hand them two or three tickets at once to emphasise something you're really pleased with. At the end of the lesson, they place their tickets into a box ready for a draw. The more tickets they have, the better their chances of winning. The outcome of the draw may be to offer an inexpensive gift.

How do I include children who consistently display highly disruptive behaviours?

When running a handpicked or 'targeted group' of students, the presence of some troublesome behaviours is expected in the beginning. This is a consequence of everything being new. Some will struggle to work out how they fit in, how they can be noticed and valued, what's going to happen, and where the boundaries lie. Disruptive behaviours usually settle.

Consider which behaviours deserve immediate attention, and which behaviours can be left to work on individually and privately, at the end of the lesson. We suggest you stay closer to the student, provide an increase in friendly eye contact, provide more consistent positive feedback when they're on track, and keep the group warmly connected to you and the group values. If there is more than one facilitator, one might whisper encouraging comments into the ear of the student who is struggling. When a student's disruptive behaviour has dominated a lesson, talk to them about it privately afterwards. Explain what the group needs from them. Discuss exactly what they need to do to achieve the goal next time. It may also be wise to recruit advice from their parents or past educators. If the difficulty persists, please consider the following:

- How long can the group sustain this bombardment of difficult behaviour?

- How much damage will occur to the cohesion of this friendship group?

- Is the child genuinely up to this?

- Is the situation too dynamic or too challenging for them?

- Might they be better off doing some individual work around *What's the Buzz?* for six months before re-entering a new group?

Is training recommended?

You will find everything you need to run a successful program in this book. Training is desirable as it helps to ensure the highest quality of SEL couched within a framework of positive education. For training, contact Mark Le Messurier (mark@ marklemessurier.com.au) or Madhavi Nawana Parker (madhavi.james@icloud. com) directly. A comprehensive online training option that offers accreditation is available at www.whatsthebuzz.net.au

I see that a *What's the Buzz?* website with online resources is available – do I need these resources?

The website companions the book to provide deeper relational and strategic insights. It also contains a wealth of positive education ideas and resources when it comes to working with our trickier and more vulnerable young adolescents. There are two sections to the website.

First, there's access to the program's development, structure and content, opportunities for training, background readings about children's social and emotional development, links to other reputable like-minded programs, and options to purchase *What's the Buzz?* books, *Archie's BIG BOOK of Friendship Adventures* and *Archie's POSTERS*. Books and posters can be purchased at www.whatsthebuzz.net. au/main-menu/to-purchase-whats-the-buzz

Second, for a fee, online registration as a 'site licence' is available. Each person at your school or in your organisation can access the website resources using their own name and password. The site offers four online training modules for potential facilitators. These bring the training to you and take about two hours to complete. On completion, you can print your own certificate of online accreditation. In addition, registration permits direct access to the full-colour Archie images from all *What's the Buzz?* programs. There are two Archie images for each lesson. These will fill your electronic whiteboard and have students absorbed as they listen to and watch the stories. Online registration also delivers four social skills games for children to play, role-play cards, skill cards, with compliment cards, certificates, worksheets, pre- and post-group social functioning surveys, and access to a specialised tracking facility to children's progress.

I'd like to run the program – are there a few start-up tips?

Tip 1: Who makes an ideal facilitator?

Those who wish to facilitate, and have been trained in circle time or embrace the values of it, are ideally positioned to run *What's the Buzz?* (Roffey, 2006). The role of a facilitator is someone who can lead through positive engagement and encouragement – someone who can optimistically work with the group to develop their own solutions rather than being too controlling, too critical or too severe.

Tip 2: Can I run the program with a mainstream class or a smaller 'targeted group'?

Yes, the program is designed to benefit all children in all kinds of ways. When we deliberately work within a social and emotional context, two critical things occur. First, we strengthen our relationship with children. Second, we build natural opportunities to engineer a better emotional tone between students in both mainstream and targeted groups.

Tip 3: Should I let parents/caregivers know that their child is participating in *What's the Buzz?*

When running the program with a mainstream class, formal notification to parents probably isn't necessary. However, do let parents know, and follow up with *After the Buzz: Social thinking ideas for parents and caregivers* at the back of each lesson or available online. When running a smaller handpicked 'targeted group', it is good practice to capture the interest of parents by sending home the *Introductory letter and consent form* – adjust it to suit your requirements. A guide is located at the end of this introduction and can also be downloaded from www.whatsthebuzz.net.au/main-menu/content-whats-the-buzz-with-teenagers

Tip 4: Is there a way to measure the progress of students?

Yes. *Parent, teacher and student pre-group social functioning surveys* are available online (www.whatsthebuzz.net.au/main-menu/content-whats-the-buzz-with-teenagers) in the introduction to establish baseline data for more complex students. You'll also find the *Parent, teacher and student post-group social functioning surveys* online in lesson 15 (http://whatsthebuzz.net.au/main-menu/content-whats-the-buzz-with-teenagers). These surveys are not available in this book. The data collected from the surveys can be compared to provide evidence of progress or where future work lies. The website also offers a specialised data-tracking facility that graphs comparisons between the indicators in the *pre-group* and *post-group* surveys.

Tip 5: Can parents sit in on lessons with students?

We do not recommend this as a parent can remain the focus of a student's attention. Social and emotional literacy is best learned between peers when opportunities are provided for them to practise and refine the skills together without this kind of distraction. By doing so, we set them up to continue to connect and use new skills in environments outside the immediate teaching space.

Tip 6: How can I use *After the Buzz: Social thinking ideas for parents and caregivers*?

These are located at the end of each lesson and may be photocopied. They are also available from www.whatsthebuzz.net.au as a Word document. Feel free to print these for parents as they expand on the lesson's content with practical ideas parents can use at home to build further skills and deepen connections. Many schools and organisations use these as part of their newsletter. It's critical to tune parents into the complexities of raising young adolescents, and this section offers such encouragement.

Tip 7: Should I run information sessions for parents?

This is optional, but when working with a smaller handpicked 'targeted group' we recommend inviting parents to a one-hour 'parents-only' meeting early in the program. This allows a dedicated time to give a little background about the program and receive additional information about each child. This is a friendly way to get that little extra investment from parents. Towards the end of the program, perhaps in weeks 14 or 15, we suggest you run a final 'parents-only' meeting to discuss each child's progress. This is a great way to optimistically conclude the program.

Tip 8: How do I give parents feedback?

When working with small 'targeted groups' of children in our private practices, we have parents nearby waiting for their children. Parents are always keen to know how their child did. Most are happy with a smile, a thumbs up or a small anecdote from the session. Occasionally, we will linger longer to give more detailed feedback or follow through on an issue that may have arisen in the lesson. We also invite parents to call or email should they have questions at any stage. When running 'targeted groups' of children at school, we'd suggest staying in touch with parents so they have a sense about how their child is doing and what they can do to help.

Tip 9: I run a small handpicked or 'targeted group' of students at my school – how important is the involvement of the students' class teachers?

If you find yourself facilitating small groups of handpicked students, it is essential to get their class teachers on board by doing some follow-up within their class setting. Occasionally, swap roles with class teachers and encourage them to become the facilitator for your 'targeted group'. This will naturally inspire them to learn more about their students' social and emotional world. Without this collaborative support, you are more likely to feel unappreciated, and gains for these students will be much harder to achieve.

Tip 10: I want to run a *What's the Buzz?* lunchtime program – what do you think?

Students, just like us, are at their learning peak early in the day and early in the week. Consequently, it's ideal to run programs during these times. However, the demands of life mean that not everything can be scheduled at the perfect time. Lunchtime sessions may prove problematic because everyone else is free to play and students doing the program may feel disadvantaged. On the other hand, if children see lunchtime sessions as safe, engaging and as a warm learning refuge, it may be perfect. When programs are run privately outside of school, they are usually offered after school. This means facilitators will need to offer extra support in response to their fatigue. Fresh bottles of water, a healthy snack at the beginning and encouragement from facilitators makes a world of difference to enthusiasm.

Tip 11: Must I insist that every child participates in every activity?

Some students will take several sessions before feeling safe enough to contribute. Allow participants to say 'pass' on an activity if they're feeling anxious or contrary. Some learn and gain confidence through observation. Occasionally, a child will insist on sitting outside the social circle but will stay near the group. We usually accept this in the early stages, but make it clear we'd prefer them to be part of the social circle. Work on a progressive plan to support the student's entry into the circle over time.

Tip 12: How long should a lesson take? Should I do every activity in the lesson?

Structure lessons to suit the unique needs of your students. If you know your group struggles with being engaged for more than 15 minutes, then break the lesson down into 15-minute grabs over a week. Most educators run a lesson for about 40 minutes. *What's the Buzz?* is built to be delivered with pace and enthusiasm, so we'd prefer you to deliver selected parts of a lesson and keep the interest of your students rather than slavishly following every bit of a lesson. Our best advice: learn what your group is capable of and then flexibly adjust your delivery to meet their needs. Be flexible and discerning; choose the parts within each section that most appeal to you and to the group.

Tip 13: How should I arrange my group?

The best arrangement is to have students and the facilitator(s) sitting in a social circle on chairs. In this way, everyone can see, hear and participate. Keep in mind that children always feel more settled walking into an environment that is organised the same way every time. If you're doing this with a larger mainstream class, position the children into a 'goldfish bowl arrangement'. This is where there are an inner and outer circle of chairs. Children in the inner circle participate and those seated in the outside circle observe. Every so often, they swap over. It's fun and will keep everyone engaged!

Tip 14: How many children do I place in a group?

Keep 'targeted groups' of children small. We recommend four or five students when there is one facilitator and groups of six to eight with two facilitators. Choose your groups wisely. Bringing the right composition of students together is the difference between running a satisfying friendship group or feeling as though you're stomping out wildfires each lesson!

Tip 15: Must I use name tags?

Building a 'name-rich' environment is essential because names are personal, meaningful and assist quality interactions. Only use name tags until the children know each other's names. And don't forget to warmly and persistently encourage the group to use each other's names.

Tip 16: Why ask the group to say 'goodbye' to each other?

At the end of each lesson, encourage participants to say goodbye to one another. Ask each student to move around the social circle to say goodbye to each person. Encourage them to use their name, give a gentle high five, offer a smile and perhaps a compliment. Your coaching will be needed early on, but just watch this valuable skill grow!

Tip 17: What other approaches are likely to expand the SEL skills of my group?

We have learned that when young people listen to stories and are guided to participate in directed conversations and discussions that analyse the behaviour and emotions of characters, they develop their empathic or 'social and emotional mind-reading' abilities (Dewar, 2015). Likewise, researchers have measured that empathy can be taught and enhanced through role play because it has the scope to spark conversations about the feelings of others, display how a character handled their feelings, explore what drove those feelings, and heighten more positive ways to express feelings (Nelis et al., 2009).

Also, there are card games that provide opportunities for social and emotional growth. The game 'Awkward moment', for example, places players in delightfully awkward moments. They must try to impress 'the decider' by offering their best empathic response! The research tells us that compared to students in a control group, the young people assigned to play this game showed improvements in their ability to imagine another person's perspective (Kaufman and Flanagan, 2015). There are also empathy-styled card games that are backed by research

(Coughlin, 2016). In 'The empathy game', players simply draw a card. Each card has a provocation or a question on it that prompts them to reveal something about themselves or to see things more empathically from another's point of view. It's a safe and playful way to explore and teach empathy.

In a similar vein, there are board games with a focus on empathy, feelings and improving social competence. The board game Empathy (https://boardgamegeek. com/boardgame/135427/empathy) is worth exploring. Finally, there's a new genre of video games designed to support children and teens to understand how other people think, feel and behave. We have enjoyed *Quiplash 2, Trivia Murder Party, Guesspionage, Tee K.O.* and *Fakin' It* by Jackbox Games (http://jackboxgames.com/project/jbpp3/).

Closing words

Beyond seeing young people trial new ways to self-regulate, broaden self-awareness, better manage relationships and have a go at positive problem-solving, there is one other benefit that consistently arises from *What's the Buzz?* The creation of this thoughtful and predictable space provides opportunities for children and young adolescents to build new relationships and feel a sense of belonging and fun with peers. This is so heartening because many of the participants find it difficult to build friendships in the highly dynamic school environment.

References

Attwood, T. (2007) *The Complete Guide to Asperger's Syndrome*. London: Jessica Kingsley.

Coughlin, S. (2016) *What Couples Who Communicate Well Do Differently*. Available at: www.refinery29.com/2016/03/105447/happy-couples-listening-and-empathy-study (accessed June 2018).

Cornelius-White, J. (2007) Learner-centered teacher–student relationships are effective: a meta-analysis. *Review of Educational Research*, 77(1): 113–143.

Dewar, G. (2015) *Evidence-Based Ideas to Help Kids Communicate, Connect, Empathize, and Read Minds*. Available at: www.parentingscience.com/social-skills-activities.html (accessed June 2018).

Diekstra, R.F. (2008) *Effectiveness of School Based Social and Emotional Education Programmes Worldwide*. Available at: www.fundacionbotin.org/89dguuytdfr276ed_uploads/EDUCACION/ANALISIS%20INTERNACIONAL/2008/ingles%202008/Results2008.pdf (accessed June 2018).

Durlak, J.A., Weissberg, R.P., Dymnicki, A.B., Taylor, R.D. and Shellinger, K.B. (2011) Enhancing students' social and emotional learning promotes success in school: a meta-analysis of school-based universal interventions. *Child Development*, 82(1): 405–432. Available at: www.casel.org/wp-content/uploads/2016/06/meta-analysis-child-development-1.pdf (accessed June 2018).

Godfrey, J., Pring, T. and Gascoigne, M. (2005) Developing children's conversational skills in mainstream schools: an evaluation of group therapy. *Child Language Teaching and Therapy*, 21(3): 251–262.

Hattie, J. (2009) *Visible Learning: A Synthesis of Over 800 Meta-Analyses Relating to Achievement*. New York: Routledge.

Hay, D., Payne, A. and Chadwick, A. (2004) Peer relations in childhood. *Journal of Child Psychology and Psychiatry*, 45: 84–108.

Jenkins, H.J. and Batgidou, E. (2003) Developing social strategies to overcome peer rejection of children with attention deficit hyperactivity disorder. *Australian Journal of Learning Disabilities*, 8(1): 16–24.

Kaufman, G. and Flanagan, M. (2015) A psychologically 'embedded' approach to designing games for prosocial causes. *Cyberpsychology: Journal of Psychosocial Research on Cyberspace*, 9(3).

Kenworthy, L., Anthony, L.G., Naiman, D., Cannon, L., Wills, M.C., Luong-Tran, C., et al. (2014) Randomized controlled effectiveness trial of executive function intervention for children on the autism spectrum. *Journal of Child Psychology and Psychiatry*, 55(4): 374–383.

Koning, C., Magill-Evans, J., Volden, J. and Dick, B. (2013) Efficacy of cognitive behaviour therapy-based social skills intervention for school-aged boys with autism spectrum disorders. *Research in Autism Spectrum Disorders*, 7: 1282–1290.

Nelis, D., Quoidbach, J., Mikolajczak, M. and Hansenne, M. (2009) Increasing emotional intelligence: (how) is it possible? *Personality and Individual Differences*, 47(1): 36–41. Available at: www.sciencedirect.com/science/article/pii/S0191886909000567 (accessed June 2018).

Pace, K. (2013) *Sequenced, Active, Focused and Explicit Programs Contribute to Kids' Social and Emotional Learning*. Available at: http://msue.anr.msu.edu/news/sequenced_active_focused_and_explicit_programs_contribute_to_kids_social_an (accessed June 2018).

Payten, J., Weisberg, R., Derlak, J., Dyminicki, A., Taylor, R.D., Shellinger, K.M., et al. (2008) *The Positive Impact for Social and Emotional Learning for Kindergarten to Eighth Grade Students: Findings from Three Scientific Reviews*. Available at: www.casel.org/wp-content/uploads/2016/08/PDF-4-the-positive-impact-of-social-and-emotional-learning-for-kindergarten-to-eighth-grade-students-executive-summary.pdf (accessed June 2018).

Steiner, C. and Perry, P. (1997) *Achieving Emotional Literacy*. London: Bloomsbury.

Roffey, S. (2006) *Circle Time for Emotional Literacy*. Thousand Oaks, CA: Sage.

Tse, J., Strulovitch, J., Tagalakis, V., Meng, L. and Fombonne, E. (2007) Social skills training for adolescents with Asperger syndrome and high functioning autism. *Journal of Autism and Developmental Disorders*, 37: 1960–1968.

Verduyn, C.M., Lord, W. and Forrest, G.C. (1990) Social skills training in schools: an evaluation study. *Adolescence*, 13: 3–16.

What's the Buzz with Teenagers?

01 Introductory letter and consent form for parents and caregivers

Date ....

Dear ....

We're pleased to offer (student's name) .... inclusion in *What's the Buzz with Teenagers? A Universal Social and Emotional Literacy Resource*, a highly regarded program now used in many countries to build the social and emotional awareness and resilience of young people.

Over 10 lessons, students become immersed in a variety of 'getting along' and 'positive problem-solving' skills. In each lesson, students discuss, research, role-play and share opinions about Archie's social and emotional problems. Archie is the central character in the program who presents the very same issues that young adolescents face in their everyday lives. As they work together through the lessons and activities, they'll learn how to become more flexible thinkers and build better social resilience.

The aim is for your child to participate with a small group that offers warmth, explicit teaching and opportunities to connect to other students. *What's the Buzz with Teenagers? A Universal Social and Emotional Literacy Resource* covers the following topics:

1 The ins and outs of friendships

2 What is a friend?

3 Switching on positivity

4 Wellbeing and social media

5 Empathy

6 Resilience

7 Dealing with disappointment (loss and grief)

8 Handling anxiety

9 Responding to dominating behaviours

10 Being hurt, trolled or abused online

What's the Buzz with Teenagers?

01 Introductory letter and consent form for parents and caregivers *continued . . .*

What can you do?

We welcome your interest and contact. So that you know what your child is experiencing in lessons, notes with the heading *After the Buzz: Social thinking ideas for parents and caregivers* will be sent home via a link to the website or as a hard copy. These contain useful advice about the social and emotional development of young adolescents and how you can add value to what your child is learning with us.

In the meantime, would you kindly fill out and sign the consent form below.

Your child's *What's the Buzz?* facilitator(s) will be ....
....

Their contact(s) ....
....

Cut here, sign and return ....
....

What's the Buzz with Teenagers?

We seek your permission for (child's name) ....
to be involved in *What's the Buzz?*

By signing this, we assume you have read the information attached and give permission for information to be shared, respectfully and confidentially, between teachers and facilitators during this time.

Parent/caregiver's name ....

Parent/caregiver's signature .... Date ....

02 Group values

Be friendly

Ask for help

Help others

Do your best

What's the Buzz with Teenagers?

03 Thumbs up feedback cards

What's the Buzz? Thumbs up! 	**What's the Buzz?** Thumbs up! 	**What's the Buzz?** Thumbs up! 	**What's the Buzz?** Thumbs up!
What's the Buzz? Thumbs up! 	**What's the Buzz?** Thumbs up! 	**What's the Buzz?** Thumbs up! 	**What's the Buzz?** Thumbs up!
What's the Buzz? Thumbs up! 	**What's the Buzz?** Thumbs up! 	**What's the Buzz?** Thumbs up! 	**What's the Buzz?** Thumbs up!
What's the Buzz? Thumbs up! 	**What's the Buzz?** Thumbs up! 	**What's the Buzz?** Thumbs up! 	**What's the Buzz?** Thumbs up!

04 Group values feedback cards

What's the Buzz? Group values: feedback	**What's the Buzz?** Group values: feedback	**What's the Buzz?** Group values: feedback	**What's the Buzz?** Group values: feedback
What's the Buzz? Group values: feedback	**What's the Buzz?** Group values: feedback	**What's the Buzz?** Group values: feedback	**What's the Buzz?** Group values: feedback
What's the Buzz? Group values: feedback	**What's the Buzz?** Group values: feedback	**What's the Buzz?** Group values: feedback	**What's the Buzz?** Group values: feedback
What's the Buzz? Group values: feedback	**What's the Buzz?** Group values: feedback	**What's the Buzz?** Group values: feedback	**What's the Buzz?** Group values: feedback

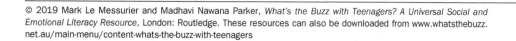

The ins and outs of friendships

"New beginnings"

Key social and emotional principles (learning intention)

Friendships are dynamic and complex. Sometimes differences of opinion, dishonesty, confusions, jealousy, fearfulness and mistakes can threaten them. There are, of course, many ways to repair a friendship providing a willingness for restoration exists. Friendships always change over time, and can become deeper and richer. However, other friendships fade and disappear. This lesson explores one of the many complexities that can threaten a friendship, and how to go about repairing it.

Materials required for this lesson

- Name tags.

- Chairs arranged in a social circle for students to sit on.

- Whiteboard/butcher's paper/screen and markers.

- Create a simple outline of the lesson on the whiteboard/butcher's paper/ screen for students to follow.

- Display the *What's the Buzz?* group values (located in the introduction or at www.whatsthebuzz.net.au/main-menu/ content-whats-the-buzz-with-teenagers).

- Organise feedback and reminder cards, or similar, to strengthen responsive behaviours (located in the introduction or at www.whatsthebuzz.net.au/ main-menu/content-whats-the-buzz-with-teenagers).

- Have Archie's story ready to read to students. This can be done directly from this lesson. Or, for a small registration fee, you can download the 16 Archie stories as you want them. Each story contains text, audio in the form of the authors reading to your students, and two large illustrations in full colour that will fill your screen. Access is available at www.whatsthebuzz.net.au/ main-menu/content-whats-the-buzz-with-teenagers

- A pencil, pen, paper or an iPad for students to do the activities in Part 1 of *Show me the Buzz*.

- Print the role-play cards for 'The ins and outs of friendships' in Part 2 of *Show me the Buzz* (located at the end of the lesson or at www.whatsthebuzz.net.au/ main-menu/content-whats-the-buzz-with-teenagers, ready to print).

- Print 'The ins and outs of friendship circles' activity in *The Buzz* (located at the end of the lesson or at www.whatsthebuzz.net.au/main-menu/ content-whats-the-buzz-with-teenagers).

- A pencil and a blank A4 sheet of paper for each student to record on when playing the game 'What do friends have in common?' in *The Buzz*.

- Prepare handouts for parents(s):

    One copy of this lesson for each parent to read.

    One copy of *After the Buzz: Social thinking ideas for parents and caregivers* to send home (located at the end of the lesson, ready to photocopy, or at www. whatsthebuzz.net.au/main-menu/content-whats-the-buzz-with-teenagers).

Lesson 1

Explanation

Friendship connects us to others. It provides us with a sense of worth, value and belonging. It is the essence of sound mental health, now and into the future.

Yet the fundamental skills of friendship take years to refine. Just think about them. There's trust and loyalty that hinges on one's own esteem, poise and ability to know when to go with the flow; there's sharing, helping, asking for help, initiating a social interaction and holding a conversation, the ability to deal with frustration and positively problem-solve, giving compliments, taking turns, saying please and thank you, showing empathy, a sense of humor, and being able to understand dynamic social contexts, to mention just a few. For children to flourish emotionally, parents and caregivers need to pack the early years with abundant opportunities for children to feel loved and stimulated, to be physically and emotionally available for them, and to keep them safe by building predictable boundaries into their lives. Even with this foundation in place, it takes years of exposure to socialising and deliberate guidance for children to enjoy the art of friendship. But it is a very different story for children who have not received this advantage. Children who have suffered the disadvantages of uncertainty, neglect, too much sadness, displacement from home countries, and trauma, or are dealing with disability, battle to establish and maintain friendships.

This lesson looks at what friendship is and how differences of opinion are a natural part of it. Its goal is to get young people thinking and discussing how friendships must be flexible because – most certainly – they'll be tested and change over time. While some can handle the ups and downs of friendships, like water off a duck's back, others feel threatened when new individuals or challenges emerge.

Also, young adolescents are now defining themselves in more complex ways. Today, a great deal of social interaction and communication takes place through social media sites. This can be both a real helper and a challenge. It can offer information, support and community for teens. Most experts agree that social media is more likely to be a force for good rather than harm. The best advice is to help young people proceed gently and gather suitable tools and supports. Ongoing discussions about what is appropriate, moral and legal to text, film, photograph and forward are vital. While online communication is a social world, we also want to encourage natural opportunities for young people to build social emotional literacy skills face-to-face. Interestingly, the research guides us to understand that when young teens have internet access up to one hour a day, their contentment is boosted, but more than this spent on social media is an attribute of an unhappier person (McFall and Garrington, 2011).

The early teen years is a time where children begin to show their individuality and show varying degrees of opposition to authority figures, mostly parents and educators. It is often a time of misperception and confusion for young people, making them reliant on our understanding, empathy and composure. With explicit teaching, these skills can be learned, but getting along with others is a lifelong process, and no one gets it right all the time.

1. *What's the Buzz?*

Actively greet students as they enter. Provide chairs in a social circle for them to sit on and have a brief lesson plan on the whiteboard/butcher's paper/screen for students to see. As students are settling, hand each of them a 'Thumbs up' feedback card to highlight their thoughtful behaviour and using the group values.

Let's begin

To begin the lesson, we start by highlighting the key social and emotional principles or the learning intention. Learning to be a good friend isn't easy. It takes time and practice, and even with the best intention a friendship may not run perfectly well. What is most important is that we develop the willingness and skills to repair friendship problems when they occur. There are many things that cause friendship difficulties. Ask your group if they can guess the ten listed here:

1 Feeling left out, lonely, rejected or bullied.

2 General unhappiness about learning and school.

3 Jealousy.

4 Dealing with a tough home life.

5 Lack of sleep because it wrecks a person's tolerance, flexibility, organisation, memory and ability to learn.

6 No breakfast, no drink, no energy and low mood.

7 Lack of practice and not being sure what to do.

8 Friends betraying you.

9 Previous troubles with a friend.

10 Sickness.

To be a good friend means we must improve our 'mind-reading' abilities. In other words, we must learn to tune in to the emotions of others because our general wellbeing depends on it. The one certain thing about friendships is that they will change. A few become deeper, richer and lifelong. Other friendships go well for a while and gradually fall by the wayside.

05 Archie's story: "New beginnings" – first image

Lauren Eldridge Murray

This image can be downloaded from http://whatsthebuzz.net.au/main-menu/content-whats-the-buzz-with-teenagers and will fill your screen in colour. There is also the option to have the authors read the story to students.

Archie's story: "New beginnings"

Archie arrived at Castle Rock Middle School early today. He liked getting there early because he enjoyed sitting with his friends and talking light-heartedly before the seriousness of lessons started.

A lot had happened over the last few weeks. Most of his friends had moved across from Castle Rock Primary to the middle school. While Archie had expected the lessons, the homework, the teachers and the school to be different, he'd been surprised by the changes in his friendships. Oliver, who in earlier years had been obsessed by Lego, had become dazzled by a new group of kids who loved all things robotics. They were still friends, but it was different. He felt like he'd lost Oliver, who'd reinvented himself as a brainiac. The other difference was that no one ran around playing at break times any longer. Everyone hung about in groups messing around and talking. Some people were loud and talked too much. Archie knew it was their way to be noticed so they'd be liked, but it was annoying. Others were too quiet. Every few days, a new person would join the group and another would drop out. Everything felt shifting and random. He missed the old days because he knew where he stood.

As he walked up to his group, he noticed a stranger standing with them. He greeted everyone and hung back, wanting to learn a bit more about this person. Within a few moments, Archie learned his name was Ayman, and he seemed friendly without being loud or demanding. He was new to the city and lived with his family – his dad and a younger brother and sister. He loved soccer, basketball, reading and collecting crystals. His mother had passed away three years ago from motor neurone disease, and this meant Ayman did a lot to help at home. Archie thought this was a brave thing to say to a new group. He also thought how lonely Ayman must feel without any of his old friends.

The bell sounded, and everyone headed to home group. Archie and his closest friend, Tobias, walked with Ayman. Archie sensed that Ayman may become a good friend. They unpacked their bags and walked into class together. The home group teacher, Mr Messma, gently nudged and guided Ayman and Archie to sit together.

Mr Messma asked everyone to form pairs. Archie thought this would be a chance to get to know Ayman better, so decided to work with him. They got on with the task together. Later, Archie glanced across the classroom towards Tobias. Tobias was staring at them. His face looked stony, almost angry, and his arms were folded. He looked switched off and shut down. Archie could tell something was wrong.

06 Archie's story: "New beginnings" – second image

Lauren Eldridge Murray

This image can be downloaded from http://whatsthebuzz.net.au/main-menu/content-whats-the-buzz-with-teenagers and will fill your screen in colour. There is also the option to have the authors read the story to students.

Home group finished, and the boys walked together to the next lesson. It was an awkward walk because Tobias was so quiet. Then he got closer to Archie and said, "What happened in home group? You just forgot about me, Arch. How do you think that made me feel?" Archie could see that Tobias was teary. This took Archie by surprise. He never meant to hurt Tobias' feelings, but now he knew he had. Archie felt an impulse to defend himself and argue back. His instinct urged him to say, "Hey, Tobias, you've got it wrong! You're being jealous and trying to control me. All I was doing was being friendly to Ayman."

Strangely, the language around 'smart thinking' jumped into his head. He'd had years of teachers such as Ms Marshall saying, "Before you say or do anything, take three deep breaths because it gives your emotions the best chance to calm and allow the upstairs part of your brain to solve the problem." This was the moment for self-control, and not for fast, hurtful words.

Archie shot a glance at Ayman. Ayman's face was flushed with embarrassment. He didn't want to cause any trouble but could see what was happening. Tobias continued to stare at Archie and time froze. Archie felt paralysed. Then Tobias turned and walked away, leaving Archie with Ayman. Archie felt misunderstood by Tobias. He felt angry because Tobias should know better and trust him.

Discussion based on the questions and statements below will occur later in *Do you know the Buzz?* For now, simply read them to get students thinking. Encourage them to listen and respond to each question by putting their thumb up if they 'agree' or think 'yes', thumb down if they think 'no', and thumb to the side if they think 'maybe'. Move very quickly through them. No verbal responses are required.

Your thoughts on these statements and questions?

- Oliver had reinvented himself. Do you know what this means? Have you ever reinvented yourself? Is it okay?

- Did Archie do anything wrong?

- Was he thoughtless or unkind towards Tobias?

- Did Tobias do anything wrong?

- Was he too sensitive?

- Do you agree that Tobias should have trusted Archie and just gone with the flow?

- Is it okay to make new friends without checking in with existing friends?

- Does allowing new people into a group make friendships stronger?

- Does allowing new people into a group threaten old friendships?

- Can you think of a reason why Tobias was feeling unsure about his friendship with Archie?

- Do you think Ayman handled the situation well?

- Should Ayman have been more respectful of Archie and Tobias' friendship?

- Can you see a way that Archie and Tobias can solve this problem?

2. *Show me the Buzz*

Show me the Buzz provides students with the opportunity to discuss a variety of social and emotional ideas, absorb the thoughts of others, debate them, create role plays and receive feedback from the group. We have learned that this approach heightens understandings and the transference of skills. There is always a Part 1 and a Part 2. Choose one activity from either Part 1 or Part 2, depending on what appeals to you, the time you have and your group's likely preferences. There's plenty of content in *Show me the Buzz*, so the lesson can be revisited time and time again while continuing with this same topic.

Part 1

1. Group discussion

(a) Explain two ways Archie could restore his friendship with Tobias.

(b) Explain two ways Archie could further damage his friendship with Tobias.

(c) What two things could Tobias do to restore his friendship with Tobias?

(d) What could Ayman do to heal the rift between Archie and Tobias?

2. Write a script

Write your own ending to Archie's story. It may be one that shows friendship and tolerance, or a conclusion that highlights the lack of maturity needed for repair.

3. Make a role play or short film

Consider any of the ideas above and turn them into a role play or short film.

Part 2: Role plays – the ins and outs of friendships

The role plays are in the photocopiable section at the end of this lesson. They are also available online at www.whatsthebuzz.net.au/main-menu/content-whats-the-buzz-with-teenagers – you may either read them to students, or print them and hand each group a role play. Help students to form small groups. Each role-play card states the number of students required. It does not matter if the same role play is given to several groups. Give students a few minutes to rehearse, and move between groups to provide plenty of coaching and enthusiasm.

Next, ask each group to perform their role play. If a student does not wish to perform, allow them to pass. So much can be learned through observing. Always perform role plays in the middle of the social circle. Consider capturing the action on video or photo by using your iPad, camera or smartphone. Encourage others to give constructive feedback after each role play.

3. *Do you know the Buzz?*

Do you know the Buzz? is a lively group 'discussion time' where students briefly respond to a series of questions and statements highlighted by Archie's story. The goal is for them to exchange ideas, and in the process 'mind map' their way more empathically through the complexities of social and emotional situations. This should also provide facilitators with an insight into the depth of student understandings. To do this, have students sitting on chairs in a social circle.

Your thoughts on these statements and questions?

- Oliver had reinvented himself. Do you know what this means? Have you ever reinvented yourself? Is it okay?

- Did Archie do anything wrong? What?

- Was he thoughtless or unkind towards Tobias? In what way?

- Did Tobias do anything wrong? What?

- Was he too sensitive? Did he have a right to feel jealous?

- Do you agree that Tobias should have trusted Archie and just gone with the flow?

- Is it okay to make new friends without checking in with existing friends? Why or why not?

- Does allowing new people into a group make friendships stronger?

- Does allowing new people into a group threaten old friendships?

- Can you think of a reason why Tobias was feeling unsure about his friendship with Archie?

- Do you think Ayman handled the situation well?

- Should Ayman have been more respectful of Archie and Tobias' friendship?

- Can you see a way that Archie and Tobias can solve this problem?

4. *The Buzz*

The Buzz is an opportunity for the group to play games that strengthen their relationships and the skills central to the lesson.

Game: Friend or foe (moderately exciting)

Divide the room into three sections. One section is where friendship lives. The second part is where the behaviour of foes, rivals or enemies live. The third section is in the middle and indicates a complication. When a player chooses to stand in this middle section, they will be expected to give an explanation to explain why it's not always easy to say someone is simply 'for' or 'against' us.

Let the group know that you're about to call out everyday events that happen between people. Their job is to listen. Then move to the section they feel best explains the behaviour you've read out.

Friend or foe questions:

- A person rolls their eyes at you when you speak.

- Someone who smiles at you most days when they see you.

- This person is often around but rarely talks to you.

- A person who whispers about you to others.

- Someone who laughs at your jokes, even when others don't.

- This person is your friend when they have no one else to be with.

- Someone who invites you over to their house but spends most of the time gaming and hogging the controller.

- This person often invites you to go to a movie.

- A person who willingly gives you half their snack when you look at them with hunger in your eyes.

- Someone who never shares.

- A person who ran off with your bag.

- A person who listens to you, offers advice and cares.

- Someone who sticks up for you.

- This person cheers you up when you're sad.

- A person who encourages you and notices your strengths and interests.

- A person who doesn't make eye contact with you and is very quiet.

- Someone who talks about you behind your back and gives your personal information away.

- Someone who shows off about how much stronger/smarter/better they are than you.

Game: What do friends have in common? (passive)

This game invites easy conversations with the aim of breaking down any biases students may have about each other. First, arrange students into groups of three or four. Be sure to mix them with peers they do not usually have much contact with. Each student will need a pencil and a blank A4 sheet of paper to record on. The goal is for each person in the group to find five things they have in common with others in their small group. These may be common experiences, foods, likes, dislikes, fears, accomplishments, embarrassments and so on. Give them five to ten minutes to do this, and ask someone from each group to report back their findings to everyone.

Game: A good friend is . . . (passive)

This game is played a little like the old favourite, "I went to the shops and I bought a . . ." To begin, position the group into a social circle and ask what makes a good friend. As soon as you receive a few classic friendship qualities, let them know that they're ready to play.

You might start by saying, "A good friend is . . . (name a friendship quality)." The person next to you follows by saying, "A good friend is . . . (names the friendship quality you stated and adds theirs)." The next person says, "A good friend is . . . (names the previous friendship qualities stated and adds theirs)." And so the game continues!

There are two ways you can play this game. First, you can choose to play it highly competitively, where each player must independently remember the friendship qualities stated and they are out of the game when they cannot remember. Or you play for friendship, where the group works collectively to support each other, and the goal is to see how many times you can get around the circle.

Game: The ins and outs of friendship circles (passive)

This is a visual approach to sort out who your friends are and how close they are at the moment. This exercise shows there's a world of difference between someone you chat to at your locker and someone you share loads of personal things with – but both are necessary to live a happy connected life. Also, friendships change, sometimes for the better, sometimes unexpectedly and sometimes for the worse. When this happens, it's smart to change our expectations of them. They can remain as a friend, but we need to check the level of trust and loyalty we should give them.

First, download or photocopy the 'Friendship circles' resource at the end of this lesson. Hand one to each student and ask them to write their name in the middle circle. Their task is to discreetly write each of their friends' names in one of the three concentric circles. Please explain that this work is sensitive. Impress the value of privacy and respectfulness. Do your best to ensure that no student feels hurt, upset or shamed by participating in this exercise. Before beginning, read the descriptions below to students:

- *Concentric circle 1*: These are core friends. They are true friends because they like being with you and always want to know more about you. They know what you like, what you don't like, even what scares you! You know the same things about them. You trade trust, loyalty and time with each other, and because of this your friendship is strong and continues to grow. You may have history together too. They may not be family, but it feels just as close.

- *Concentric circle 2*: These are reasonable friends. They are part of a wider group of friends you see most days and chat with on social media. You would not share everything with them as you would with a core friend, but you value them enough to invite them to your birthday party. Your friendship with them is good, and some may become closer to you in the future. These might include people you've only recently met, so naturally your expectations of them are moderate.

- *Concentric circle 3*: These are acquaintances, and our relationship with them sits on the fringe of friendship. You get along with them, you see them most days, you chat sometimes and there's some contact through social media, but that's all! You wouldn't invite them to your home or to your party, but you do catch up at other people's parties. What you get from them – and give back – is pleasant and safe conversation. This group holds the possibility of friendship in the future and should be cared for.

Follow-up discussion

So, how many friends does a person need? Not many. Most of us can identify one or two in in the closest circle, two or three in the next circle, and two, three or four in the outermost circle. That's all it takes!

Are level 1 friends better than level 3 acquaintances? No. And this is not what the exercise is about. What's most important is to be able to identify the different levels of friendships around you. All relationships need nurturing. Remember, a level 3 relationship can grow into a core friendship, and sometimes core friends need to be respectfully moved to levels 2 or 3. Ask students, "Why might you decide to move a core friend to level 2?"

As this has been an exercise in awareness about friendship, there is no need for students to keep their 'Friendship circles' worksheets. The safest idea is to collect them up so privacy is respected.

Lesson 1

After the Buzz: Social thinking ideas for parents and caregivers

Lesson 1: The ins and outs of friendships

Key social and emotional principles (learning intention)

Friendships are dynamic and complex. Sometimes differences of opinion, dishonesty, confusions, jealousy, fearfulness and mistakes can threaten them. There are, of course, many ways to repair a friendship providing a willingness for restoration exists. Friendships always change over time, and can become deeper and richer. However, other friendships fade and disappear. This lesson explores one of the many complexities that can threaten a friendship, and how to go about repairing it

After the Buzz presents further ideas for parents, guardians and educators to encourage the generalisation of the social and emotional thinking students have touched on during the lesson. All children rely on us to consolidate these skills by positively modelling them, and emphasising the language and ideas used in the lesson. Here are a few practical ideas.

Do you model what a friend looks like?

Our children mimic us. Parents who consciously live happy, well-connected, balanced lives send a potent message about how to live life to their children. The best thing we can do for our children is to show them how to handle their feelings by aptly handling our own. Children are always listening, and if they overhear you talking to friends or your spouse about others in adverse ways, they are likely to start doing the same. They are our greatest imitators! Do whatever it takes to keep your own social and emotional life harmonious and in check.

Time to step in or time to listen?

As a parent, it is hard not to dive right in when your child is faced with a problem or their feelings are hurt. In general, children will experience distance, conflict and nastiness within their friendships. They are still developing the ability to manage their impulses and behave appropriately when upset. A perfect way to approach this is to think about what you need when you're facing a problem. Usually, it is for someone to listen to you and show confidence that things will work out. If you show too much concern or start doing the problem-solving for your child, you might unintentionally give your child the message they are facing a crisis, and that it can't be resolved without you. This can make a child feel helpless and can also lead them to blow things out of proportion. Your job is to listen and show your confidence in them to work things out. Attempt to validate their feelings, reflect to them what they have shared, express your care and let them know you're always happy to listen to them. If they ask for advice, give it, but try to bring it back to them and their ideas. Give them the sense they have a voice and that their thinking can make a difference.

Active listeners ask questions

Active listening is a prized parenting tool as it helps kids cope with tough situations without them feeling as though the adult is rescuing or judging them. To do this, simply rephrase back to them what they have just said as a statement validating their thoughts or as a question for them to ponder. Use a tone that soothes and offers dignity. This helps them feel comforted and may well diffuse a potential meltdown! Focus exactly on what your child is saying – this is *active listening*. The approach helps them to clarify their thoughts:

- What did they say to you?

- Wow, how did you feel? I would have felt the same.

- What did you say back?

- How do you think he felt when you said that?

- Do you think that made things better or worse? I agree. I can see why you said that.

- So, what do you think he should do to make this better?

- What can you do to help fix this? Good idea.

- How can I help you to do that? (Be very clear as to how much you should buy into this.)

This is such a steadying approach for anyone wrestling with intense feelings. It sounds strange, but the immediate objective isn't to fix your child's problem; it is much more about leading them to see that they can process tricky feelings, think their way through the dilemma and work out solutions.

After the Buzz . . . Lesson 1

Celebrate your children's friends

The quality of a mother and father's connection with each of their children is crucial to their intellectual, social and emotional development. Just as important is your child's connection to peers. This doesn't mean you must become obsessed by arranging endless play dates for your child. But actively compliment them on their choice of friends. Let them know how pleased you are that they have so many great kids in their lives. You may not completely embrace each of their friends, but it is important to show your child you have confidence in their choice of relationships. When you blatantly criticise, control and manipulate who they socialise with, they'll know they don't have your confidence, and this will affect their relationship with you. Interestingly, what helps kids aged 10 to 15 years be happier and more resilient? Besides having good friends and a stable home life, having a friend over for a meal once a fortnight is rated highly (McFall and Garrington, 2011).

Keep your expectations high

Keep your expectations about how your child communicates and treats others high, whether your child has a disability or not. Let them know how much you value their likeable style. Make no mistake – the way your kids present themselves to you, to friends, other parents, school staff, sports coaches, extended family and so on will influence how their lives turn out. Their likeability, or lack of it, will influence how much care and interest they receive from others in the future. When your child is behaving unreasonably or badly, hold them accountable. Children need boundaries from their parents, and if you make excuses for their poor behaviour things are likely to get much worse for them socially and emotionally as life goes on.

Create time to develop 'mind-reading' abilities in your teens

While sitting together at the dinner table, you can build your child's emotional intelligence by telling a simple story and asking a few basic questions about it. Here's an example:

> It was late on a Saturday afternoon, and Jade had started to watch a great movie at home. Dad comes in and says he's had some good news and wants to take the family out to a favourite restaurant for dinner. Jade bitterly complains. She doesn't want to leave the couch or her movie. She gets nasty and refuses to go. Her mum, dad and younger brother don't take long and give in to her. Instead, dad and her brother make spaghetti bolognaise while she keeps watching her movie alone. When dinner is ready, Jade pauses the movie and eats dinner with the family, but everyone is disappointed and very quiet.

- How did Jade act? Which words best describe it?

- Did she show any empathy towards the others?

- Come up with other ways Jade could have handled this.

- Did Jade think about dad's needs or feelings?

- What else could Jade have said to dad?

- Jade got her way, but I think she missed out on something more important. Do you?

- Her mum and dad did not fight her. What does this suggest to you?

Stop toxic friendships

If your child is friends with someone who is toxic to their wellbeing, you must call it and act authoritatively. You're not going to win your child's affection in moments such as this, but make it clear you're always willing to protect them from harm. Try to communicate openly about the specific behaviours you're concerned about, how they're affecting them and have the potential to affect how others perceive them. Be sure to point them in the direction best to focus on, and this is, of course, towards friends who are constructive and help them to grow.

Welcome your child's friends into your home

While the sanctity of family time must be valued, as children embark into the teen years they need their peer group around too. If you can, make your home open to your child's friends on weekends. The bonus is that you'll get to know them and gain an insight into the young people your child chooses to spend time with. Give them plenty of space but be present so they know you are there if needed. The time they spend socialising is often double-edged. While it's energising and relaxing, it also helps to keep them in an emotionally happy place to take on the challenges and commitments offered by school.

Use the friendship circles idea from this lesson with your kids

This circle idea is a way to sort out who one's friends are, as well as their loyalty and trustworthiness. This exercise is an approach to show there's a world of difference between someone you chat to sometimes and someone you rely on and share loads of personal things with. Yet both are friends. Also, friendships change, sometimes for the better, sometimes unexpectedly and sometimes for the worse. When this happens, it's smart to readjust our expectations of them. They can remain a friend, but we need to check the level of trust and loyalty we should give to them.

After the Buzz . . . Lesson 1

Keep it simple by drawing four large concentric circles on a blank piece of A4 paper. Hand one to each of your children and be sure to do one for yourself. Ask them to write their name in the middle circle. Next, ask them to write each of their friends' names in one of the concentric circles. To help them place the names accurately, read the descriptions below:

- *Concentric circle 1*: These are core friends because they like being with you and always want to know more about you. They know what you like, what you don't like, even what scares you! You know the same things about them. You trade trust, loyalty and time with each other, and because of this your friendship is strong and continues to grow. You may have history together too. They may not be family, but it feels just as close.

- *Concentric circle 2*: These are reasonable friends. They are part of a wider group of friends you see most days and chat with on social media sometimes. You would not share everything with them as you would with a core friend, but you value them enough to invite them to your birthday party. Your friendship with them is good, but not as deep as your core friends. However, some may become closer to you in the future when you get to know them better.

- *Concentric circle 3*: These are acquaintances, and our relationship with them sits on the fringe of friendship. You get along with them, you see them most days, you chat sometimes and there's some contact through social media, but that's all! You wouldn't invite them to your home or to your party, but you do catch up at other people's parties. What you get from them – and give back – is pleasant conversation. This group holds the possibility of friendship in the future and should be cared for.

Follow-up discussion

So, how many friends does a person need? Not many. Most of us can identify one or two in the closest circle, two or three in the next circle, and two, three or four in the outermost circle. That's all it takes! Are level 1 friends better than level 3 acquaintances? No. And this is not what the exercise is about. What's most important is to be able to identify the different levels of friendships around you. All relationships need nurturing. Remember, a level 3 relationship can grow into a core friendship, and sometimes core friends need to be respectfully moved to levels 2 or 3. Ask students, "Why might you decide to move a core friend to level 2?"

This is an exercise in awareness about friendship, and because friendships change keep this record and compare it to another you might do together in several months' time.

Impulse control: 'Hot cognition' versus 'cold cognition'

As children grow, they gradually receive improved brain connections, and these result in better processing powers. In fact, most young adolescents have decision-making skills like adults – except in the heat of the moment when their 'cold cognition' abandons them. 'Cold cognition' is rational decision-making that is thoughtful, planned and purposeful. Information is processed in a factual way. 'Hot cognition' is fast, 'in the moment' thinking. It may include a little logical reasoning, but is overwhelmed by social and emotional factors in a fateful moment.

To illustrate this, while your young teen knows never to get into a car with a driver they don't know or trust, it becomes different when they are in 'that' moment. In that moment, they must rapidly deal with their own emotions, their friends' emotions, their friends' expectations and the social pressures surrounding the situation itself. Don't be scared by this. It is the way it is, and the way it's always been. In calm and connected moments, discuss these kinds of situations, and the idea of 'hot and cold cognition', and how it can play out. By discussing this in the right moments, you safeguard your teen's future decision-making by mentally rehearsing future complexities.

Teach your children how to repair upsets and hurts

The word 'sorry' when used honestly can rescue many a tricky situation. So, have fun role-playing situations where sorry might be helpful. Try sorry with a smile, a gesture, a wink, a handshake, a rub on someone's arm or a hug. As they have fun practising with you, they also pull together a few vital skills. Without showing empathy and digging deep to find a little courage, emotional resilience and social emotional literacy will remain in scant supply.

References

McFall, S.L. and Garrington, C. (2011) *Understanding Society: Early Findings from the First Wave of the UK's Household Longitudinal Study*. Available at: http://repository.essex.ac.uk/9115/1/Understanding-Society-Early-Findings.pdf (accessed June 2018).

After the Buzz . . . Lesson 1

07 Role-play cards: The ins and outs of friendships

Role play 1

Follow on from Archie's story. One of you is Archie and the other is Tobias. It's recess time and you both decide to talk. You're both keen to fix this, even though you feel hurt in different ways. Show us how you could have an honest conversation and solve this. (A pair – Archie and Tobias)

Role play 2

Your friend has made a new friend. Now they can't meet you on the weekend as planned because they're going to do something with this new friend. You feel annoyed. You've had this catch-up planned for ages. In this role play, be honest and calmly talk to your friend about how you feel. Keep your words focused on finding a positive solution. (A pair – you and your friend)

Role play 3

Your friend is going through a tough time and you're tired of them complaining. Without thinking, you blurt out, "Give it a rest! Lighten up." Your friend is shocked and replies, "What? I thought you understood what I'm going through?" Instantly, you feel bad and want to repair this. But you also want your friend to know how hard it is being around their grumpiness. Show how you could constructively handle this in a conversation together. (A pair – you and your friend)

07 Role-play cards: The ins and outs of friendships *continued . . .*

Role play 4

You walk out into the yard to catch up with your friends. They aren't where they usually are. Then you spot them in the distance. As you walk towards them, they seem to look at you and wander away. Show how you would stay calm, not jump to conclusions and find out what is going on. So, what is going on? (A group of four – you and three friends)

Role play 5

You discover one of your closest friends has just told others about something private you shared with them. You are not happy. You ask your friend why they did it. They shrug their shoulders and say, "It's no big deal. Lots of parents split up, and it's better that your friends know." It is a big deal for you because you weren't ready to share it with other people yet. Your friend has broken your trust. Is this a reason to end the friendship, or a time to clear the air and work things out? Whatever you choose, do it with thoughtfulness and self-control. (A pair – you and your friend)

Role play 6

There's a new kid, about your age, who has just moved into your street. They've just started at your school too. Every time you go past their place, they wave and say hi to you. You're just not sure about them. They may be fine, and it might be your anxiousness playing tricks on you. A few days later as they walk past, they invite you in to meet their family. You decide to do it. Let's see what happens. (A group of four – you, the new kid and their parents)

07 Role-play cards: The ins and outs of friendships *continued . . .*

Role play 7

You and your friend have known each other since kindy. You've always been close and have shared similar interests. Lately it feels different. You don't feel as close to them and they've been spending more time with others. It's like your friend is looking for other things and more than you can offer. This doesn't feel good. Show how you could talk to your friend and carefully deal with it. We'd like to listen to your conversation. (A pair – you and your friend)

Role play 8

At school, your long-time friend wants to be with you some days and seems less interested on other days. It's not that they're wanting to be with others; they're just distant and a bit shut down. You sense something isn't right for them, but it is still a good friendship. In this role play, let's see you sharing your concerns with your friend. Speak openly and honestly and encourage them to do the same. (A pair – you and your friend)

Role play 9

You had a heated argument with a friend and you both said some hurtful things. You both said the friendship is over. A few days have passed, and you've cooled down and want to repair the damage. You know the chance of becoming close again is low, but you're keen to patch things up so you can get along with them. In this role play, we want you to be brave, approach your old friend and talk through your feelings so the relationship feels better. (A pair – you and your friend)

What's the Buzz with Teenagers?

08 Friendship circles

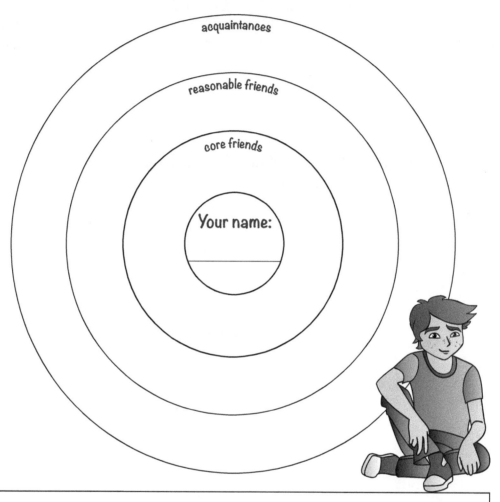

acquaintances

reasonable friends

core friends

Your name:

Concentric circle 1 - these are core friends. They are true friends because they like being with you and always want to know more about you. They know what you like, what you don't like, even what scares you! You know the same things about them. You trade trust, loyalty and time with each other and because of this your friendship is strong and continues to grow. You may have history together too. They may not be family, but it feels just as close.

Concentric circle 2 - these are reasonable friends. They are part of wider group of friends you see most days and chat with on social media. You would not share everything with them as you would with a core friend, but you value them enough to invite them to your birthday party. Your friendship with them is good, and some may become closer to you in the future. These might include people you've only recently met, so naturally, your expectations of them are moderate.

Concentric circle 3 - these are acquaintances and our relationship with them sits on the fringe of friendship. You get along with them, you see them most days, you chat sometimes and there's some contact through social media, but that's all! You wouldn't invite them to your home or to your party, but you do catch up at other people's parties. What you get from them, and give back, is pleasant and safe conversation. This group holds the possibility of friendship in the future and should be cared for

What is a friend?

"A good friendship, it's bigger than being popular"

Key social and emotional principles (learning intention)

This lesson highlights the essential skills required to build friendships and become a friend. It focuses on the qualities of friendship: What makes a good friend? What does a good friend say and do? How many friends does one need? What should we expect from a friend as we get older? What's the difference between a good friend and an acquaintance?

Materials required for this lesson

- Name tags.

- Chairs arranged in a social circle for students to sit on.

- Whiteboard/butcher's paper/screen and markers.

- Create a simple outline of the lesson on the whiteboard/butcher's paper/ screen for students to follow.

- Display the *What's the Buzz?* group values (located in the introduction or at www.whatsthebuzz.net.au/main-menu/ content-whats-the-buzz-with-teenagers).

- Organise feedback and reminder cards, or similar, to strengthen responsive behaviours (located in the introduction or at www.whatsthebuzz.net.au/ main-menu/content-whats-the-buzz-with-teenagers).

- Have Archie's story ready to read to students. This can be done directly from this lesson. Or, for a small registration fee, you can download the 16 Archie stories as you want them. Each story contains text, audio in the form of the authors reading to your students, and two large illustrations in full colour that will fill your screen. Access is available at www.whatsthebuzz.net.au/ main-menu/content-whats-the-buzz-with-teenagers

- Pencils, pens and paper for students to do Part 1 of *Show me the Buzz*.

- Organise several slips of coloured construction paper, a texta and staples for each student to play the game 'Friendship chain' in *The Buzz*.

- Organise 20 large flathead nails and a two-metre length of twine for each pair to play the game 'Nail hang' in *The Buzz*.

- A set of building blocks, or similar, per pair. Alternatively, a cheap deck of playing cards per pair and scissors for each person to play the game 'Cooperative building' in *The Buzz*.

- Prepare handouts for parents(s):

  One copy of this lesson for each parent to read.

  One copy of *After the Buzz: social thinking ideas for parents and caregivers* to send home (located at the end of the lesson, ready to photocopy, or at www. whatsthebuzz.net.au/main-menu/content-whats-the-buzz-with-teenagers).

Lesson 2

Explanation

As children get older, they begin to appreciate that friendship is more than simply knowing a few or a lot of people. There is a yearning to connect more deeply and feel emotionally closer. Friendship drives us to spend time together and make our friends' lives emotionally richer. A good friendship nurtures and enriches each other's lives.

Each person holds a slightly different view about what a good friendship should look like, but we all agree that good friendships are important to our happiness and wellbeing. Studies repeatedly tell us that having friends, and being a friend to others, is one of the most important mental health protective influences (Chopik, 2017). Friendship is invaluable. So, how many friends does one need? Is there a checklist of qualities a good friend should have? What might the checklist look like? Does a friend have to have every quality on the checklist to be a good friend? Can friends fall into different categories, such as acquaintances, casual friends, school friends, family friends, friends who live in my street, loyal friends or forever friends? And, on this note, it is essential to stress that friendships change – they grow, they stall, they diminish and they can finish. One thing is for sure – friendship is dynamic and ever-shifting.

Friendship begins with a few basics around body language. The way we sit, stand, our physical proximity, the way we use eye contact, as well as the tone of our voice, will make or break our likeability and the possibility to cement deeper friendships. Knowing how to use positive body language, an inviting voice tone and a willingness to participate provides every human being with a vital social edge. Yet the qualities of friendship run deeper than just the instrumental steps around connected body language. Our friends also expect us to develop stronger social connections, which eventually allows for more complex emotional interactions. So, being a friend is an evolving process where we need to be deliberately arranging opportunities to deepen connections along the way.

If you treat others with care and empathy, then you're off to a good start to build friendships with them. But there are no guarantees because being a good friend also depends on many things outside of our direct control.

1. *What's the Buzz?*

Actively greet students as they enter. Provide chairs in a social circle for them to sit on and have a brief lesson plan on the whiteboard/butcher's paper/screen for students to see. As students are settling, hand each of them a 'Thumbs up feedback card' to highlight their thoughtful behaviour and using the group values.

Let's begin

Always frame the lesson by introducing the key social and emotional principles, or the learning intention. Today, ask students, "What do you think makes a good friend? What qualities do you look for?" Encourage the group to develop a list of 10 qualities they feel are essential to find in a friend. Record these on the whiteboard/ butcher's paper/screen. Their list will be like this:

- accepts you for who you are;

- cares for you;

- will not judge you;

- is kind;

- is respectful;

- is loyal;

- is trustworthy;

- is honest;

- is enjoyable or fun to be with;

- sticks up for you or has your back;

- laughs and makes you smile;

- is a good listener; and

- can show empathy and comfort you.

Once you've listed the 10 vital qualities for friendship, pose these questions to the group. No response is required – just allow them to think:

- Which of these qualities do you do best with your friends?

- Which of these qualities do you have trouble showing to your friends?

> Archie's story: "A good friendship, it's bigger than being popular"
>
> The wellbeing teacher was explaining *What's the Buzz?* day, and the activities that went with it, to Archie's class. He said that when we have just a few people in our lives who are interested in us, we feel happier and are better protected from sadness or loneliness. Asking a friend or an acquaintance, "Hey, what's the Buzz?" is a great place to start a conversation to improve a connection.
>
> In the first activity, each student was asked to create a card and a small gift for three others. Most had made something from origami

09 Archie's story: "A good friendship, it's bigger than being popular" – first image

Lauren Eldridge Murray

This image can be downloaded from http://whatsthebuzz.net.au/main-menu/content-whats-the-buzz-with-teenagers and will fill your screen in colour. There is also the option to have the authors read the story to students.

because the wellbeing teacher loved all things origami and had set up online tutorials. Archie decided to make a shark for Tobias, his long-time friend, and an opening and closing heart for Joanna for obvious reasons! He'd also decided to make a robot for Oliver because their friendship wasn't as tight as it once was. Archie thought giving something to Oliver was a good way of saying he still appreciated having him in his life.

Now it's time to introduce Prisha. She was part of Archie's larger friendship group. Prisha is popular and always busy chatting and enjoying others. She's smart, pretty, fun to be with, sporty and a cross-country running champion. She's good at everything, has a massive number of friends and is always kind. Not only does she invite loads of people to her birthday parties, but she remembers the birthdays of most people and gives them a small gift on the day. You're probably thinking, "So what's wrong with Prisha?" The answer is: nothing. She's a great person and no one at school has as many friends as she does.

But something unexpected happened during this activity.

Prisha didn't receive a card or gift from anyone. There was nothing for her. She looked confused, and so did her teachers, because they thought the system they had used would stop something embarrassing such as this happening. Before it got any worse for Prisha, Tobias suddenly launched into action. He leant across to Archie and said, "Arch, I'm going to give your card and shark to Prisha and say it's from me. I'll make the gift work and can change the card. Nice words – thanks! Are you okay if I do it?"

Archie had already tuned in to what was happening, and replied, "Yes. Just do it fast before she loses it."

With that said, Tobias hurriedly made the switch and took the card and gift to Prisha. As she saw him approaching, her face lit up. "I'm sorry I took so long to get my gift to you, Prisha. I hope you like it." He explained that he'd made a shark because he loved them as a species, plus they never stop moving – just like Prisha! Tobias sat with Prisha for a while to make sure she was feeling okay.

Pause and invite a few answers to this question . . .

Prisha has everything going for her, so why didn't she receive a card and gift from anyone?

Continue Archie's story

As Archie, Tobias and Joanna walked home from school, they discussed why Prisha had missed out.

"I'm glad you did some quick thinking, Tobias. I think I know why Prisha missed out," commented Joanna.

10 Archie's story: "A good friendship, it's bigger than being popular" – second image

Lauren Eldridge Murray

This image can be downloaded from http://whatsthebuzz.net.au/main-menu/content-whats-the-buzz-with-teenagers and will fill your screen in colour. There is also the option to have the authors read the story to students.

"Me too," answered Archie, "She's so great at everything, and with everyone, we all just thought she'd be the popular pick."

"Nope, that's not what I'm thinking," replied Joanna.

"I know what you're thinking, Joanna," chipped in Tobias. "You're thinking all the boys think she's too good-looking to give a gift to, and all the girls are jealous of her."

"That's not so crazy – it might be. But it wasn't what I was thinking," responded Joanna. "Here's the thing. I think Prisha spends so much time being friendly to everyone that she hasn't got any close or true friendships. All she's got is a massive bunch of contacts!"

"I wouldn't mind being a close friend to her," joked Tobias. "Maybe I'll start tomorrow and spend some time with her. I'll give her a chance to become my true friend! Who knows how that might work out, for her and for me!"

"So," said Archie, "if you want close friends, you have to put the time in. You can't be a close friend to everybody because you can't spread yourself that far."

"Yeah, a good friendship, it's bigger than being popular," agreed Joanna.

Discussion based on the questions and statements below will occur later in *Do you know the Buzz?* For now, simply read them to get students thinking. Encourage them to listen and respond to each question by putting their thumb up if they 'agree' or think 'yes', thumb down if they think 'no', and thumb to the side if they think 'maybe'. Move very quickly through them. No verbal responses are required.

Your thoughts on these statements and questions?

- When we're with friends, we often feel happier.

- Was it a bit weak of Archie to give Oliver a present? After all, Oliver is an ex-friend.

- It's best to forget old friends, move on, and enjoy new ones.

- Is making friendships more than just knowing a bunch of people?

- What Prisha had wasn't friends, just lots of contacts.

- Do you agree with Archie when he said, "If you want close friends, you have to put the time in with them"?

- Would you talk to your closest friends most days?

- Can you think of one thing you'd do with a close friend but you would not do with an acquaintance?

- Did Prisha miss out because the boys thought she's too good-looking and the girls were jealous of her?

- Have you seen that happen before?

- Do you think Prisha missed out because everyone thought she'd be popular, so they didn't need to bother?

- Do you think Tobias was courageous?

- Would you do what Tobias did?

- Do you agree with this statement? "Popular people don't really have close friendships."

2. *Show me the Buzz*

Show me the Buzz provides students with the opportunity to discuss a variety of social and emotional ideas, absorb the thoughts of others, debate them, create role plays and receive feedback from the group. We have learned that this approach heightens understandings and the transference of skills. There is always a Part 1 and a Part 2. Choose one activity from either Part 1 or Part 2, depending on what appeals to you, the time you have and your group's likely preferences. There's plenty of content in *Show me the Buzz*, so the lesson can be revisited time and time again while continuing with this same topic.

Part 1

1. Group discussion

Archie, Tobias and Joanna discussed several reasons why Prisha was forgotten in the activity. Why do you think she was forgotten? What will she need to do to build closer friendships? Discuss this in small groups, then as a larger group.

2. Create a friendship recipe

Write a 'friendship recipe' with a 'method' that explains how to be a good friend. Then list the 'ingredients' needed to be a good friend. Place the most important 'ingredients' at the top. This can be done with a large group to tune everyone in, and then smaller groups can design and build their own recipes, capturing their priorities.

3. What makes a friend?

Assist students to fold a piece of A4 paper into thirds. At the top of each third, write one of these headings: "I like a friend who . . ." or "Things I do for my friends . . ." or "Things I like to do with my friends . . ." Spend time encouraging students to share their thoughts.

4. Group discussion

Discuss the meaning behind these statements:

> True friendship is when you walk into their house and your Wi-Fi connects automatically.
>
> Author unknown

> Don't walk behind me; I may not lead. Don't walk in front of me; I may not follow. Just walk beside me and be my friend.
>
> Albert Camus

> I don't need a friend who changes when I change and who nods when I nod; my shadow does that much better.
>
> Plutarch

> Sometimes being a friend means mastering the art of timing. There is a time for silence. A time to let go and allow people to hurl themselves into their own destiny. And a time to prepare to pick up the pieces when it's all over.
>
> Octavia Butler

5. Watch and discuss

Play the clip 'Big Bang Theory: the friendship algorithm' (www.youtube.com/watch?v=k0xgjUhEG3U). Then discuss these questions:

- Is Sheldon on to a good idea?

- How did Sheldon's friend Kripke help?

- Might a flow chart be a useful way to understand the complexity of friendships?

- Are there parts of friendship that a flow chart could never explain? Like what?

Part 2: Before the role play

When friendship is at its best, the interaction between people tells all. Here are some key skills. Share this information with the group.

A smile and a little eye contact

A smile is a powerful thing, and it's done with our eyes and mouth. A smile invites connection, and as this occurs neurotransmitters are released that make the other person feel good. So, show me your best smile? Eye contact also delivers a powerful non-verbal message. Too much and it turns into an awkward stare, and too little signals you are not interested. Best advice – keep eye contact as simple as a series of long glances. Don't overthink it.

Active listening

Friendly listeners are interested. They lean into the conversation, nodding their head in understanding or agreement; they'll validate a person's feelings and ask questions. Quality listening is the difference between building a deeper respect and trust, or feeling as though you've been short-changed.

A responsive body

To spark a connection, you want your body to work with your words. When chatting with someone, or talking in a group, we subtly present three areas of our body: the nape of the neck, the tummy area and the upper legs. We try not to block or cover these with our hands. And without being fake, we mirror the posture and the actions of the person or people we're with. This helps to build a bond. Be careful, though – don't overdo it!

Matching energy levels

Each student has a natural energy that can vary from boisterous and loud to timid, quiet and cautious. Also, the setting we find ourselves in influences the energy we project. For example, you'd use a much stronger energy level to work with a group of friends in the gymnasium than you would when you're having a personal discussion with someone in the library. The most effective way to build rapport is to match your energy so it's close to the person or people you are with.

Contact

Research shows most people appreciate being lightly touched, occasionally, during an interaction. A brief and gentle touch on the arm suggests warmth and is a physical reminder of the relationship you're keen to build. Be careful not to overdo it and appreciate that a few people will not like it. Additionally, hugging close friends or a high five or handshake is a great way to show you care for them because physical contact is comforting.

Choose the right words

Deliberately greet your friends with warmth in your voice. Move towards them and say something: 'hi', 'hello', 'hey there', 'good morning' or 'great to see you'. Let them know that you're happy to be with them. Alternatively, ask a question: "How are you?" "How was your weekend?" "What did you do last night?"

Part 2: The role play – guess what skill is missing in my friendly role play?

Help students to form groups of two, three or four. Their task is to create a friendly scene where the group meets up and begins to talk to each other. Imagine it's a Monday morning and there are things to share. Encourage them to use the friendly connecting ideas just discussed! However, choose *one* person who will be friendly but omits using one of the friendly skills. It may be obvious or subtle. As the group watches each role play, they will need to be great emotional detectives. Their job is to guess which person has left out a skill, and which skill it is. Have fun. Give students a few minutes to rehearse, and move between groups to provide plenty of coaching and enthusiasm.

Next, ask each group to perform their role play. If a student does not wish to perform, allow them to pass. So much can be learned through observing. Always perform role plays in the middle of the social circle. Consider capturing the action on video or photo by using your iPad, camera or smartphone. Encourage others to give constructive feedback after each role play.

3. *Do you know the Buzz?*

Do you know the Buzz? is a lively group 'discussion time' where students briefly respond to a series of questions and statements highlighted by Archie's story. The goal is for them to exchange ideas, and in the process 'mind map' their way more empathically through the complexities of social and emotional situations. This should also provide facilitators with an insight into the depth of student understandings. To do this, have students sitting on chairs in a social circle.

Your thoughts on these statements and questions?

- When we're with friends, we often feel happier.

- Was it a bit weak of Archie to give Oliver a present? Oliver is an ex-friend; don't you think Archie should move on?

- Isn't it best to forget old friends, move on, and enjoy new ones?

- Is making friendships more than just being with a bunch of people?

- What Prisha had wasn't friends; they were lots of contacts or acquaintances.

- Do you agree with Archie when he said, "If you want close friends, you have to put the time in with them"?

- How much time? Would you chat to your closest friends most days?

- Can you think of one thing you'd do with a close friend but you would not do with an acquaintance?

- Did Prisha miss out because the boys thought she's too good-looking and the girls were jealous of her?

- Have you seen that happen before?

- Or did she miss out because everyone thought she'd be popular, so they didn't need to bother?

- Do you think Prisha was brave? After all, she kept her disappointment together!

- Do you think Tobias was courageous?

- Would you do what Tobias did?

- Do you agree with this statement? "Popular people don't really have close friendships."

4. *The Buzz*

The Buzz is an opportunity for the group to play games that strengthen their relationships and the skills central to the lesson.

Game: Friendship chain (passive)

To begin, brainstorm a list of qualities essential in friendship. Record these for the group to refer to. Next, give each student several long slips of coloured construction paper. On their paper, they write what they believe is the most important quality in friendship. Next, ask them to combine their slips to make a chain by stapling each person's slip together. The friendship chain can be hung and referred to throughout the year.

Game: Nail hang (passive)

Divide students into pairs. Then ask them to run a very tight twine between two chairs or desks. Their goal is to sit with each other and work together to hang 20 large flathead nails from the twine. This is a lovely activity and provides the scope for students to chat as fingers stay busy to achieve a goal. Later, mix the pairs up so new relationships can be built.

Game: Student interviews (passive)

Break students into pairs. Do this strategically so the students you want to be together are together. Ask them to face their partner and discuss the following: things they like to do, a hobby or interest, a passion, a talent, a special experience, a personal strength, a dream they might be chasing, or a favourite book or movie. Also ask them to chat about things they do not like: a fear or phobia, a dislike, a worry, something annoying, or a bad experience they've had. Their task is to find something they have in common for the things they like to do and for the things they do not like.

Game: Random things about us (passive)

Display the questions below on to a screen or on a sheet of paper for students to see. Their task is to work in pairs and exchange answers to these questions:

- Is there a surprising, nifty or unexpected thing about you?

- On a scale of 1–10, how strict are your parents?

- Who has been your favourite teacher? Why?

- If you could only choose one, would you choose to be so good-looking, a genius, famous for doing something great, or yourself?

- If you could change one thing about yourself, what would it be?

- Name someone you admire.

- What are you most proud of?

- Where's the most beautiful place you've ever been, or would like to go to?

- What are your three favourite movies?

- What tricks would you get up to if you were invisible for a day?

- Would you rather live for a week in the past or the future? Why?

- Would you live as yourself or someone else?

- What's your best childhood memory?

- If you could eat only three foods for the rest of your life, what would they be?

These questions are located at the end of the lesson in the photocopiable section or at www.whatsthebuzz.net.au/main-menu/content-whats-the-buzz-with-teenagers, ready to print.

Game: Cooperative building (moderately exciting)

We know that when people team up to build something together, there are improvements in their social interactions and confidence, and the benefits last for years (Legoff and Sherman, 2006; Owens et al., 2008). So, organise your students into small groups and set them a building challenge using building blocks or bricks, Mobilo, K'Nex, Ringo or Lego. On the other hand, you might like this favourite of ours. Supply a cheap deck of playing cards to each group. Also supply them with scissors they can use, but don't dare say how they may use them. The goal is to build a tall tower using every card in the deck. It must stand for one minute following completion. Set a time limit of 10 minutes! Students can use the scissors to place small incisions in the cards, so they lock together. In this way, they can build a tall stable tower together.

Lesson 2

After the Buzz: Social thinking ideas for parents and caregivers

Lesson 2: What is a friend?

Key social and emotional principles (learning intention)

This lesson highlights the essential skills required to build friendships and become a friend. It focuses on the qualities of friendship: What makes a good friend? What does a good friend say and do? How many friends does one need? What should we expect from a friend as we get older? What's the difference between a good friend and an acquaintance?

After the Buzz presents further ideas for parents, guardians and educators to encourage the generalisation of the social and emotional thinking students have touched on during the lesson. All children rely on us to consolidate these skills by positively modelling them, and emphasising the language and ideas used in the lesson. Here are a few practical ideas.

Parenting styles: Authoritarian as opposed to authoritative

Studies prove that children who are parented in an authoritarian style are more likely to be excluded by their peers (Dewar, 2018). An authoritarian approach is characterised by levels of empathy, the very ingredient required to build relationship, loyalty and connection. An authoritarian parent tends to be highly controlling, and relies on aggressive and confrontational ways to achieve what they want. They discourage open discussion, are critical and control behaviour through punishment. Sadly, children raised this way are less likely to develop an internalised sense of right and wrong because all they've experienced is being controlled. Children exposed to harsh punishments also tend to show more hostility and aggression (Bender et al., 2007).

On the other hand, an authoritative management style is most effective for raising well-adjusted kids.

This style embodies descriptors such as respectfulness, leadership, relational, mutual, influential, decisive, emotionally reliable, trustworthy, solid, steady and so on. An authoritative parent values honest communication and expects cooperative behaviour but knows their kids won't always get it right. When they make mistakes, they'll let them know without an 'I told you so', and are prepared to walk alongside them, offering just enough guidance as it's needed. They understand the balance between building independence, smothering them, offering too much advice and being overly critical. Studies show that authoritative parents raise kids who are less aggressive, more self-reliant, more self-controlled and better accepted by peers (Myers, 2014).

Challenge: Say hello to 10 people each day for a week

Set this challenge for everyone in the family. The greeting must be in person, to friends, acquaintances, teachers, neighbours and newcomers. Many who've accepted this challenge say it made them feel happier and didn't cost a thing! What's not surprising is that saying hello opens opportunities to have new conversations with new people as well. We dare you to accept the challenge!

Friendship recipes

It's one thing to meet new people, but it takes an entirely different set of skills to maintain a friendship. These recipes are invaluable and worth spending time on with your young teen. One idea may be to create a poster based on these, but adapt what you do so it becomes more personalised. This visual reminder may provide the impetus you're trying to create.

Recipe for *making* friends

- Introduce yourself.

- Smile!

- Say your name and look at them as you speak.

- Ask them a question about themselves.

- Wait, and listen to their answer.

- Find something in common you share and talk about it.

- Be kind, and use a gentle voice and thoughtful words.

- Make the best impression you can.

Recipe for *keeping* friends

- Show you care.

- Always share.

After the Buzz . . . Lesson 2

- Talk, listen and ask questions about them.

- Build opportunities to be together.

- Allow them to have friendships with others too.

- Give positive feedback. Say what it is you like about them.

- Think before you speak – not all things should be shared.

- Friendships are not perfect – things will go wrong.

- When something goes wrong, always look for a way to fix it.

- Friendships can grow, weaken or strengthen. That's normal!

Play 'friendship detective'

Ask your child to name a person they think shows friendly behaviours. List this person's friendly behaviours, and – if you agree – comment that these are the qualities that others look for in friendship. These are the qualities worth growing! As you identify children with the friendliest behaviours, you immediately connect your child to better role models. Ask them to observe how this person gets along with others and the kind of things they say and do. If, on the other hand, your son or daughter chooses a person who shows some dubious qualities around friendship, it opens the scope for an even richer conversation.

Investigate community clubs, groups and associations

Despite everyone's best intentions, school is not always the easiest place for all children and teens to find happiness and contentment in friendship. For many, the best source of social connection takes place outside of school, where they can capitalise on a natural interest they can share with like-minded others. There are a myriad of clubs, groups, associations and societies within the local community worth exploring. These situations are usually organised and overseen by adults who want young people to connect over an interest, hobby or fascination. They foster friendship, develop interests and provide opportunities for children and adolescents to exercise their social and emotional muscle. The best place to start is to ask friends and teachers, go to your local council, or do an online search.

What makes a friend?

When it comes to the ins and outs of friendship, practice really does help! Discuss the behaviours below. They are all friendly. However, look at them and discuss situations when each is appropriate or inappropriate. And, if appropriate, how often?

After the Buzz ... Lesson 2

- Make time to catch up outside of school.

- Give in. Just 'go with the flow' and do what they want to do.

- Invite them home.

- Go to the movies together.

- Do what they ask you to do.

- Give them a massage.

- Ask, "Are you okay?" if you notice they're not okay.

- Buy gifts for them.

- Lend them money

- Offer to carry their bag.

- Say thank you.

- Keep their secrets.

- Sit and talk with them.

- Give them a big hug.

- Give them a kiss.

- Help with homework.

- Ask them to help you with homework.

- Help them with their chores at home if you're visiting.

- Ask a question and be a great listener.

- Help them walk their dog.

- Invite them over for dinner.

- Message them.

- Smile.

Engage in and monitor your children's social life

As children become adolescents, it is natural for them to look towards and be more influenced by peers than ever before. This natural change of guard really throws some parents. Some personalise this beautiful time of maturation and decide to feel abandoned, hurt or obsolete. What these parents fail to grasp is that their connection is even more valuable during this time; it simply needs tweaking and requires greater sophistication. Children at this stage will, from time to time, rebel against the constraints of family life in their search for independence. That's to be

After the Buzz ... Lesson 2

expected. Most valuable is that they need family for security, reassurance and a sense of belonging. Family is the quintessential touchstone for them to draw their strength and confidence to take on the world. So, they need you to invest in them by continuing to parent, know their friends and know what they're up to. Teens are always better off when their parents tactfully monitor their social activities.

References

Bender, H., Allen, J., Boykin, K., McElhaney., Moore, C., O'Beirne, K., et al. (2007) Use of harsh physical discipline and developmental outcomes in adolescence. *Development and Psychopathology*, 19(1): 227–242.

Chopik, W. (2017) Are Friends Better for Us Than Family? Available at: https://msutoday.msu.edu/news/2017/are-friends-better-for-us-than-family/ (accessed June 2018).

Dewar, G. (2018) *The Authoritarian Parenting Style: Little Nurturing, Lots of Psychological Control*. Available at: www.parentingscience.com/authoritarian-parenting-style.html (accessed June 2018).

Legoff, D. and Sherman, M. (2006) Long-term outcome of social skills intervention based on interactive LEGO play. *Autism*, 10(4): 317–329. Available at: http://journals.sagepub.com/doi/10.1177/1362361306064403 (accessed June 2018).

Myers, R. (2014) *What Type of Parenting Style Do You Best Fit?* Available at: https://childdevelopmentinfo.com/parenting/type-parenting-style-best-fit/#.WysR6_ZuI2w (accessed June 2018).

Owens, G., Granader, Y., Humphrey, A. and Baron-Cohen, S. (2008) LEGO therapy and the social use of language programme: an evaluation of two social skills interventions for children with high functioning autism and Asperger syndrome. *Journal of Autism and Developmental Disorders*, 38(10): 1944–1957. Available at: www.ncbi.nlm.nih.gov/pubmed/18566882 (accessed June 2018).

After the Buzz . . . Lesson 2

What's the Buzz with Teenagers?

11 Game: Random things about us

Together, ask each other these questions and exchange answers:

- Is there a surprising, nifty or unexpected thing about you?

- On a scale of 1–10, how strict are your parents?

- Who has been your favourite teacher? Why?

- If you could only choose one, would you choose to be so good-looking, a genius, famous for doing something great, or yourself?

- If you could change one thing about yourself, what would it be?

- Name someone you admire.

- What are you most proud of?

- Where's the most beautiful place you've ever been, or would like to go to?

- What are your three favourite movies?

- What tricks would you get up to if you were invisible for a day?

- Would you rather live for a week in the past or the future? Why?

- Would you live as yourself or someone else?

- What's your best childhood memory?

- If you could eat only three foods for the rest of your life, what would they be?

Switching on positivity

"This is the last place I want to be"

Key social and emotional principles (learning intention)

This lesson focuses on positivity, and how to switch it on, because sometimes when faced with tricky situations and challenges, we hear the chatter of doubt and negative self-talk in our minds. Most human beings share this peculiarity, so it's liberating to learn how to change gears from our negative state to a healthier and more optimistic gear. Switching on positivity is so much more than a warm and fuzzy idea. Without it, our negative chatter prevents us from performing at our best, finding pleasure from being in the moment and giving life a go.

Materials required for this lesson

- Name tags.

- Chairs in a social circle for students to sit on.

- Whiteboard/butcher's paper/screen and markers.

- Create a simple outline of the lesson on the whiteboard/butcher's paper/ screen for students to follow.

- Display the *What's the Buzz?* group values (located in the introduction or at www.whatsthebuzz.net.au/main-menu/content-whats-the-buzz-with-teenagers).

- Organise feedback and reminder cards, or similar, to strengthen responsive behaviours (located in the introduction or at www.whatsthebuzz.net.au/ main-menu/content-whats-the-buzz-with-teenagers).

- Have Archie's story ready to read to students. This can be done directly from this lesson. Or, for a small registration fee, you can download the 16 Archie stories as you want them. Each story contains text, audio in the form of the authors reading to your students, and two large illustrations in full colour that will fill your screen. Access is available at www.whatsthebuzz.net.au/ main-menu/content-whats-the-buzz-with-teenagers

- Plenty of pencils, pens and paper for students to do activities from Part 1 of *Show me the Buzz*.

- Cellophane, pipe cleaners, scissors and sticky tape to make two sets of pipe cleaner glasses in Part 1 of *Show me the Buzz* (www.youtube.com/ watch?v=JA8Xmjd9Rps).

- Print the cards required for the activity 'Battle lines' in Part 1 of *Show me the Buzz*. Alternatively, this game can be used as a game in *The Buzz*. These are located at the end of this lesson.

- Print the role-play cards for 'Switching on positivity' in Part 2 of *Show me the Buzz* (located at the end of the lesson or at www.whatsthebuzz.net.au/ main-menu/content-whats-the-buzz-with-teenagers).

- One large blanket, or similar, to play the game 'Shrinking blanket stand' in *The Buzz*.

- Plenty of blank A4 paper and pencils or pens to play the game 'Negative thought toss' in *The Buzz*.

- Prepare handouts for parents(s):

   One copy of this lesson for each parent to read.

   One copy of *After the Buzz: Social thinking ideas for parents and caregivers* to send home (located at the end of the lesson, ready to photocopy, or at www. whatsthebuzz.net.au/main-menu/content-whats-the-buzz-with-teenagers).

Lesson 3

Explanation

It's so much easier to be optimistic and cheery when everything is going well, but positive thinking is a saviour in the moments when we need it most. It's timely to teach young adolescents how to switch to a positive style of thinking to solve everyday problems, because when we choose to take a moment, regroup our emotions and find a constructive way forward, we give our brain the best chance to think clearly and make the best choices.

When faced with a problem, a person who employs a negative attitude is likely to think, "I'm stupid. I'll never try that again," or "This is boring," or "I hate this," or "It just gets worse and worse," or "I should have never come." Suddenly, the outcome is likely to mirror this same negative style of thinking. On the other hand, someone who chooses to think positively is more likely to approach a challenge by thinking, "It's my choice whether I give in or not," or "I'll try this again, but can do it differently," or "I'll take this step by step." Optimists keep going, and when they succeed they try even harder. When they fail, they try again.

We have also learned that even if you're not completely feeling it, try to 'fake it until you make it', because by acting more positively you're likely to become more engaged and achieve better outcomes. And, while on achievement, remember that failure can always be turned into a learning experience. By reframing it and analysing it, we can learn and grow from any experience.

According to abundant amounts of research, as well as lifelong observations, we know positive thinkers are more inclined to plan, persist, take healthy risks, arrive at better decisions and find greater success in all kinds of ways (Scheier, 1986; Scott, 2002; Seligman, 2006). People who learn to think positively are not only healthier, but live longer than pessimists (Brody, 2017). In fact, a Yale study indicates a positive attitude is likely to keep you alive for an extra seven and a half years on average (Winerman, 2006). In addition, research has revealed that switching on positive thinking, which includes identifying negative self-talk, impacts favourably on anxiety and life satisfaction (Guidi, 2016). Those who make this transition to thinking more positively gradually become expert in accessing an assortment of skills essential for lifelong emotional resilience. In a very real way, practice makes perfect!

So, teach young people to surround themselves with friends who think optimistically because this habit can be learned and strengthened. Alert teens to think about each of their friends, and rate them in terms of their positive outlook on life. Those with pessimistic and cynical styles of thinking are best avoided, and if they can't be avoided, develop protective strategies that minimise impact.

1. *What's the Buzz?*

Actively greet students as they enter. Provide chairs in a social circle for them to sit on and have a brief lesson plan on the screen, whiteboard or butcher's paper for students to see. As students are settling, hand each of them a 'Thumbs up feedback card' to highlight their thoughtful behaviour and using the group values.

Let's begin

As usual, frame the learning intention by asking:

- Do you know what a positive and negative state of mind is? Explain.

- Which is more useful? Why?

- What do you do to switch positive thinking on when you need it?

We create positive thoughts by using words, sometimes in our head, and sometimes out loud. This is because language is more than words; we think and plan with it too. As we talk to ourselves, our bodies tend to relax, and our brain believes it can better handle the situation. This switches us to rational mode, rather than feeling as though our only choices are to flee, fight or freeze. Ask students, "Can you give me an idea of what positive thinking or self-talk sounds like?"

- "I can handle this."

- "I'm smart enough to deal with this."

- "I can't control the things others do, but I can control me."

- "I can stay and look calm."

- "I'll just tackle one thing at a time."

- "Everything will be okay because it usually is in the end."

Ask, "Can you give me an idea of what negative thinking or self-talk sounds like?"

- "I'm useless."

- "I'm dumb."

- "No one ever believes me."

- "There's nothing I can do."

- "This stuff always happens to me."

- "I hate them."

- "Who cares, I hate them anyway."

- "I'm ugly."

- "I'll pay them back tomorrow."

- "I'll never do that again."

- "I'm an idiot."

- "I'm a failure."

Archie's story: "This is the last place I want to be"

It was late Saturday afternoon, and Archie, Joanna, Tobias and Prisha were at Ayman's house. They were helping Ayman and his father hold a 6-year-old birthday party for Ayman's brother, Tarik. You might remember that since Ayman's mother passed away, Ayman had taken on a lot of family responsibility. The planning for the party had been intense, with each of the friends organising a party game. Tarik's friends were due to arrive at 4 p.m., pizzas would arrive at 5 p.m. and the party would wrap up by 6 p.m. The hope was that everything would run like clockwork and they'd give the kids the best time ever.

Soon it was 4 p.m. and the young guests started to fill the house with their bodies, noise and excitement. All nine of them were bouncing off the walls! What was unexpected was that Archie's old friend, Oliver, arrived with his youngest brother, Connor. Connor sometimes had anaphylactic reactions to a few foods. Just to be sure he was safe, his parents had asked Oliver to keep an eye on him as he knew what to do if Connor had an allergic reaction. You might remember that Oliver was the Lego-mad kid that Archie stole the Lego dump truck from years ago when they were at Castle Rock Primary School. You also might remember that their friendship had cooled recently. They were fine with one another, but were no longer as close.

Oliver was standing next to Archie and sighed, "This is the last place I want to be. These kids are so annoying."

Archie was surprised by his comment. While being with a bunch of madly excited 6-year-olds wasn't Archie's first choice for great things to do, it felt good helping them to be happy. Archie didn't have a chance to respond as it was the moment for him to organise his party game, so he moved away and started to explain the rules for the sack race. But before he could finish, the kids grabbed the sacks, slid into them, helped others to get into them and were lined up ready to start. Archie was impressed by how switched on and helpful 6-year-olds can be.

As Archie was running the sack race, Joanna moved closer to her good friend Oliver. He glanced at her and repeated what he'd said to Archie before: "This is the last place I want to be. It's bad."

12 Archie's story: "This is the last place I want to be" – first image

Lauren Eldridge Murray

This image can be downloaded from http://whatsthebuzz.net.au/main-menu/content-whats-the-buzz-with-teenagers and will fill your screen in colour. There is also the option to have the authors read the story to students.

As you know, Joanna is no longer the shy girl she once was. These days, she calls it how it is: "Are you serious? Why would you not want to be part of their fun?"

"I've just got better things to do than this," replied Oliver.

"Like what?"

"Like anything!"

"Oh, Oliver. Really? You need to stop taking yourself so seriously and being so judgy," groaned Joanna. "Life's not all about you. Just fake it!"

Luck fell on Oliver because Joanna was called to organise her party game. However, Tobias had been listening to the conversation between them, and in typical Tobias style he'd already hatched a plan. His plan was to tackle Oliver's lack of enthusiasm in a different way.

Tobias called to Oliver, "Hey, Ollie. Can you help me drag this rope for tug of war on to the lawn over there?"

Together, they dragged it and laid it out straight on the lawn ready for tug of war.

"So, Ollie. It was going to be me against all the 6-year-olds. But look at them, they're bigger than I imagined. You're helping me. Okay?" stated Tobias.

"A little healthy competition never hurt anyone!" responded Oliver.

About half an hour later, Tobias and Oliver were giving a lot of good-spirited grunt and lip to the young tug of war team. Everyone was cheering and having fun. It was a well-matched competition, but the older boys made sure that the younger boys worked hard for their win.

Afterwards, Joanna just couldn't help herself. She edged up to Oliver and quietly said, "Well, that didn't kill you. You managed to shake off being Mr Grumpy Sour Pants and had some fun with them."

"Okay, you were right. I just had to make an effort and get into the zone. It feels better than being your Mr Grumpy Sour Pants," smiled Oliver.

Soon the pizzas were delivered and eaten, the candles on the cake were lit, happy birthday was sung, and the party guests were leaving with smiles on their faces and with bulging loot bags. As Archie and Joanna walked home very slowly together, Archie popped a question to her.

"Oliver was in a bad mood when the party started. How did you get him to change channels?"

"Do you want the truth or a lie?" replied Joanna.

"The truth," said Archie.

"The truth is that I had a go at him for being Mr Grumpy Sour Pants. Tobias did the trick. He helped put Oliver in the moment, so he could feel what the kids were feeling."

Lesson 3

13 Archie's story: "This is the last place I want to be" – second image

Lauren Eldridge Murray

This image can be downloaded from http://whatsthebuzz.net.au/main-menu/content-whats-the-buzz-with-teenagers and will fill your screen in colour. There is also the option to have the authors read the story to students.

Discussion based on the questions and statements below will occur later in *Do you know the Buzz?* For now, simply read them to get students thinking. Encourage them to listen and respond to each question by putting their thumb up if they 'agree' or think 'yes', thumb down if they think 'no', and thumb to the side if they think 'maybe'. Move very quickly through them. No verbal responses are required.

Your thoughts on these statements and questions?

- Have you ever felt like Oliver and got stuck thinking negatively about something?

- Can you pick out Oliver's negative talk about the party?

- Are you the sort of person that can snap yourself out of a bad mood or negative thinking?

- Have you got a strategy or something you do to get away from that feeling?

- Are you more likely to stay in a negative mood and be more like a Mr Grumpy Sour Pants?

- Is it your right to be negative if you feel like it?

- Or do you have a responsibility to spare your friends from your grumpiness?

- Have you ever seen someone being negative and sulky, and thought they do it to get attention?

- Do you know what Oliver's problem was?

- Do you think Joanna was fair calling Oliver on his negative attitude?

- Do you understand why Joanna said, "Just fake it!" to Oliver?

- Do you know why Oliver's negative attitude bothered Joanna so much?

- Afterwards, Oliver said, "I just had to make an effort and get into the zone." Who knows what he means?

- Is there a lesson to be learned from Oliver?

- Is there a lesson to be learned from Tobias?

2. *Show me the Buzz*

Show me the Buzz provides students with the opportunity to discuss a variety of social and emotional ideas, absorb the thoughts of others, debate them, create role plays and receive feedback from the group. We have learned that this approach heightens understandings and the transference of skills. There is always a Part 1 and a Part 2. Choose one activity from either Part 1 or Part 2, depending on what appeals to you, the time you have and your group's likely preferences. There's plenty of content in *Show me the Buzz*, so the lesson can be revisited time and time again while continuing with this same topic.

Part 1

1. Rewrite the ending

Archie's story had a positive ending for Oliver. Rewrite it, or tell it, with a negative outcome for Oliver. Be sure to include how Oliver's negative thinking and words affect others at the party. Pick up the story when Tobias asks Oliver to join him with the tug of war.

Alternatively, use the story as a basis for a role play, and ask one group to highlight Oliver using a positive attitude where he 'fakes it till he makes it'. They can duplicate what happened in the story and use a little artistic licence to take it in their own creative direction. Ask another group to develop a role play with Oliver acting on his negative self-talk and how it badly affects others. These very different role plays show us that there is a world of difference between these mindsets. You might decide to film these role plays.

2. Research 'flipping your lid' and 'upstairs/downstairs brains'

Ask students to take their thumbs and place them in the middle of their palms and close fingers over the top to make a fist. Explain that your thumb represents your feelings, and your feelings are supported when the cerebral cortex is online. You can see how the fingers are supporting your feelings. The cerebral cortex (the fingers in this model) is often called the higher part of the brain because it allows us to think, be rational, reason, and find positive solutions to a problem or crisis. We find this area right behind the forehead.

Sometimes, for all sorts of reasons, emotions can rise from the brainstem and limbic areas and overpower the cerebral cortex. This is when we 'flip our lids' and lose it! To show this, spring your hand wide open, and what do you see? The feelings have sprung out of control as they are no longer supported by the clever cerebral cortex. In these moments, we cannot self-regulate our feelings. Our positive energy, thinking and self-talk gives way to negative energy, thinking and self-talk. The amygdala, which is the primitive threat centre, takes over, and while this is bossing the brain the 'flipping out' and negative thinking continues. At this point, it's time to walk away and take a break. Even just naming your feelings can tame runaway feelings and bring the prefrontal cortex back online. As you say this to students, bring your fingers gradually back down, slowly tuck in your thumb and cover it with your fingers to show the cerebral cortex back online.

To consolidate this and strengthen what happens in the brain to cause positive and negative styles of thinking, watch Daniel Siegel present a hand model of the brain at www.youtube.com/watch?v=gm9ClJ74Oxw.

Next, introduce the idea that brains are just like a house, with an upstairs and a downstairs. This following clip will be useful ('Why do we lose control of our emotions?'): www.youtube.com/watch?v=3bKuoH8CkFc.

You and your students can make up your own stories about the sorts of characters that live upstairs and those who live downstairs. Enjoy assigning nifty names that suit the characters! Those who live upstairs, such as Calm Clare and Cool Cal, are thinkers and positive problem-solvers. They tend to plan, keep their emotions steady, and try to be flexible and empathic. To do this, they usually process their thoughts and feelings in their prefrontal cortex, which governs deeper reasoning, insight and positive problem-solving.

Those who live downstairs, such as Angry Alby and Sulky Sally, often let their strong emotions kick in fast. This is because what's happening is being processed in the threat centre of the brain. The amygdala is useful when it comes to fighting or fleeing, but useless when solving complex people problems. Suddenly, a loud alarm screams at them in their head, and before they know it they're 'flipping out' or are ready to fight, run or hide.

Motivate students to draw their own pictures of their upstairs and downstairs brains, and encourage them to assign names to the characters living upstairs and downstairs. To stimulate ideas, Google images of 'upstairs and downstairs brains'. Alternatively, get them to draw a picture of themselves 'flipping their lid' and use captions to show what happens when their amygdala becomes the boss of them! Again, you'll find plenty of ideas if you Google images of 'flipping the lid brain'.

3. Group discussion

Break students into groups of three or four. Each group will need a blank A4 sheet of paper and a pen or pencil for a recorder to write. Draw a vertical line down the centre of the page. At the top of the page on the left-hand side, write the heading 'Negative self-talk statements'. And at the top of the page on the right-hand side, write the heading 'Positive self-talk statements'. The group's task is to come up with as many words and phrases as possible under each of these headings. If time permits, share with the larger group.

Similarly, ask students to retell a time when they or someone they know used positive self-talk to overcome a tricky situation. What kind of situation was it? Was it a horribly long fun run that was no fun, was it extra schoolwork, starting at a new school, a new sport, learning to play a new musical instrument or caring for a sick member of their family? What words were used to help? Did they do it for themselves or for someone else? To model, you might begin by sharing something appropriate from your own life.

4. Pipe cleaner glasses

To highlight the difference between looking at a situation either positively or negatively, make two sets of pipe cleaner glasses (www.youtube.com/watch?v=JA8Xmjd9Rps). Organise students to make two sets of glasses – a rose-coloured set and a black set – by using cellophane, pipe cleaners, scissors and sticky tape. Once they have their two sets of glasses, display an image on a screen of a person or

Lesson 3

people facing a challenge or a risk. Ask them to put on the rose-coloured glasses and be that person. The rose-coloured glasses represent an optimistic person. So, what is this person (or people) in the image likely saying to themselves and to each other. Let's hear the style of positive self-talk as they navigate their way through the challenge. Next, put on the black glasses and remind students these represent a pessimistic person's style. Let's hear their negative self-talk, and what eventuates is that they are unlikely to navigate their way through the challenge.

5. Self-talk translations

Once students begin to spot their negative self-talk, help them to translate it. Explain that negative self-talk always has a deeper meaning, and it's their job to interpret what it's really saying. The first step is to work out how they might be feeling as the negative chatter enters their head. Are they feeling shocked, disappointed, embarrassed, scared, annoyed, fearful, sad or overwhelmed? What's really driving the negative self-talk? Our job is to be a detective and translate this, so we can go beyond it. Here are some everyday examples:

The negative self-talk . . .	The likely feeling . . .	The translation . . .
"I'm an idiot."	Embarrassed	I don't want others to think I'm stupid.
"Why bother?"	Overwhelmed	This is too much to do! Where do I start?
"I'm not good at this. Never will be."	Fearful	I'm not sure what to do. I don't think I've learned this.
"That's stupid anyway."	Annoyed	I can't believe she's giving more work to us!
"This is boring."	Worried	What do I do? Where do I start? Can I even do it?
"I hate them."	Hurt	They're awful to me. They ignore me. It hurts!

6. Battle lines

Here's an opportunity to switch on positive thinking. Let's play! The idea is for students to battle a *negative* thought with a *positive* thought, because the more we practise, the more natural it becomes. To begin, the facilitator places each of the 12 negative thought cards on the floor, face up for all to see. Next, choose students, one at a time, to draw a positive thought card from the group you are holding face down in your hand. As they draw it, ask them to flip it over and read this positive thought to the group. The students' task is to use this positive thought card to battle its negative counterpart on the floor. When they think they've found the right one, they place this positive thought card on top of the negative thought card to cancel it out! If their choice is incorrect, take back the positive thought card and place it back in your hands with the others. Continue until every negative thought card has been covered by a positive thought card.

Another way to play this game is to place all 12 negative thought cards on the floor, face up, so they can be seen. Then place the appropriate positive thought card next to each, also face up. Urge students to take notice and remember. Next, turn all of the positive thought cards face down and mix them up out of sequence so they no longer indicate accurate solutions. The group's task is to return the order of the cards so the negative and positive thought cards match once again.

Part 2: Role plays – switching on positivity

The role plays are in the photocopiable section at the end of this lesson. They are also available online at www.whatsthebuzz.net.au/main-menu/content-whats-the-buzz-with-teenagers. You may either read them to students, or print them and hand each group a role play. Help students to form small groups. Each role-play card states the number of students required. It does not matter if the same role play is given to several groups. Give students a few minutes to rehearse, and move between groups to provide plenty of coaching and enthusiasm.

Next, ask each group to perform their role play. If a student does not wish to perform, allow them to pass. So much can be learned through observing. Always perform role plays in the middle of the social circle. Consider capturing the action on video or photo by using your iPad, camera or smartphone. Encourage others to give constructive feedback after each role play.

3. *Do you know the Buzz?*

Do you know the Buzz? is a lively group 'discussion time' where students briefly respond to a series of questions and statements highlighted by Archie's story. The goal is for them to exchange ideas, and in the process 'mind map' their way more empathically through the complexities of social and emotional situations. This should also provide facilitators with an insight into the depth of student understandings. To do this, have students sitting on chairs in a social circle.

Your thoughts on these statements and questions?

- Have you ever felt like Oliver and got stuck thinking negatively about something?

- Can you pick out Oliver's negative talk about the party? Tell me.

- Are you the sort of person that can snap yourself out of a bad mood or negative thinking?

- Have you got a strategy or something you do to get away from that feeling? What is it?

- Are you more likely to stay in a negative mood and be more like a Mr Grumpy Sour Pants?

- Is it your right to be negative if you feel like it? Why can't you just be yourself?

- Or do you have a responsibility to spare your friends from your grumpiness?

- Have you ever seen someone being negative and sulky, and thought they do it to get attention?

- Do you know what Oliver's problem was? Tell me.

- Do you think Joanna was fair calling Oliver on his negative attitude? Would you do this to a friend?

- Do you understand why Joanna said, "Just fake it!" to Oliver? Explain.

- Afterwards, Oliver said, "I just had to make an effort and get into the zone." Who knows what he means?

- Is there a lesson to be learned from Oliver? What was it that switched his negative state of mind to a positive one? Here's a hint – it wasn't Tobias.

- Is there a lesson to be learned from Tobias? What did he do that helped switched Oliver's negative feelings to a more positive outlook? Is this something you could do with your friends?

4. *The Buzz*

The Buzz offers students the opportunity to play lively games to strengthen the newly acquired ideas. Today, three games are planned.

Game: Shrinking blanket stand (exciting)

Lay a blanket on the floor. Ask a group of five, six or seven students to stand on the blanket, and tell them no part of their body can touch the floor surrounding the blanket. At this stage, the task is easy, so once done congratulate the group.

Next, ask them to step away while you fold a third of the blanket over itself, which makes it smaller. Invite them back on to the blanket, being sure that they help support each other to stay on it. Suddenly, this game becomes cooperative and requires a little optimism and creativity! Once done, ask them to step off the blanket, and then fold it so it becomes slightly smaller. Invite them to step back on and help each other to stay on the blanket for at least five seconds. Keep on going to a point where the group can be proud of their cooperative efforts. Congratulate them!

If time permits, you may like to try this variation. Ask the group to stand on the blanket. Once they've settled, ask them to turn the blanket over so that the underside becomes the top. However, the players cannot step off the blanket while they do this.

Game: The 10 glads game (passive)

This game teaches how to switch on positivity! One person brings up a negative thought or situation, such as, "Guess what? I've just smashed my laptop's screen. This is a disaster!" Other players, in turn, try to rework the statement with optimism. The first may say, "Glad you got all your data back." The next could say, "Glad it was old!" or "It probably needed replacing anyway!" A third person might say, "Glad it was covered by insurance!" Play until '10 glads' have been stated. If you have a large group, let them know that not everyone will get a turn to say a negative situation.

Game: Negative thought toss (moderately exciting)

We agree that this group activity may sound odd, but the research tells us it works and it's fun (Brinol et al., 2013). Researchers have found that by recording two or three of one's common negative thoughts about themselves on to paper, discussing them with others, and tossing them away into a rubbish bin does temporarily clear the mind of them. Apparently, it's all in the doing! This is an activity that can be revisited from time to time. It's also very therapeutic to hear that others are plagued by negative self-talk too! It's a great way to normalise the impact of negative self-talk and take a little temporary control over it.

After the Buzz: Social thinking ideas for parents and caregivers

Lesson 3: Switching on positivity

Key social and emotional principles (learning intention)

This lesson focuses on positivity, and how to switch it on, because sometimes when faced with tricky situations and challenges, we hear the chatter of doubt and negative self-talk in our minds. Most human beings share this peculiarity, so it's liberating to learn how to change gears from our negative state to a healthier and more optimistic gear. Switching on positivity is so much more than a warm and fuzzy idea. Without it, our negative chatter prevents us from performing at our best, finding pleasure from being in the moment and giving life a go.

After the Buzz presents additional ideas for parents, guardians and educators to encourage the social and emotional thinking students have touched on during the lesson. As always, here are a few practical ideas to help young adolescents liberate themselves from negative feelings and self-talk to a healthier and more optimistic gear.

Teach the positive thinker's formula: $E + P = O$

E represents the events that occur in our lives. First, it's vital to discuss which things we can and can't control in our lives. We may not be able to control time, the weather, which movies are released and when, or the actions of others, but we can control our own feelings, thoughts and behaviour. As we take greater control of ourselves, we add P to the formula. P represents switching on our positive energy and optimistic reactions to the typical problematic events and challenges that happen in life. How well we do this gives us O, which is the outcome. The point here is to take charge of our own world instead of allowing the world to boss us!

Identify the optimism-sucking vampires

Just as we consciously surround ourselves with friends who think positively and make a positive difference to our wellbeing, teach young people to do the same. No one needs 'optimism-sucking vampires' around them because a big part of switching on positivity is being with others who also value and live it. In conversations with your kids, or with students, suggest they give each of their friends a one- to five-star rating in terms of their general positivity. Apparently, Gandhi once said, "I will not allow anyone to walk through my mind with their dirty feet." Those with pessimistic styles of thinking are best avoided, and if they can't be avoided, work at developing protective strategies that limit exposure and minimise impact.

A word on sensitive feelings

We all have feelings, but some of us experience them more often and more deeply. Being sensitive is not a weakness. Over time, it may become a great asset. However, what can be a problem is an individual's inability to find positive ways to express disappointed or hurt feelings, and this, of course, is where our work lies. Make a clear distinction between the good fortune of having sensitive feelings and the inability to find constructive ways to express them.

Role-model the 'silver lining'

All children need to know that when they stay calm, they give their brain the best chance to think and make the best choices. So, when something goes wrong, try to find the 'silver lining' or a lesson in it. For example, if your car runs out of petrol and you have to walk you might say, "Running out of petrol was bad, but it gave me a chance to walk and talk with you." Similarly, show how to draw on humour when things go wrong. As *Monty Python* once said, "Always look on the bright side of life!" Do what you can to guide your child or students to see other perspectives.

Explicitly teach positive self-talk

Most of us use positive self-talk when we find ourselves tackling a tricky situation. We might say, "I'll find a way to work this out." Let your children catch you modelling it because positive self-talk is a reliable way to stay in control, think, persist and find a solution. Together, brainstorm a list of positive sayings. Here are a few starters:

- "I can handle this."
- "I think best when I stay calm and give my brain a chance to think."
- "Just one thing at a time."
- "This doesn't have to get me down."
- "I can talk to someone about it."
- "I'm smart enough to get through this."
- "It will be okay."
- "I can do this."
- "I'll have a chat to my dog about it."
- "There are a million ways to solve a problem, and I just need to choose one."

From these, choose three or four that resonate. Print and laminate them, and keep them at home in a pencil case or as a bookmark as a reminder.

Develop a positive saying of the week and discuss it

It's surprising how some will seize on an optimistic saying and use it as an aid. The best sources for these are inspiring little books often found at the local news agency or the internet. They are wonderful resources:

> Attitudes are contagious. Are yours worth catching?
>> Dennis and Wendy Mannering

> Wherever you go, no matter what the weather, always bring your own sunshine.
>> Anthony J. D'Angelo

> I had the blues because I had no shoes until upon the street, I met a man who had no feet.
>> Ancient Persian saying

> Attitude is a little thing that makes a big difference.
>> Winston Churchill

> Every day may not be good, but there's something good in every day.
>> Author unknown

> Happiness is an attitude. We either make ourselves miserable, or happy and strong. The amount of work is the same.
>> Francesca Reigler

> I don't like that man. I must get to know him better.
>> Abraham Lincoln

Practise being in the present

Avoid pondering for too long on past experiences that haven't gone so well. If you've experienced a tricky, awkward or uncomfortable situation, work out what went wrong, and do what you need to do to move forward. Too much obsessing over past events tends to paralyse people and see them remain stuck in despair or regret. Also, when we dwell on negative things that haven't happened and may never happen, we take away the pleasure we should be getting from being in the moment.

"Fake it till you make it!"

In an acclaimed 2012 TED Talk, Amy Cuddy, a Harvard social psychologist, shared her findings that adopting a powerful posture affects your body chemistry (www.youtube.com/watch?v=RVmMeMcGc0Y). She explained that in her

After the Buzz . . . Lesson 3

study, she had subjects who adopted either a power stance or a meek pose for just two minutes. Those who maintained the power poses showed a decrease in the stress hormone cortisol and an increase in testosterone, a hormone related to confidence. Her experiment concludes, "Our non-verbals govern how we think and feel about ourselves. Our bodies change our minds." So, what do we take away from this research? This isn't about being superior, arrogant or not being true to oneself. It's all about trusting your own capacity, adapting to a new situation and going with the flow. This is an attitude that has the potential to unlock success.

Focus on the positive

Encourage your child, or students, to keep a daily journal of the good things that happen in their life. Younger children can simply draw the positive experiences from the day. While this activity helps to end the day on a strong, positive note, it also provides a space for young people to see that a mix of things happen throughout the day, and one unfortunate experience doesn't mean it has to be a bad day. This is yet another way to build the notion of 'growth mindset', the idea of expanding one's thinking beyond a limited or unrealistic comfort zone.

Be kind to yourself

Coach kids of all ages to be alert about how they talk to themselves: "I'm useless," "There's nothing I can do," "This stuff always happens to me," "I deserve this," "They all hate me," "I'm ugly" or "I'm an idiot." Remind them that they would never allow a friend to talk about themselves in this way, so there's no way we should ever be this unkind to ourselves! To change this pattern, the first step is to recognise this negative chatter in our minds and say, "This negative self-talk of mine isn't good enough and will take me nowhere good."

References

Brinol, P., Gascó, M., Petty, R. and Horcajo, J. (2013) Treating thoughts as material objects can increase or decrease their impact on evaluation. *Psychological Science*, 24: 41–47.

Brody, J. (2017) *A Positive Outlook May Be Good for Your Health*. Available at: https://www.nytimes.com/2017/03/27/well/live/positive-thinking-may-improve-health-and-extend-life.html (accessed June 2018).

Guidi, M. (2016) *5 Scientific Studies That Prove the Power of Positive Thinking*. Available at: www.linkedin.com/pulse/5-scientific-studies-prove-power-positive-thinking-mark-guidi (accessed June 2018).

Scheier, M.F. (1986) Coping with stress: divergent strategies of optimists and pessimists. *Journal of Personality and Social Psychology*, 51(6): 1257–1264.

Scott, D. (2002) *Stress That Motivates: Self-Talk Secrets for Success*. Scarborough: Nelson Education.

Seligman, M. (2006) *Learned Optimism*. New York: Pocket Books.

Winerman, L. (2006) A healthy mind, a longer life: can the right attitude and personality help you live longer? *Monitor on Psychology*, 37(10). Available at: www.apa.org/monitor/nov06/healthy.aspx (accessed June 2018).

After the Buzz . . . Lesson 3

What's the Buzz with Teenagers?

14 Battle lines cards

What's the Buzz?	BATTLE LINES	POSITIVE Thought Card	
"This is hard, but I can do it."			

What's the Buzz?	BATTLE LINES	POSITIVE Thought Card	
"Maybe he's painful because he needs friends."			

What's the Buzz?	BATTLE LINES	POSITIVE Thought Card	
"I'll give this a try. I'll start it and see how it goes."			

What's the Buzz?	BATTLE LINES	POSITIVE Thought Card	
"I could say, 'Sorry Mum' and tell her the truth."			

What's the Buzz?	BATTLE LINES	POSITIVE Thought Card	
"I'll try to join in. It will probably make me happier."			

What's the Buzz?	BATTLE LINES	POSITIVE Thought Card	
"I should just make a start. It might be worthwhile."			

What's the Buzz?	BATTLE LINES	POSITIVE Thought Card	
"I'll wait, do something for Mum and Dad, then ask again."			

What's the Buzz?	BATTLE LINES	POSITIVE Thought Card	
"I need to think. Anger isn't going to help."			

What's the Buzz?	BATTLE LINES	POSITIVE Thought Card	
"Homework is boring. It's got to be done. I'll do it, bit by bit."			

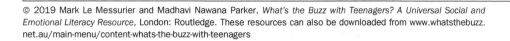

What's the Buzz with Teenagers?

14 Battle lines cards

continued . . .

What's the Buzz?	BATTLE LINES	**POSITIVE** **Thought Card**
"Maybe I was out. I should just go with the flow."		

What's the Buzz?	BATTLE LINES	**POSITIVE** **Thought Card**
"I can't control what she said, but I can control me."		

What's the Buzz?	BATTLE LINES	**POSITIVE** **Thought Card**
"I can see what she does. She lies to impress people."		

What's the Buzz?	BATTLE LINES	**NEGATIVE** **Thought Card**
"This is too hard for me. I'll never do it."		

What's the Buzz?	BATTLE LINES	**NEGATIVE** **Thought Card**
"He's such a pain. I hate him."		

What's the Buzz?	BATTLE LINES	**NEGATIVE** **Thought Card**
"I'm not doing this. She can't make me."		

What's the Buzz?	BATTLE LINES	**NEGATIVE** **Thought Card**
"Mum never believes me, so I won't tell her."		

What's the Buzz?	BATTLE LINES	**NEGATIVE** **Thought Card**
"I deserve to be lonely."		

What's the Buzz?	BATTLE LINES	NEGATIVE Thought Card	
"Who cares? It's not worth it."			

What's the Buzz?	BATTLE LINES	NEGATIVE Thought Card	
"Mum and Dad never let me do what I want."			

What's the Buzz?	BATTLE LINES	NEGATIVE Thought Card	
"I'm so angry. I'll show them. I'll smash their stuff."			

What's the Buzz?	BATTLE LINES	NEGATIVE Thought Card	
"I hate homework. It's boring and gets in the way."			

What's the Buzz?	BATTLE LINES	NEGATIVE Thought Card	
"I was not out. I will not go out. Try and make me!"			

What's the Buzz?	BATTLE LINES	NEGATIVE Thought Card	
"She had no right to say that. I'll pay her back."			

What's the Buzz?	BATTLE LINES	NEGATIVE Thought Card	
"She's a liar. She's always lying."			

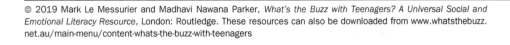

15 Role-play cards: Switching on positivity

Role play 1

Your computer shuts down. It saves but cannot be restarted. Your assignment is due tomorrow and you already have an extension. You will not be able to print out your work until the computer is repaired, and this may take two weeks. Show your positivity, and let's see how you'd approach your teacher and explain the situation. Then, replay it showing how events would look and probably work out using a negative mindset. (A pair – you and your teacher)

Role play 2

An older kid at school has threatened you by bumping you into a wall. They make you feel frightened, and so do their friends. This is the second time it's happened this week. In this role play, show us a possible positive solution, even though you're feeling scared. Then replay it showing how events would look and probably work out using negative talk. (A group of three or four – you, the person threatening you, a teacher or a friend)

Role play 3

You've studied and prepared well for this test, but as you start to read it you realise that you studied the wrong unit of work. You have some idea about the questions, but it isn't good. Role-play a possible positive solution, even though this is a tough situation. If time permits, replay it showing what might happen if you used a negative mindset and negative self-talk. (A pair – you show the actions and another person can speak as your internal self-talk)

15 Role-play cards: Switching on positivity

continued . . .

Role play 4

You've just received a text from your girlfriend/boyfriend. They're breaking up with you. It feels awful and you didn't see it coming. You're shocked! In one scenario, show us how a positive mindset might help to keep you calm and reach out for help from close friends. In another scenario, present how angry thinking drives you to react badly and encourage others to act badly. (A group of three – you and two friends)

Role play 5

Kim is a good long-term friend, but is different to you. You're into friends, fun and gaming. Kim is quiet, loyal to you, doesn't have many friends, works part-time in a pet rescue centre and adores coding. A few of your friends have started to comment about Kim's quirkiness. In your role play, show how you respond to your friends' negative comments about Kim with clever positivity, which allows them to appreciate more about Kim. (A group of three or four – you and friends)

Role play 6

You are frustrated with your parents because it seems their favourite word to you is 'no'. There's a party coming up that you really want to go to. In this role play, show us how you'd approach and discuss this with your parents to find a positive solution. Then replay it showing how things would probably work out if you chose to use a negative attitude and aggressive talk. (A group of three – you and your parents)

---

15 Role-play cards: Switching on positivity

continued . . .

Role play 7

You've received a low grade in the test you just got back. In the first scenario, you and a friend talk. The conversation illustrates how a positive attitude helps you to see that there's no such thing as a 'bad day'. It's just that this thing hasn't turned out well, and you can fix it next time by doing something differently. In the second scenario, you and a friend are talking, but this time we see your negative mind catastrophising and turning it into a disaster. (A pair – you and your friend)

Role play 8

One of your friends confidentially tells you that they've been trying marijuana some days over the last week or so. Obviously, this really worries you because you care for them and know the risks. In the first role play, we watch the most positive you – a great listener and a wise friend. In the second role play, you allow yourself to become negative and fearful and completely overreactive. (A pair – you and your friend)

Wellbeing and social media

"Archie, get off your phone! You're addicted to it!"

Key social and emotional principles (learning intention)

Wellbeing is a mindset, a way of thinking. It is deeper than happiness. It is reflected by a prevailing attitude to regulate our feelings as we face the tribulations of life. We build wellbeing by valuing healthy relationships with friends and family, being keen to find positive solutions to problems, sharing complications with valued others, and striking a healthy balance between all things in life. When we fail to balance these things, our sleep, fitness, memory, emotions, tolerance, learning and relationships are worse off.

Materials required for this lesson

- Name tags.

- Chairs in a social circle for students to sit on.

- Whiteboard/butcher's paper and markers.

- Write a simple outline of the lesson on the whiteboard/butcher's paper for students to follow.

- Display the *What's the Buzz?* group values (located in the introduction or at www.whatsthebuzz.net.au/main-menu/content-whats-the-buzz-with-teenagers).

- Organise feedback and reminder cards, or similar, to strengthen responsive behaviours (located in the introduction or at www.whatsthebuzz.net.au/main-menu/content-whats-the-buzz-with-teenagers).

- Have Archie's story ready to read to students. This can be done directly from this lesson. Or, for a small registration fee, you can download the 16 Archie stories as you want them. Each story contains text, audio in the form of the authors reading to your students, and two large illustrations in full colour that will fill your screen. Access is available at www.whatsthebuzz.net.au/main-menu/content-whats-the-buzz-with-teenagers

- Pencils, pens and paper for students to do Part 1 of *Show me the Buzz*.

- Arrange students into pairs, with a device to share and with an internet connection, to complete 'Group research and presentation' and 'Lead students to explore technology designed to promote mindfulness' in Part 1 of *Show me the Buzz*.

- A set of coloured pencils and the task sheet 'Which mindfulness activity is best for you?' in Part 1 of *Show me the Buzz* (located at the end of the lesson or at www.whatsthebuzz.net.au/main-menu/content-whats-the-buzz-with-teenagers).

- Prepare handouts for parents(s):

    One copy of this lesson for each parent to read.

    One copy of *After the Buzz: Social thinking ideas for parents and caregivers* to send home (located at the end of the lesson, ready to photocopy, or at www.whatsthebuzz.net.au/main-menu/content-whats-the-buzz-with-teenagers).

Lesson 4

Explanation

The pursuit of wellbeing has continued over the centuries. We have a good idea that it was being taught around 2,500 years ago in China, Greece and India with great thinkers such as Confucius, Socrates and Buddha, respectively. These thinkers saw the virtues of goodness, compassion, tolerance and integrity as the real wealth in human beings. Today, we refer to this state of thinking as 'wellbeing', and understand it as the basis for human beings to flourish.

Wellbeing is a mindset to live a balanced physical, emotional and psychological life. It is beyond simply being happy or having good health. It gives us a framework to:

- discover and explore our strengths;

- build meaning into life;

- find happiness and contentment;

- foster good relationships with those we love, as well as with outsiders who cross our paths;

- develop altruism and contribute to a greater society;

- lose ourselves in things we find challenging, enjoyable and rewarding;

- cleverly self-manage our emotions;

- build social supports and self-efficacy; and

- emerge from setbacks knowing we have a resiliency to cope with adversity.

Wellbeing is the 'guardian' of our mental health. It places us in a position to enrich the emotional lives of others, and appreciate them, as they enrich ours. Yet many struggle to keep the poise in their lives that creates healthy wellbeing. If it's so good for us, how do we improve wellbeing or get more of it? The experts often promote five keys to wellbeing, and they are based on the evidenced-based principles of positive psychology:

1 *Connect with people.* Having a minimum of three people who are supportive, encouraging and loyal is highly protective. Quality people are more important than sheer numbers of connections.

2 *Be active, and eat and sleep well.* We all know that higher levels of physical activity, even daily walking, protects against feelings of depression and

anxiety at every age. Studies also show that people who eat a balanced diet (especially fibre and fresh fruit and vegetables) have lower rates of mental illness as adults and adolescents. Diet also affects the gut microbiota, which in turn affects our mental health (Bertrand and Jackson, 2017). Evidence suggests the relationship between sleep problems, anxiety and depression is entwined. On the one hand, higher levels of worry while trying to fall asleep makes it difficult to get enough sleep, and, on the other hand, not getting enough sleep causes more anxiety (Anxiety and Depression Association of America, 2017).

3 *Connect yourself to the environment, and become aware about what you're sensing, feeling and thinking.* Consider redesigning your home or workspace so it gives a heightened sense of freedom, connection and choices. This is where mindfulness begins. The more in touch we are with our environment, the better we'll feel and the better our wellbeing. As Winston Churchill famously said, "We shape our buildings; thereafter they shape us." More and more educators understand that students' wellbeing and optimal learning outcomes cannot be separated. Teachers are now building comfortable, engaging and respectful spaces in classrooms that invite students to interact and learn in a variety of ways. It's a delight to walk through some of these new and soothing classrooms:

wooden pallets, stacked, clipped together and finished beautifully to make low, wide tables with cushions scattered around them;

groups of tall tables for students to stand at while they work;

egg chairs hanging from the ceiling;

pot plants, mini gardens on wheels, PVC pipe planters that bring nature into the classroom;

small stools, tall stools, traditional chairs, cushions, couches, armchairs and fitness balls as seating options;

spaces and opportunity for quiet times or meditation;

classroom designs that offer visual tranquillity and feel inviting;

groups of working spaces, balanced with plenty of flexible floor space;

small Balinese huts built as reading or quiet spaces filled with large cushions;

both fixed and portable technologies;

tepees and tents that encourage withdrawal for quiet moments, to chat, work or read; and

large and mini Zen spaces with mats on the floor so students can peacefully refocus as they design the garden using patterns and textures.

In addition, specific mindfulness activities are offered to help students engage in the now, rather than obsessing over something that just happened and becoming anxious, angry or destructive. It is a type of self-awareness and self-regulatory training that takes no special skills, and is so flexible and utterly valuable.

4   *Keep on learning because learning lifts human beings.* First, it connects us socially. Second, it boosts our sense of worth and confidence. Third, achievement promotes wellbeing. When we choose and chase goals that match our values and interests, the more engaged we feel about learning and life too.

5   *Wellbeing is improved when we do something for someone else.* Evidence shows that committing an act of kindness, even once a week, helps us improve our levels of wellbeing. So, get out and do things for others! Start with a smile.

Young adolescents have a lot to juggle. It's a time when the brain and body are rapidly changing and adapting, along with a serious surge of hormones. Also, social media has added a new dimension. While it brings many advantages, it is a medium that is too alluring for some. For a few, it virtually replaces face-to-face social settings. And it is the nature of social media to expose young people to the superficial social lives of too many, which is not always real, appropriate, inclusive or safe. So, what is a parent, caregiver or teacher to do? Our best advice is to continue to be available to parent and teach at all stages of adolescence. Yes, they will rebel against our constraints at home and at school in their search for independence, but they need our certainty, security and reassurance. Because the pull to peers is strong, most adolescents do not do well with adults who are too controlling or get steamed up too fast. At every stage, adolescents are not children, but they are not wired as adults for a very long time.

1. *What's the Buzz?*

Actively greet students as they enter. Provide chairs in a social circle for them to sit on and have a brief lesson plan on the whiteboard or butcher's paper for students to see. As students are settling, hand each of them a 'Thumbs up feedback card' to highlight their thoughtful behaviour and using the group values.

Let's begin

Ask students if they know what wellbeing means. Take a few responses, but do not comment. Explain that you have a 'fact or myth' quiz to test their understanding about wellbeing. To play, they will need to stand up when they hear a fact about wellbeing and stay seated if they think the statement is a myth. Warn them to be focused because you'll move fast!

Statements – fact or myth?

1 Wellbeing is a new, trendy idea.

2 You can buy wellbeing at a health shop.

3 Not getting enough sleep or eating badly can harm your wellbeing.

4 Wellbeing comes when you have heaps of money, great cars, a mansion and you're popular.

5 There's nothing you can do to get wellbeing because it is genetic.

6 Wellbeing is just being happy. So, make yourself feel happy!

7 Happiness comes and goes. Wellbeing is bigger.

8 Wellbeing improves with the number of likes you get on Facebook.

9 Wellbeing is living a balanced life that also allows us to enrich the lives of others.

10 Wellbeing is big. It's psychological, emotional, social, physical, cognitive, spiritual and environmental.

11 You can be physically well but have poor wellbeing.

12 You can have a lot of money but have poor wellbeing.

13 Wellbeing changes. In one situation, you might feel happy, connected and confident, but not the same way in another situation.

14 There are things you can do to improve your wellbeing.

Archie's story: "Archie, get off your phone! You're addicted to it!"

It was Friday afternoon, school was finished, and holidays had begun. Archie needed the break. He felt sluggish and heavy, from his tired mind right through to every exhausted muscle. He hadn't been getting enough sleep and had stopped walking his whippets because he always had schoolwork to do. He missed his old freer life that he had back at primary school.

Early tomorrow morning, he was flying off with his family for their first overseas holiday. The plan was to be up at 4 a.m. and ready for an 8 a.m. flight. He felt excited about it but had planned to stay in touch with his friends through Instagram and Facebook. Both of these social media platforms, as well as YouTube, had become important for Archie because he could follow the things he loved and now it was all at his fingertips! Top of his list was music and musicians, some hilarious YouTubers, then Ninja Warrior competitions, the whippets doing flyball at Crufts dog show, drone aerial competitions

16 Archie's story: "Archie, get off your phone! You're addicted to it!" – first image

Lauren Eldridge Murray

This image can be downloaded from http://whatsthebuzz.net.au/main-menu/content-whats-the-buzz-with-teenagers and will fill your screen in colour. There is also the option to have the authors read the story to students.

and amazing drone photos. Archie loved to grab his phone, find a comfy spot and scroll through his favourite feeds. Before he knew it, hours flew by.

Social media helped Archie and his friends to stay in touch, swap ideas and amuse themselves. Together, they had set up a group account on Instagram to organise catch-ups and share. Friendships were the backbone of his life. Being connected to them kept him feeling that life was good. They held him accountable when his decisions were dodgy, and he did the same for them.

Archie's mum didn't understand what it felt like to be part of this new way of being connected to friends and to the world. "Archie, get off your phone!" "Archie, you're addicted to it!" "Archie, you're a slave to your phone!" she'd shout repeatedly. Archie wished she could understand just how important his phone was. He wasn't addicted or a slave to it – he just liked it and needed it! Lately, he'd started taking his phone to bed to check his feeds as he fell asleep, and this is when the unthinkable happened.

It was about 9 p.m. and he was in bed to grab a few hours of sleep. As he was scrolling through his feeds, a message from Rafi came through. Then another from Tobias, then one from Ayman, then Joanna, Daisy and more from others he knew at school. Archie couldn't believe it. Message after message, photo after photo, about a party they were all at. Archie knew nothing about it. No one had bothered to tell him.

A million questions raced through his head. "Why wasn't I invited?" "Why didn't someone say something to me?" "Don't they realise I can see all this?" "Are they trying to tell me to get lost?" "Do they realise this is upsetting?" "I'd never do this to them." Archie felt disappointed, angry and lonely. It left him with so many unanswered questions. All he wanted to do was to respond and let them know how mean they were. But he didn't do that. He cared too much about his friends to do it. By 1 a.m., the messaging had stopped and he drifted into a restless sleep. Even asleep, his mind replayed every happy message and party photo that had been sent between his friends.

At 4 a.m., his mother tiptoed into his room and turned on the lamp. "Good morning darling – it's time to get up, get moving and get to the airport."

"Go away," he grunted from under his pillow.

Archie froze. Did he just tell his mum to 'go away' at the start of a family holiday? He hated what he just said to Mum because he knew it hurt her feelings. He didn't mean it. Then the deeper misery of last night flooded back. He desperately wanted to stay under his quilt.

17 Archie's story: "Archie, get off your phone! You're addicted to it!" – second image

Lauren Eldridge Murray

This image can be downloaded from http://whatsthebuzz.net.au/main-menu/content-whats-the-buzz-with-teenagers and will fill your screen in colour. There is also the option to have the authors read the story to students.

Discussion based on the questions and statements below will occur later in *Do you know the Buzz?* For now, simply read them to get students thinking. Encourage them to listen and respond to each question by putting their thumb up if they 'agree' or think 'yes', thumb down if they think 'no', and thumb to the side if they think 'maybe'. Move very quickly through them. No verbal responses are required.

Your thoughts on these statements and questions?

- Do you and your friends use social media to stay in touch?

- Do your parents nag you to get off your phone?

- Do they think you're addicted?

- Who takes their phone to bed like Archie?

- Is there anything wrong with taking your phone to bed?

- Who knows they spend a bit too much time on their phone?

- Does the time you spend on social media and gaming make it hard to balance other things in your life?

- Have you had a bad experience using social media?

- Did Archie overreact to what he saw on Instagram?

- Should Archie's friends have told him about the party?

- Can you think of a positive reason why his friends did not tell him?

- Was he wise to not respond and have a go at them? Would you have held back or let them have it?

- If you have a party and not everyone is invited, would you still openly talk about it in a group chat?

- Can you think of a private way Archie could find out more about the party and why he wasn't invited?

- Who has taken their frustration out on a parent like Archie did? Why are we more likely to behave like this with our parents?

2. *Show me the Buzz*

Show me the Buzz provides students with the opportunity to discuss a variety of social and emotional ideas, absorb the thoughts of others, debate them, create role plays and receive feedback from the group. We have learned that this approach heightens understandings and the transference of skills. There is always a Part 1 and a Part 2. Choose one activity from either Part 1 or Part 2, depending on what appeals to you, the time you have and your group's likely preferences. There's plenty of content in *Show me the Buzz*, so the lesson can be revisited time and time again while continuing with this same topic.

Part 1

1. In pairs or individually, continue writing Archie's story as a series of text messages

Archie has a trusted group of friends, so it's obvious they meant no harm to him. Most likely, they chose not to tell him about the party because they respected he was going away, needed to pack and had to get some sleep. Start the story as Archie snaps at his mother. What should he say next to her? Then once he arrives at the airport, should he send a group text to express his upset to the group? Or is it better to privately message someone? Who should he send a private message to?

Let's see a series of text messages trying to sort this out. Also keep in mind that his friends included him in the group texting, and this was a vote of confidence in the strength of their relationship with him. After all, they didn't try to keep anything a secret!

2. Group discussion and problem-solve

As a group, brainstorm five *possible* reasons (positive and negative) why Archie was not invited to the party. Record these for students to see. Then next to each reason, write *likely* or *not likely* using all the information and history you have about Archie and his friends. Take a group vote to decide. Discard the *not likely* reasons and do not act on them, just as we do in life. Next, discuss thoughtful ways Archie could deal with each *likely* situation and record the idea. Now the stage is set to take this to the next level! Organise groups of two, three or four to role-play each scenario. Consider filming the role plays. It is a good idea to encourage several role-play groups to use the same idea, so personal positive variations can be seen.

3. Explore the term 'wellbeing'

Initially, break students into pairs. Each pair will need a blank A4 sheet of paper and a pen or pencil to record with. Set the pairs of students up with a tablet or laptop, access to Google, a dictionary and a thesaurus, and encourage them to draw on their own collective vocabularies. Their task is to generate as many words as possible that are linked to wellbeing. Here are a few: healthy, happy, successful, balanced, advantage, good fortune, protection, satisfaction, robustness, contentedness and wellness. Give students 15 minutes to do this, and then collate everyone's answers, so a comprehensive list is shared. The intention is for students to grasp the vast scope of this term, and to see that wellbeing is the 'guardian' of our mental health. Without our wellbeing, we have little else!

4. Group research and presentation

First, arrange students into pairs with a device to share and an internet connection. Ask them to choose one of the topics below, or you can assign topics to them.

Remind students that they will be presenting their findings to the class in a subsequent lesson:

- Use the websites below to find a meaning of wellbeing that you like and understand. Record it, show where it came from, and explain why you like it.

  1 www.betterhealth.vic.gov.au/health/healthyliving/wellbeing

  2 www.blackdoginstitute.org.au/clinical-resources/wellness/general-wellbeing

  3 www.habitsforwellbeing.com/what-is-wellbeing/

- Review the websites below. The task is to choose two that are especially useful for teens. Show the class the positive highlights from these websites and explain why you ranked these as the best.

  1 www.abc.net.au/health/

  2 https://familydoctor.org/understanding-your-teens-emotional-health/

  3 https://youngminds.org.uk/

  4 http://raisingchildren.net.au/articles/mental_health_teenagers.html

- We know that wellbeing has been talked about for centuries. Great thinkers such as Confucius, Socrates and Buddha made many statements around wellbeing. Collect six of their statements that capture good ideas about how to live a healthy life. Record them and be ready to explain the ones you most appreciate.

  1 www.habitsforwellbeing.com/20-wise-quotes-from-confucius/

  2 https://simplelifestrategies.com/wisdom-from-socrates-inspiring-quotes/

  3 http://quotesnsmiles.com/quotes/calming-buddha-quotes/

- What is mindfulness? How is it connected to wellbeing? Find five mindfulness-styled activities that you like. Explain these five and then teach one to the class. Remember to organise instructions, images and resources. The best teachers always do a little practice first!

  1 https://au.reachout.com/articles/how-to-practice-mindfulness

  2 http://mindfulnessatwork.ie/what-is-mindfulness/

  3 www.telegraph.co.uk/lifestyle/wellbeing/diet/4124815/Health-advice-50-ways-to-boost-your-wellbeing.html

- When we feel stressed, our breathing rate and rhythm changes as part of our fight or flight response. Research shows that if we control our breathing, we manage our response to stress much better. Your task is to find several ways, some novel, to use controlled breathing. Choose one or two to teach the rest of the class. YouTube is helpful – begin with these:

Lesson 4

1 Square breathing technique – www.youtube.com/watch?v=mgzh KW08bMQ

2 Feeling anxious? Take deep breaths in sync with this! – www.youtube.com/watch?v=Wdbbtgf05Ek

3 Take 5 breathing – www.youtube.com/watch?v=sh79w9pn9Cg

4 Playful ways to teach deep breathing – www.encourageplay.com/blog/playful-ways-to-teach-deep-breathing

- Research 'progressive muscle relaxation'. This is a process where you tense up muscles and then relax them. The exercise helps to lower tension and stress levels, especially anxious feelings. Find more detailed information to share with the group. Prepare to take the group through a 'progressive muscle relaxation' exercise so they can experience it. Start your learning with these:

1 A six-minute mindful progressive muscle relaxation – www.youtube.com/watch?v=9x3tl81NW3w

2 Deep muscle relaxation technique – www.youtube.com/watch?v=Dz7isY92LzM

3 Progressive muscle relaxation – www.adolescentwellness.org/wpcontent/uploads/2011/06/Relaxation_Exercises_for_Adolescents_and_Adults.pdf

5. Which mindfulness activity is best for you?

Let's view mindfulness as a set of tools or strategies that soothe jangly feelings. There's a huge variety. Their job is to bring us into a more peaceful state of mind by encouraging the threat centre of the brain to stand down while the prefrontal cortex comes back online, allowing us to think more rationally. The best results occur when we continually use the same two or three ideas. Through repetition, our favourite ideas become embedded, and consequently become our 'go-to'. The worst approach is to never practise them and expect someone to use them when they're stressed! In this exercise, each student will need a printed sheet called 'Which mindfulness activity is best for you?' and a set of coloured pencils. This activity can be printed from the photocopiable section at the end of this lesson. Direct students to work in small groups, so they can discuss their choices with each other. First, suggest they colour the kaleidoscope in a classic symmetrical pattern. As they are colouring, ask the group to choose their top 10 mindfulness activities and strongly shade these areas.

6. Group discussion: How might we redesign our classroom so it adds to our wellbeing?

After all, wellbeing and optimum learning outcomes cannot be separated. Ask students to contribute ideas to make the classroom more inviting, more interactive and better cater for individual learning preferences. Here are a few clips to help introduce quality into the discussion:

- Innovative learning environments: form follows function – www.youtube.com/watch?v=8lOKS8Mv-8M

- Flexible learning environments – www.youtube.com/watch?v=O_x4OLsfReQ

- Flexible classroom seating – www.youtube.com/watch?v=I5p_88Pb_G0

- Flexible classrooms: making space for personalized learning – www.youtube.com/watch?v=jQkL5efkViw

- Flexible classrooms: providing the learning environment that kids need – www.youtube.com/watch?v=4cscJcRKYxA

In these clips, there are many ideas that could be easily developed in your own situation. Which ones appeal to you and your students? List them and see what you can implement!

7. Lead students to explore technologies designed to promote mindfulness

There are many emerging programs and apps that supplement the cultivation of good mental health. For this activity, students will require a device and an internet connection. Assign one of the programs below to each of them. Or you may encourage them to work in pairs. Give them plenty of time to explore, experiment and form a critical opinion. Their goals are:

1   Rate the activity using a five-star rating system (5/5 = brilliant, 3/5 = okay, 1/5 = poor). Justify the rating.

2   Briefly demonstrate how the activity works.

3   Critically review what's good and what's not so good.

It is a good idea to have several groups reviewing the same program so multiple perspectives are given:

- *Monument Valley* (www.monumentvalleygame.com): A tranquil puzzle game inspired by the joy of exploration. Relaxing and therapeutic.

- *Viridi* (www.icewatergames.com/viridi): A meditative app. Nurture a small pot of succulents that grow in real time. Here's a safe haven and a beautiful place to return to peace and quiet.

- *Thomas Was Alone* (www.mikebithellgames.com/thomaswasalone): Enjoy the social journey, the relaxing narrative and visuals. It is a platform puzzler accessible to all ages, and works well as a friendly distraction and introduction to social issues.

- *Prune* (www.prunegame.com): A serene puzzle with stunning visuals. It emphasises cultivating good mental health ("Cultivate what matters. Cut away the rest"). Play and discuss.

- *Smiling Mind* (www.smilingmind.com.au): An Australian mindfulness meditation smartphone app with versions for adults, teens and kids. It's free, has soothing colours, a simple design and is enjoyable to use. Each age group is given a set of guided meditations designed to bring users from a beginning level to a 'mindful master' level over time.

- *Breath of Light* (www.manymonkeysdev.com/breathoflight): A meditative Zen flow puzzle game. Players rearrange mystical stones to guide light through a mysterious world and bring it back to life. No timing or scoring, just the wish to solve puzzles as beautifully as possible.

- *Minecraft* (www.minecraft.net/en): A place of relief and creativity. Players build their own world in their own way. They can complete quests and battle or choose to have complete safety to create their own private world.

- *GoNoodle* (www.gonoodle.com): It's deep! GoNoodle is best presented to a class on an interactive whiteboard. Choose a game. It walks students through introductions, warm-up routines and the game itself. A tally in the dashboard keeps track of the minutes of each activity, points gained and medals won. While it's a great way to give students a quick burst of physical activity, there are plenty of those quieter mindfulness-styled activities too.

8. Make Zen gardens

The effort to create a Zen garden (meditation garden) brings calm, concentration and focus to people of all ages. The Zen garden originated in Japan over 1,000 years ago. Usually, it features an enclosed area of coarse sand or fine gravel, which represents the ocean, and the rocks or other objects create islands. A mini rake is used to create the waves in the gravel. As always, a picture is worth a thousand words, so Google images of 'small Zen gardens on trays' and you'll be inspired. Share some of these images (http://smallgarden-ideas.com/miniature-zen-garden) with students too. There's also a great app called iZen Garden for iPad. Wooden trays are a perfect container to build a Zen garden, and bamboo mini rakes are inexpensive.

Part 2: Role plays – wellbeing and social media

The role plays are in the photocopiable section at the end of this lesson. They are also available online at www.whatsthebuzz.net.au/main-menu/content-whats-the-buzz-with-teenagers. You may either read them to students, or print them and hand each group a role play. Help students to form small groups. Each role-play card states the number of students required. It does not matter if the same role play is given to several groups. Give students a few minutes to rehearse, and move between groups to provide plenty of coaching and enthusiasm.

Next, ask each group to perform their role play. If a student does not wish to perform, allow them to pass. So much can be learned through observing. Always perform role plays in the middle of the social circle. Consider capturing the action on video or photo by using your iPad, camera or smartphone. Encourage others to give constructive feedback after each role play.

3. *Do you know the Buzz?*

Do you know the Buzz? is a lively group 'discussion time' where students briefly respond to a series of questions and statements highlighted by Archie's story. The goal is for them to exchange ideas, and in the process 'mind map' their way more empathically through the complexities of social and emotional situations. This should also provide facilitators with an insight into the depth of student understandings. To do this, have students sitting on chairs in a social circle.

Your thoughts on these statements and questions?

- Do you and your friends use social media to stay in touch? Which platforms do you prefer?

- Do your parents nag you to get off your phone?

- Do they think you're addicted?

- Who takes their phone to bed like Archie? Is there anything wrong with taking your phone to bed?

- Who knows they spend a bit too much time on their phone?

- Does the time you spend on social media and gaming make it hard to balance other things in your life?

- Have you had a bad experience using social media?

- Did Archie overreact to what he saw on Instagram?

- Was he wise to not respond and have a go at them? Would you have held back or let them have it?

- Should Archie's friends have told him about the party?

- Can you think of a positive reason why his friends did not tell him?

- If you have a party and not everyone is invited, would you still openly talk about it in a group chat?

- Can you think of a private way Archie could find out more about the party and why he wasn't invited?

- Who has taken their frustration out on a parent like Archie did? Why are we more likely to behave like this with our parents?

4. The Buzz

The Buzz is an opportunity for the group to play games that strengthen their relationships and the skills central to the lesson.

Game: Widen the network (passive)

We have learned that people with strong family or social connections generally have better levels of wellbeing than those who lack support networks. It's vital to encourage students to understand what support networks are and how to develop them. This activity does just that! Sit together on seats, side by side, in a straight line. Frame the activity by reminding the group how important healthy relationships are to maintaining good wellbeing. Let them know you'll be calling out the names of various people, places and organisations that offer guidance, good advice, friendship and support. Explain that if they see value in the idea, they are to stay seated. If the idea does not appeal to them, they are to stand up, take five steps away from their chair, and turn and face the students who are still sitting. Ask students who remained seated to volunteer why they value the networking option just mentioned. Once the volunteers have given their opinion, the students who are standing return to their seats and the activity continues.

Here are the networking options: "Who has found value in using . . .

- . . . the school counsellor/psychologist/social worker/youth worker/chaplain?"

- . . . their GP?"

- . . . a teacher, past or present?"

- . . . your mother?"

- . . . your father?"

- . . . a brother?"

- . . . a sister?"

- . . . an aunt?"

- . . . an uncle?"

- . . . a cousin?"

- . . . a grandma?"

- . . . a grandpa?"

- . . . a family friend?"

- . . . a school friend?"

- . . . a friend outside of school, such as a neighbour?"

- . . . a friend's mother?"

- . . . a friend's father?"

- . . . a sports coach?"

- . . . a youth group?"

- . . . a youth group leader?"

- . . . Scouts, Guides or Rangers?"

- . . . a neighbour?"

- . . . an online friend?"

- . . . a kids helpline, a teen line or something like that?"

Game: How would you know, and what would you do? Prove it! (moderately exciting)

This is a group challenge where the students are to imagine that the wellbeing of a good friend is at risk. The group must work together to complete this two-part challenge within four minutes. First, they must identify 10 revealing or telltale signals that warn us a friend may be struggling with their wellbeing (signals may include talking less than usual, not joining in as much, flatter/less energetic, not looking after their personal hygiene, looking sad, more emotional, teary, arguing more often, not turning up to school or things they said they would, and so on). Second, they must come up with 10 simple ideas to support this friend.

Before you begin timing, be sure the group understands the challenge, and set yourself up with a marker and whiteboard ready to record their responses. Give the group a chance to begin thinking, then it's ready, set, go!

Game: Share jokes together (passive)

Everyone enjoys a good laugh, and we're beginning to see that laughter has wonderful benefits for our wellbeing.

Laughter boosts happiness, relationships, memory, learning and resilience. Encourage your group to remember a favourite joke or two they can share with the group. Make sure you have a couple to contribute too! Then enjoy taking turns. If you have a group likely to be missing the spontaneity of joke-telling, take the initiative and bring in a selection of joke books for them to peruse together first.

Game: "Come back!" (passive)

Often our mind wanders, and we suddenly catch ourselves being too caught up in a worry about the future, or guilt or regret about something from the past. Introduce a therapeutic idea called "Come back!" because it can wash away unwanted thoughts that randomly creep into our minds. To begin, ask the group to share one of their happiest memories – places, people or events that give them happy, connected and safe feelings. Begin by sharing a special one of your own. Once they have shared and listened to each other, introduce the idea of "Come back!" Explain that when they notice worrying thoughts reappearing, they simply say to themselves, "Come back!" as a cue to take several deep breaths and refocus on this soothing thought for a few moments.

Game: Body scan (passive)

The body scan nudges people away from feeling too anxious, upset or angry by encouraging them to be in the present. Use it lying down or sitting up. Ask your group to find a space on the floor and sit or lay. Have them listen to this three-minute guided meditation, produced by UCLA's Mindful Awareness Research Center (MARC): http://marc.ucla.edu. It can be played and down-loaded from MARC's website. To do so, use this link: http://marc.ucla.edu/mindful-meditations. Also, the transcript can be printed if you prefer to read it to your students. Research suggests that using this mindful exercise before sleep reduces problems getting off to sleep, as well as problems with fatigue and depression (Essig, 2015).

After the Buzz: Social thinking ideas for parents and caregivers

Lesson: Wellbeing and social media

Key social and emotional principles (learning intention)

Wellbeing is a mindset, a way of thinking. It is deeper than happiness. It is reflected by a prevailing attitude to regulate our feelings as we face the tribulations of life. We build wellbeing by valuing healthy relationships with friends and family, being keen to find positive solutions to problems, sharing complications with valued others, and striking a healthy balance between all things in life. When we fail to balance these things, our sleep, fitness, memory, emotions, tolerance, learning and relationships are worse off.

After the Buzz presents further ideas for parents, guardians and educators to encourage the generalisation of the social and emotional thinking students have touched on during the lesson. All children rely on us to consolidate these skills by positively modelling them, and emphasising the language and ideas used in the lesson. As always, here are a few practical ideas to help children build wellbeing.

Do you know what makes a happy and resilient teen?

A comprehensive study on life satisfaction and material wellbeing on children in the UK identified:

- Having good friends.

- Having friends over for dinner once a fortnight.

- Playing sport.

- Those who went swimming once a month were also happier with their lives than those who did not.

- An emotionally stable home life.

- Those who had their own bedroom, a bike or other leisure equipment.

- Those experiencing a healthy lifestyle.

- A sense of belonging to community through sporting, religious or special interest groups.

- Good behaviour from their classmates during lessons.

There was little difference in the average life satisfaction score of children in families with lower incomes compared with those living in families with higher incomes. Interestingly, access to the internet for up to one hour a day boosted contentment, but more time than this spent on social media became a feature of an unhappier teen (Gundi, 2013).

Keep calm and build an emotionally stable home

The link between too much stress in the lives of children and mental health problems is now well established. When stressed, there's a release of chemicals in our bodies. First is the release of adrenaline, which provides an increased heart rate because that's what's needed to escape a bully, a frightening situation or a rampaging parent. If the threat continues, our body advances to a new state of high alert, and a stress hormone called cortisol kicks in to help with the fight or flight response to the perceived threat.

Unfortunately, the symptoms of too much cortisol include weight gain, especially around the tummy and face, fragile, slow-to-heal skin, acne and irregular menstrual periods, as well as negative impacts on rational thinking, memory and the immune system. This constant additional input of cortisol seriously effects the way a child's brain grows. Rational thinking, memory and our immune system don't set up anywhere nearly as strongly as they should. Instead, most of the action switches to the emotional or low part of the brain. So, what we see in children growing up living with chronic stress is serious damage to their wellbeing. We witness significant increases in hyperactivity, hyper-vigilance and impulsive behaviours, all because of the way their brain has been forced to wire up in those first few precious years of life.

Praise tips the balance

Children of all ages thrive when they hear how their intention, effort or hard work has made a difference. Be sure to praise the process they have been involved in and highlight their effort by saying, "You've worked hard on this, well done!" or "You've stuck with it. Your effort has paid off!" or "Impressive. You used your stubbornness for good!" This way, your child knows you have noticed their endeavour, not simply the outcome. This is important for a young person's wellbeing as it takes the pressure off performance perfection, and allows them to enjoy the process of having a go and learning for the joy itself. From this, they gain greater self-confidence, and feel more relaxed, balanced and capable of persevering.

As if you need to be reminded, teens aren't renowned for spoiling you with help, or doing chores or getting their homework done, so when they do, be sure to offer a few encouraging words. "Thank you" and "I appreciate your help" are clear ways of showing your appreciation, and set up the best chance that they'll do this again.

Keep boundaries clear

While teenagers will always push the limits and ask for flexibility around the rules, they also need someone who is emotionally steady, who can lead and keep them safe. They look to parents and caregivers for leadership. Hearing 'no' when it's fair and reasonable is vital for emotional wellbeing. A child, a teen or an adult who doesn't know the limits is more likely to behave inconsistently and selfishly. Parents and caregivers can help by being empathetic when setting limits, being flexible when necessary, listening to their child's needs, but maintaining clear guidance around where the boundaries lie. The ideal is to find ways to involve them in establishing the rules. By doing so, you show them you trust and value their ideas and opinions. When they are involved in the process, they have an investment and are more likely to follow what has been agreed on together.

Try to lower the stress and intensity in your life

Create simple family routines – favourite outings, meals, movies, jogging, walking, or start a card or board game night at home – so a family identity is created around shared interests. Spend just enough quality time together that contributes to a healthy emotional tone. It is also wise to do things on an individual basis with your children rather than always doing everything together. For example, we have a delightful dad as a client who has a regular date with his teenage daughter to watch *The Bachelor* and *The Bachelorette* together throughout the series. There's not a lot of chat, but it's their thing, and his daughter encourages it now! In addition, be respectful that young teens require more of their own space and independence than ever before. Work with them to find a balance.

Support them to try new things

Cleverly help your young teen to find the courage to step out of their comfort zone and build new skills. Encourage them to take on challenges as they naturally occur as it builds confidence and pride. When you see they are interested in something new but are not sure how to initiate it, be available to offer moral or physical support.

After the Buzz ... Lesson 4

Focus on their strengths

Adolescents feel secure when we radiate affectionate and accepting signals about them. Each of your kids have unique qualities, such as fairness, gentleness, reliability, persistence and determination, lovingness, loyalty, honesty, kindness, and many more. Grab a sheet of paper and assign five personal qualities/strengths to each of your children.

From now on, make a pledge to yourself that when you are talking to them, freely use these adjectives. By doing so, they will begin to understand the unique qualities/strengths you see in them.

Sleep sustains wellbeing

Pre-teens and teens need between 9 and 11 hours of sleep a night to revive, download new information and be alert for the new day. If you know your son or daughter isn't getting enough sleep, talk to them and see if you can come up with a plan together. Getting too little sleep disrupts hundreds of genes that are essential for good health (Sample, 2013). These genes govern the immune system, the metabolism and the body's response to stress. Getting enough sleep is one of the most powerful ways we can protect ourselves both physically and mentally. Sleep is the best tool for organisation, tolerance, continued learning, remaining at school and for wellbeing!

Healthy eating and wellbeing

Everything we eat influences our moods, our behaviour and our general health. Healthy eating means an emphasis on a balanced diet: vegetables, fruits, whole grains and whole milk products, with a balance of lean meats, poultry, fish, beans, eggs and nuts. Most important is to balance the kilojoules we take in with the kilojoules burned through physical activity. Without this balance, it is hard to maintain a healthy weight and vigor. In fact, we do know that in countries where the population eats higher levels of fish, they have lower levels of depression (Olson, 2015). Fish contains a fatty acid called EPA, which is lacking in those more inclined towards sadness and depression. If you and the kids won't eat fish, these good fatty acids are also found in flaxseed, walnuts and chia seeds.

Help create a balanced life for them

Help your teen keep a healthy balance between study, chores or part-time work, family time, socialising, screens, and sporting endeavours. At this age, it's very easy for them to become immersed in one thing for too long, which can compromise wellbeing. Try not to fall into the 'nagging trap'. It's too easy to do and is damaging

After the Buzz . . . Lesson 4

and unproductive. Step up, be clever, and structure their life where they're naturally involved in a variety of things.

References

Anxiety and Depression Association of America (2017) *Understand the Facts: Sleep Disorders.* Available at: https://adaa.org/understanding-anxiety/related-illnesses/sleep-disorders (accessed July 2018).

Bertrand, P. and Jackson, M. (2017) *Gut Microbiota: How It Affects Your Mood, Sleep and Stress Levels.* Available at: www.sbs.com.au/topics/life/health/article/2016/10/14/gut-microbiota-how-it-affects-your-mood-sleep-and-stress-levels (accessed July 2018).

Essig, T. (2015) *Disturbed Sleep Shown to Benefit from Mindfulness Training.* Available at: www.forbes.com/sites/toddessig/2015/02/27/disturbed-sleep-shown-to-benefit-from-mindfulness-training/#616e1f575be3 (accessed July 2018).

Gundi, K. (2013) *Life Satisfaction and Material Well-Being of Children in the UK.* Available at: www.iser.essex.ac.uk/research/publications/working-papers/iser/2012-15 (accessed July 2018).

Olson, S. (2015) *Eating Lots of Fish May Reduce Risk of Depression, Plus Other Mental Health Disorders Fish May Help.* Available at: www.medicaldaily.com/eating-lots-fish-may-reduce-risk-depression-plus-other-mental-health-disorders-fish-352100 (accessed July 2018).

Sample, I. (2013) *Sleeping Less Than Six Hours a Night Skews Activity of Hundreds of Genes.* Available at: www.theguardian.com/science/2013/feb/25/sleeping-six-hours-night-activity-genes (accessed July 2018).

After the Buzz . . . Lesson 4

18 Which mindfulness activity is best for you?

When we engage in a mindfulness exercise, we give ourselves the best chance to encourage the amygdala to stand down while the prefrontal cortex comes back on line, allowing us to think more clearly. Colour the kaleidoscope in a classic symmetrical pattern. Choose your top ten mindfulness activities shading these areas more strongly.

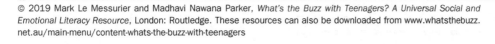

What's the Buzz with Teenagers?

19 Role-play cards: Wellbeing and social media

Role play 1

At the moment, it feels like homework is taking all evening, every evening. Your wellbeing is low because you're fed up with it. In this role play, we see you talking to two wise friends about how you're feeling. Together, you come up with several easy ideas to get homework out the way, put your life in balance and improve your wellbeing. (A group of three – you and your two wise friends)

Role play 2

Your parents are irritated by you. They say you're forgetting to do your chores and you've fallen into a habit of answering them back. You don't mean to, but the angrier they get at you, the worse your backbiting is becoming. However, you also know that your parents are struggling with money worries and this is putting the family's wellbeing at risk. In this role play, you decide to talk to your parents respectfully and warmly. (A group of four – you, your brother/sister and your parents)

Role play 3

Your friend is spending more and more time alone. They are no longer cheerful and lack energy. Also, they've opted out of catching up outside of school. You value their friendship, so in this role play you attempt to ask them, "What's going on?" They respond by saying, "Nothing. I'm fine." You know they are not fine. Even though they don't want to talk, what could you say and do that shows you care, and are there for them. (A pair – you and your friend)

What's the Buzz with Teenagers?

19 Role-play cards: Wellbeing and social media *continued . . .*

Role play 4

You're not happy, you can't sleep, you wake up tired, you're skipping meals, eating too much junk, obsessing over your phone and letting too much schoolwork slip by. You like your school counsellor, so decide to talk with them. This role play catches you and the school counsellor trying to work out what's going on. You're not surprised to realise that you have too much happening! Together, you work out what's been stressing you and a plan to get your life back into balance. (A pair – you and the school counsellor)

Role play 5

A new person has just started at school. They are spending more and more time with your group. You are the only one that knows they had a terrible time at their last school. They had to leave because they overreacted and hurt someone who had cruelly bullied them for a long time. They are very nice. Do you owe it to your friends to tell them about this person's past, or do you owe it to this person to let them make a fresh start with a great friendship group? In this role play, you decide to discuss the situation with your two older cousins. During the conversation, bring out both points of views, but the best idea is one that supports this person's wellbeing. (A group of three – you and your two older cousins)

Role play 6

Your year level is booked to do surfing lessons. Trying new things has always been tricky for you. But this is far worse because it's in the ocean. You're scared of the ocean and the sharks that are in it! You've been so distressed that you haven't slept much in the week leading up to it. The day before the surfing lessons are to begin, your teacher randomly asks how you're feeling about it. Tears well up in your eyes. In this role play, discuss how you're feeling with your teacher. Together, find a way to get through this. (A group of three – you, your friend and your teacher)

19 Role-play cards: Wellbeing and social media *continued . . .*

Role play 7

You're lying in bed and can't get to sleep because you're worrying about a disagreement you had with a close friend. It got sorted out and everything is fine. However, you feel bad because you were jealous when you really didn't need to be. In this role play, show three ways to calm your mind and fall back to sleep. (A group of four – you, laying in bed and thinking, and three others, who each become one of your positive thoughts – they act out, and say, one helpful thought each)

Role play 8

You've fallen into a habit of eating more junk food than you should. Pies, French fries and potato crisps are what you've been eating on the way to school, at recess, lunch and after school. It's making you feel sluggish and you want to do something to get your energy levels back on track. This role play shows you coming up with three brilliant ideas to make changes and eat well again. (A group of four – you and three friends trying hard to sort your food and fitness out)

Role play 9

Earlier today, your teacher asked your class two tough questions. They were "What do you believe in?" and "What puts meaning into your life?" The questions have irritated you because you don't have the answers. What annoyed you most was listening to others confidently talking about what they believe in, what their purpose in life is, and how this helps them to set goals to have the best future. This role play captures you and a group of close friends discussing these big questions in life. (A group of four – you and three friends)

Empathy

"Thanks for understanding"

Key social and emotional principles (learning intention)

Empathy is a core life skill. This lesson explores how to identify the feelings, thoughts or attitudes of others, and respond to them with a delicate balance of sensitivity and purpose. To develop empathic powers, several actions must occur. The first is to detect the emotions the other person is experiencing. Second, an empathic person communicates they understand how this person must be feeling. Finally, they do or say something to comfort them, or offer a possible solution. The goal is to lift their spirits, and this can be achieved by giving them hope. In dire situations, the only hope to be found may be the promise of an understanding and enduring friendship.

Materials required for this lesson

- Name tags.

- Chairs in a social circle for students to sit on.

- Whiteboard/butcher's paper/screen and markers.

- Create a simple outline of the lesson on the whiteboard/butcher's paper/ screen for students to follow.

- Display the *What's the Buzz?* group values (located in the introduction or at www.whatsthebuzz.net.au/main-menu/content-whats-the-buzz-with-teenagers).

- Organise feedback and reminder cards, or similar, to strengthen responsive behaviours (located in the introduction or at www.whatsthebuzz.net.au/main-menu/content-whats-the-buzz-with-teenagers, ready to print).

- Have Archie's story ready to read to students. This can be done directly from this lesson. Or, for a small registration fee, you can download the 16 Archie stories as you want them. Each story contains text, audio in the form of the authors reading to your students, and two large illustrations in full colour that will fill your screen. Access is available at www.whatsthebuzz.net.au/main-menu/content-whats-the-buzz-with-teenagers

- Pencils, pens and paper for students to do Part 1 of *Show me the Buzz*.

- Download the two or three images you require for the 'What's in a face?' activity in Part 1 of *Show me the Buzz*.

- Poster paper, textas and pencils for students to create empathy acrostic poems in Part 1 of *Show me the Buzz*.

- Gather together books, balls, shoes or jumpers ready to play 'Landmine' in Part 1 of *Show me the Buzz*.

- Print the role-play cards for 'Empathy' in Part 2 of *Show me the Buzz* (located at the end of the lesson or at www.whatsthebuzz.net.au/main-menu/content-whats-the-buzz-with-teenagers, ready to print).

- A coin to play the game 'Heads or tails?' in *The Buzz*.

- Print A4 sheets of paper and print the dots ready for students to play 'Dots and boxes' in *The Buzz*. Provide pencils too. Use this link to see how the dots on the page look: https://en.wikipedia.org/wiki/Dots_and_Boxes.

- Prepare handouts for parents(s):

    One copy of this lesson for each parent to read.

    One copy of *After the Buzz: Social thinking ideas for parents and caregivers* to send home (located at the end of the lesson, ready to photocopy, or at www. whatsthebuzz.net.au/main-menu/content-whats-the-buzz-with-teenagers).

Lesson 5

Explanation

For the purpose of this lesson, we describe empathy as the capacity to understand another person's situation, accurately assess their feelings and deliver a compassionate response that enriches their emotional situation. It is the idea of seeing a circumstance from their perspective, and in that moment, trying to feel what they must be feeling with a goal to support them.

The development of empathic skills takes time and practice. It starts with understanding our own feelings, so teaching children to identify their feelings leads them to better judge the feelings of others. The emergence of empathy is not automatically guaranteed either. Influences such as personality, temperament, intellectual ability, social/emotional opportunities, environmental circumstances, and the serendipity of positive or negative forces in one's life all contribute to shape the speed and profile of development (Stafford et al., 2016).

Some of us have well-developed empathic traits that allow us to tune into the predicaments of others more easily. As an example, a friend might explain that their mother is very sick and not responding to medical treatment. They tell you her prognosis is hopeless. While you've never lost or experienced a gravely sick parent, you can empathise. You can visualise the awful reality of not ever being able to touch, hold, talk with and confide in someone who has been there for you all your life. Your imagination is powerful enough to put yourself 'in the shoes of that other person'. Suddenly, on an emotional level, you appreciate the loss almost as if it is your loss. Your emotional responses may include sensations usually kept for when it is happening directly: a hollow, shocked feeling, tearfulness, a rise in breathing rate, disbelief or sadness. Remarkably, these feelings reflect your friend's despair.

To make things even more complicated, some of us lose our objectivity because we get so caught up in their emotion that we become ineffective. Conversely, some of us feel the dilemma facing another, and all we can do is bark tips to fix it. And there are a few who cannot echo to the emotional experiences of others. While they can intellectualise the situation, their emotional response falls short of what's really needed and expected.

Higher levels of empathy in children are a positive predictor of wellbeing and better academic achievement (Carnicer and Calderón, 2013). When a child can 'mind-read' how other people are feeling and knows how to care for them, they are less likely to bully, and more likely to build friendships, handle conflict constructively and feel better about themselves (Grühn et al., 2008). A person with empathy tends to appreciate differences in people and looks to the beauty of these differences. Those with scant supplies of empathy are more likely to be insular, reject differences, show less resilience, be defensive and act negatively about uneasy feelings (Ponischil, 2014) Finally, empathy also assists us to communicate our thoughts in a way that makes sense to another. As an empathic person is speaking, their empathy helps them to sense whether the listener is interested or not, whether they are grasping what is being conveyed and is feeling comfortable. This 'mind-reading' ability is a core life skill.

Finally, research tells us that for girls, cognitive empathy rises from the age of 13 years, and affective or emotional empathy remains relatively high and stable through adolescence. In boys, however, cognitive empathy begins rising from the age of 15 years, and there is a brief decline in emotional empathy between the ages of 13 and 16 years of age. It does, of course, improve later. The assumption is that the decline in emotional empathy among young adolescent males likely relates to a sharp increase in testosterone levels at this time. The intense rise in testosterone often inspires dominant behaviours in young males that oppose compassion, tolerance and understanding others. Also, adolescent males are influenced by social pressures telling them to 'act like a man', be tough, suck it up, and never show weakness by displaying emotions (Van der Graaff, 2014).

1. *What's the Buzz?*

Actively greet students as they enter. Provide chairs in a social circle for them to sit on and have a brief lesson plan on the whiteboard or butcher's paper for students to see. As students are settling, hand each of them a 'Thumbs up feedback card' to highlight their thoughtful behaviour and using the group values.

Let's begin

Ask the group, "Can you explain what empathy means?" and "Do you know how to do it?" Empathy is to be able to feel the world as another is feeling it. It is like acquiring a 'mind-reading' superpower that can be used to help and heal others! Ask, "Do you know the three empathic powers and their sequence?"

- *Empathic power 1*: Detect the emotions the other person is experiencing. To do this, stop, listen and tune into what's happening for this person. Ask a question or two for clarification. Listen to the feelings attached to their words. This isn't the time to offer your opinion or fix the problem. Just be in the moment with them.

- *Empathic power 2*: Say something short and simple that shows you understand how they must be feeling. You might say, "You have every right to feel so disappointed" or "I agree" (with a supportive sigh) or "I feel your frustration."

- *Empathic power 3*: Next, do or say something to comfort them, or something that gives hope. Refrain from giving a list of your ideas to fix the problem. You may lightly suggest an idea, but more empathetic is to state, "You know I'm here for you" or "What you're going through is tough, but we have your back" or "What can I do to help?"

Archie's story: "Thanks for understanding"

It was nearing the end of lunchtime, and Archie quietly moved away from his group of friends to find Joanna and spend some time with her. Catching up together had become an everyday thing as they both enjoyed being together without the others. He rounded the corner and could see Joanna waiting for him. That made him feel happy and urged him to walk with a bounce in his stride.

As Archie approached her, he sensed something wasn't right. Joanna didn't look up. She didn't shoot him the smile he loved and had become familiar to receiving from her. Instead, she stared at the ground. Her body leant forwards, her legs were drawn up to her chest and her arms were locked hard around her knees. She was gently rocking.

"Are you okay?" he asked softly as he sat down next to her.

"It's Mum. She had hyperglycaemia again and collapsed at work, but his time she hit her head and needs stitches," replied Joanna.

"What's happening now with her?" questioned Archie.

"Dad sent me a text. He's on his way to pick me up so we can see her in hospital," replied Joanna.

"I bet you're feeling shaken up," Archie commented. He moved closer, placed his arm around Joanna and drew her close to him. "You know it will be okay?"

"Sort of. But, it makes me feel scared. Makes me feel like nothing is for sure and I worry that Mum might die," shared Joanna.

"It is scary because they haven't sorted out your mum's new insulin pump yet. They said it would take time to get it right," Archie reassured Joanna.

"Yeah, and while they're trying to get it right, Mum's likely to die by splitting her head open and bleeding to death!" Joanna vented.

"Right now, it's scary, but your mum's determined to make this work. Plus, I remember you told me that 1 in 10 people have diabetes. And you know what that means, don't you? It means the doctors have had a lot a practice at treating diabetes! They'll get it right!" Archie said with a cheeky grin and a glint in his eyes.

"Thanks for being my friend. I know you're right. I just need to feel sad for a while. Want to throw me a pity party?" Joanna asked just as cheekily.

"Okay, you can have me and your pity party while we walk to the office and wait for your dad, but once he arrives he'll need your brave face," suggested Archie. Joanna smiled, and they walked to the school office together.

20 Archie's story: "Thanks for understanding" – first image

Lauren Eldridge Murray

This image can be downloaded from http://whatsthebuzz.net.au/main-menu/content-whats-the-buzz-with-teenagers and will fill your screen in colour. There is also the option to have the authors read the story to students.

After a short wait, Joanna's dad hurried into the foyer. He looked hot and stressed. Joanna took his hands and reassured him that everything would be all right. Archie noticed that Joanna had put her brave face on, ready to help her dad and her family.

Archie shook Joanna's father's hand and wished him the best, and they headed towards the door. Then, unexpectedly, Joanna turned, ran back to Archie, hugged him tightly and said, "Thanks for understanding."

As they drove off, Archie was left with one thought. Joanna had just given him the best hug ever and it felt good!

Discussion based on the questions and statements below will occur later in *Do you know the Buzz?* For now, simply read them to get students thinking. Encourage them to listen and respond to each question by putting their thumb up if they 'agree' or think 'yes', thumb down if they think 'no', and thumb to the side if they think 'maybe'. Move very quickly through them. No verbal responses are required.

Your thoughts on these statements and questions?

- Did Archie show empathy to Joanna?

- Did he use the 'three empathic powers' in the right sequence?

- Did you notice how Archie mirrored Joanna's energy? Was this the right way to go?

- Archie used a little humour. Was it appropriate?

- Do you agree with this statement? "Archie didn't fix Joanna's problem, so he failed."

- What benefits did Archie receive for showing empathy towards Joanna?

- Are you a naturally empathic person, someone who is caring and emotionally helpful to others?

- Are you empathic if you feel the feelings of another, but do nothing to help them?

- Do you agree with this statement? "Empathic people are friendlier, more predictable and safer to be around."

- Should you only show empathy to close friends and family?

- Have you ever shown empathy to someone you didn't know very well?

- Is there a difference between being 'helpful' and 'emotionally helpful'?

- Has there been a time when someone showed you empathy?

21 Archie's story: "Thanks for understanding" – second image

Lauren Eldridge Murray

This image can be downloaded from http://whatsthebuzz.net.au/main-menu/content-whats-the-buzz-with-teenagers and will fill your screen in colour. There is also the option to have the authors read the story to students.

2. *Show me the Buzz*

Show me the Buzz provides students with the opportunity to discuss a variety of social and emotional ideas, absorb the thoughts of others, debate them, create role plays and receive feedback from the group. We have learned that this approach heightens understandings and the transference of skills. There is always a Part 1 and a Part 2. Choose one activity from either Part 1 or Part 2, depending on what appeals to you, the time you have and your group's likely preferences. There's plenty of content in *Show me the Buzz*, so the lesson can be revisited time and time again while continuing with this same topic.

Part 1

1. Create a new version of Archie's story

Discuss taking Archie's story in different directions! One version might highlight Archie's lack of awareness, where we see him so excited by what's going on in his life that he's clueless about her feelings. Alternatively, we might see Archie offering Joanna a list of 'how to fix things', but in doing this he overlooks acknowledging her feelings. Be sure to show Joanna's response to both options, and the likely consequences Archie's poor empathic skills will have on their friendship. Next, break students into pairs or small groups to practise role-playing one of these versions. Later, encourage students to perform their role play to the group. Additional options are to film role plays or to write the new story up as an Archie story with a very different outcome.

2. 'Acts of kindness'

Play the video clip 'Random acts of kindness: what do you desire most' – www.youtube.com/watch?v=blRsRhb45-4.

Then ask students, "What's the message you pick up about empathy from the clip? What did this man give? What was it that he received?" These answers take us to a scientific fact: kindness is teachable and contagious. The positive effect of kindness is that it creates happiness and puts people in an emotional place where they are more likely to 'pay it forward'. This means one good deed sparks another and another and another! Finish up with the clip 'Rafael Nadal stops tennis match as distraught mother looks for her little girl lost in the crowd – www.youtube.com/watch?v=nndnElzb5cE.

Did you feel the empathy not just from Rafael Nadal, but from the entire crowd? Empathy is infectious.

To explore 'paying it forward' in a little more depth, try the clip 'Inspirational video: pay it forward' – www.youtube.com/watch?v=X3ld9_p2bS0.

3. The golden rule

The golden rule is "Do unto others as you would have them do unto you." There's also a parallel saying that says, "Whatever is hurtful to you, do not do to any other person." Living a truly empathic life is treating others in the way we'd like to be treated. Share this short video with students: 'Do unto others as you would have them do unto you' – www.youtube.com/watch?v=kLRMuYf0HEY.

Ask, "What message do you take away from the clip?"

This clip is a reminder about the courage required to live an 'open-hearted life'. It's too easy to respond aggressively when someone does or says something that is hurtful. We all instinctively seek revenge to rebalance the scales of justice. The idea of living open-heartedly, however, is refusing to get nasty when we've been wronged. It takes courage and a well-developed emotional intelligence to not get caught up in another person's anger or rant. An open-hearted person talks to the 'situation' and does not use words that blame, harm or inflame the other person. With this kind of empathy, there's a deep awareness about recognising feelings, easing stressed emotions and using a language that is helpful and uniting.

To finish up, work your way around the social circle, encouraging students to contribute words and phrases that describe how they wish to be treated by others. Generate a list together on the whiteboard. Next, let's see if it's possible to rank the list from the most important to those of lesser importance. Ask students to vote on each and tally their scores. Use this activity as a catalyst to create posters that capture the way people want to be treated.

4. What's in a face?

Empathy is described as the ability to step into someone else's shoes or the skill to enter another person's emotional world. This exercise does just this! Prior to the activity, collect three or four interesting or provoking images from Google images. To do this, type in 'close up character in people's faces'. Download the images so they are ready to display when you want them. To begin, bring up the first image on your screen for students to see. Ask:

- Tell me some things about this person – name, nationality, age, gender, religion?

- Are they likely to have children? Why do you think this?

- Are they married? Have they been married? Why do you think this?

- What kind of home do they live in? Be bold and describe it, based on their 'feel' and the way they're dressed.

- Have they suffered hardship and trauma, or had an easy and well-off life?

- Are they happy, content, sad or curious? Name the feelings you read from their face.

- Would they be a generous person?

- Would they like music? What kind of music?

- What do you guess their most precious possession is?

- How do they spend most of their time?

- Might they have any special gifts or talents?

- What do you sense this person is most worried about?

- If this person had done something remarkable, what might it be?

- What could this person's biggest regret be?

This experience offers students the chance to step into someone's shoes. Interestingly, even from a static image, we have the capacity – as human beings – to dig down and make assumptions that bring us close to empathising and appreciating another.

5. Make empathy acrostic poems

An acrostic poem is where words, phrases or sentences are chosen and written next to each letter from the special word selected. Here are some examples for EMPATHY to tune you in!

EMPATHY

Everyone

matters

people

always

trust

happiness

yeah!

(adapted from https://austinisdselblog.com/2013/
01/30/campus-and-classroom-bulletin-boards/
ridgetop-elementary-bb-4/)

EMPATHY

Extend your soul from within yourself

Meet sorrow while not fearing pain

Place your feet in others' shoes of sadness,

Accept tears as moments of emotional rain

Tire your ears as you unscramble words

Hear truly, just with your heart

You'll reach the threshold of empathy, if you're willing to try

(adapted from https://poemsfromherlife.com/2015/
01/22/empathy-an-acrostic/)

EMPATHY

Extremely observant, you are by far

My favorite person. With just a gaze,

Perceptive, you read me. With just a phrase,

All wise, you see through me.

The magic of your unending empathy

Helps enjoy life fully. The sympathy

You radiate makes my life quite wonderful.

(adapted from www.sharepoems.com/poems-english_
feelings_Your+empathy.html)

If you want to take this a step further, use online dictionaries, thesauruses and acrostic poem generator sites.

6. Pairs to perform

In this role play, students can play themselves. The role play begins as friend 1 and friend 2 start a conversation together. Friend 1 seems preoccupied and isn't right. Friend 2 stops, draws a little closer and asks, "Hey, are you okay? You're lost in thought." Then, just a Joanna did, this friend shares that a family member is back in hospital and is very sick. They are feeling scared and don't know what to do.

The goal in this role play is for friend 2 to show an empathic response. To do this, remind everyone of the three empathic powers:

- *Empathic power 1*: Detect the emotions the other person is experiencing. Ask a question or two. Listen. Be in the moment and allow them to express their thoughts and feelings.

- *Empathic power 2*: Be sure to say something that shows you understand how they must be feeling.

- *Empathic power 3*: Next, do or say something to comfort them, or something that gives hope. Suggest a helpful idea, or state, "What you're going through is tough, but I'm here for you" or "What can I do to help?"

It is wise for pairs to do the same role play because students will witness how the same scenario can be handled very differently. Tune them in to watch and listen for body language, voice tone, the actual words used, hand gestures, touch, spatial proximity, and so much more! If you want to add a little variety, then secretly whisper to a pair (or two) that you'd like friend 2 to play being less than empathetic. Sometimes the awkwardness a quality role play brings offers deeper opportunities for discussion and learning.

Lesson 5

7. Landmine

This activity hinges on trust and empathy. First, select an appropriate space to play in. Let the group watch as you scatter a range of objects (books, balls, shoes, jumpers – whatever is easiest) over the floor. They become the landmines. Next, arrange participants into pairs. Choose a pair to begin while the others watch on. The idea is that one of the pair becomes a trusted guide and the other becomes dependent on the guide because they stay blindfolded. Once blindfolded, the game begins! At this point, the guide may not touch their blindfolded partner and may only use words to direct them safely through the minefield. If the blindfolded player touches a mine, the pair must go back to the start. The idea is to make it to the other side without touching a mine. For older students, set out more mines to make the task more complex or have several pairs crossing the minefield at the same time! You may want to use this activity as a springboard into a terrible world reality. Play one of the clips below, then ask:

- Why would human beings do this to each other, especially because thousands of innocent people are maimed or killed each year?

- Does the use of landmines show a gross lack of empathy towards each other?

'Which countries still have active landmines?' – www.youtube.com/watch?v=M-3n9AngJm3c

'Landmine free 2025: BBC World News coverage' (5 April 2017) – www.youtube.com/watch?v=I-VoZbBvbMQ

8. Online empathy survey

These are intriguing and educative! They give a good guide about how empathic someone is based on their own reflections of themselves. They're fast to do as they offer a list of statements to rate how strongly you agree or disagree. There are no right or wrong answers or trick questions. One option is for each student to complete a survey by working on their device. Another is for you to complete your own survey onscreen for all to see. You might complete it for a student who is prepared to publicly declare their thoughts in front of the group.

- https://psychology-tools.com/empathy-quotient/ – The empathy quotient (EQ) is a 60-item questionnaire designed to measure empathy in adults. The test was developed by Simon Baron-Cohen at the University of Cambridge.

- www.buzzfeed.com/kellyoakes/whats-your-empathy-score?utm_term=. ievanPmnZ#.xbMPRA7RY – How empathic are you? Answer the 16 questions to see how you measure up. Primarily built for adults, but worth a play.

- https://greatergood.berkeley.edu/quizzes/take_quiz/empathy – This empathy quiz contains 28 questions to measure your level of empathy. Once done, you'll receive an empathy score, along with feedback interpreting this score and tips for strengthening your empathy skills.

Part 2: Role plays – empathy

The role plays are in the photocopiable section at the end of this lesson. They are also available online at www.whatsthebuzz.net.au/main-menu/content-whats-the-buzz-with-teenagers. You may either read them to students, or print them and hand each group a role play. Help students to form small groups. Each role-play card states the number of students required. It does not matter if the same role play is given to several groups. Give students a few minutes to rehearse, and move between groups to provide plenty of coaching and enthusiasm.

Next, ask each group to perform their role play. If a student does not wish to perform, allow them to pass. So much can be learned through observing. Always perform role plays in the middle of the social circle. Consider capturing the action on video or photo by using your iPad, camera or smartphone. Encourage others to give constructive feedback after each role play.

3. *Do you know the Buzz?*

Do you know the Buzz? is a lively group 'discussion time' where students briefly respond to a series of questions and statements highlighted by Archie's story. The goal is for them to exchange ideas, and in the process 'mind map' their way more empathically through the complexities of social and emotional situations. This should also provide facilitators with an insight into the depth of student under-standings. To do this, have students sitting on chairs in a social circle.

Your thoughts on these statements and questions?

- Did Archie show empathy to Joanna? What did he do to show it?

- Did he use the 'three empathic powers' in the right sequence? Explain the sequence.

- Did you notice how Archie mirrored Joanna's energy? Was this the right way to go? Explain.

- Archie used a little humour. Was it appropriate? How do you know it worked?

- Do you agree with this statement? "Archie didn't fix Joanna's problem, so he failed to be empathic."

- What benefits did Archie receive for showing empathy towards Joanna?

- Are you a naturally empathic person, someone who is caring and emotionally helpful to others?

- Are you empathic if you feel the feelings of another, but do nothing to help them?

- Do you agree with this statement? "Empathic people are friendlier, more predictable and safer to be around."

- Should you only show empathy to close friends and family? Why? Why not?

- Have you ever shown empathy to someone you didn't know very well? What did you do? How did it work out?

- Is there a difference between being 'helpful' and 'emotionally helpful'? Explain the difference.

- Has there been a time when someone showed you empathy? How did that feel?

4. *The Buzz*

The Buzz is an opportunity for the group to play games that strengthen their relationships and the skills central to the lesson.

Game: Heads or tails? (exciting)

This old favourite reminds us why developing our empathic powers is everything! Without well-developed 'mind-reading' skills, we go through life depending on chance rather than connecting with others, getting to know them and creating choices. So, let's play a game where 'your life in the game' is up to chance because you have no choice.

Ask the group to stand up in a social circle just in front of their chairs. You'll need a coin ready to play heads or tails. Before each flip, students must place their hands on their 'heads' or on their 'tails' to indicate which way the coin will fall. Flip the coin. Those who win remain standing. Those who lose on sit on their chair. Continue until you have just one winner. Point out that this winner wins because of chance, and those who lost, lost because of chance. But when we participate in a social and emotional world, there are so many more chances to find success. Humane connections vastly increase our chances of success.

Game: Mind-reading in four guesses (moderately exciting)

Choose a student who will be the mind-reader. They walk to someone and ask them to think of a number from 1 to 10. They are to keep this number in their head and are not to say it yet! For the moment, they can only say "higher" or "lower." The mind-reader has four guesses to discover their number. They might begin by saying "6." The person holding the number in their mind (let's say it's 7) would say "higher." Continue with two more guesses. On the fourth guess, the mind-reader must guess their number. While doing this, urge the mind-reader to study the face of the person and their reactions to help uncover clues.

Game: Mind-reading in 20 questions (moderately exciting)

Think of something. To illustrate this, let's say you think of a carrot. The group has 20 questions to guess that you are thinking of a carrot. The first player might say, "What category is it? Animal, vegetable or mineral?" In this case, you would answer, "Vegetable!" The next student might say, "Does it grow on a tree?" And so, the game continues until a participant guesses it is a carrot. The player who guesses begins the next round.

Game: Dots and boxes (moderately exciting)

'Dots and boxes' is a simple game where players are required to read the play and think ahead. To play 'Dots and boxes', provide each small group of students with pencils and an A4 sheet of paper to share with dots already printed (this link will help you see how to do it – https://en.wikipedia.org/wiki/Dots_and_Boxes).

To begin, one player draws a short vertical or horizontal line between any two dots (no diagonal lines are permitted). The next player must do the same, but the question is where will they draw it? They may choose to connect to their opponent's line and extend it to the next dot, or continue from it at right angles. They may even choose to begin a new line somewhere else on the grid. The aim of the game is to make the fourth side on as many squares as possible and claim that box. Once they claim a box, they write the letter of their first name inside it, and must take a free turn. Free turns are a bonus at the outset but a curse later in the game. And so, the game continues until every square has been claimed. Each player counts how many squares they have won, and the person who claims the most wins.

Remind participants that this game gives them a chance to practise their empathic abilities towards each other. Playing without empathy may well encourage others not to play with you again!

After the Buzz: Social thinking ideas for parents and caregivers

Lesson: Empathy

Key social and emotional principles (learning intention)

Empathy is a core life skill. This lesson explores how to identify the feelings, thoughts or attitudes of others, and respond to them with a delicate balance of sensitivity and purpose. To develop empathic powers, several actions must occur. The first is to detect the emotions the other person is experiencing. Second, an empathic person communicates they understand how this person must be feeling. Finally, they do or say something to comfort them, or offer a possible solution. The goal is to lift their spirits, and this can be achieved by giving them hope. In dire situations, the only hope to be found may be the promise of an understanding and enduring friendship.

After the Buzz presents further ideas for parents, guardians and educators to encourage the social and emotional thinking students have touched on during the lesson. Our children rely on us to consolidate these skills by positively modelling them, and emphasising the language and ideas contained within the lesson. As always, here are a few ideas to help your child, and students, develop their empathic or 'mind-reading' skills.

Do it yourself

A natural way to teach empathy is for us to model compassion ourselves, at home and in the classroom. Our children never stop watching and learning from us! Children who have been coached how to calm themselves when stressed are better at empathising with others who are experiencing stress. A beginning for being empathetic is to teach children how to do diaphragmatic breathing, box breathing, buddy breathing, finger breathing, progressive muscle relaxation, to go get a drink, sit with a friend, write in their journal, draw or talk. If a child struggles to process and regulate their own feelings, then they simply don't have capacity to process someone else's.

Active listening is empathy in action

When we feel understood, it's easier to stay calm, process our feelings and gain clarity. So, an emphasis on active listening demonstrates empathy in action. It may start by rephrasing back what they've just said as a statement or question. When we validate their feelings, we offer them a chance to keep their dignity. We might say:

- What did he say to you?
- How did you feel?
- Yes, I would have felt the same.
- How do you think he felt when you said that?
- Do you think that made things better?
- So, what do you think you could do to make this better?
- That's a good idea!
- How can I help?

It sounds strange, but the immediate goal is not to fix the problem. It is more about giving ourselves to be in the moment and listening to them.

Empathy begins by being able to name one's own feelings

Help young people of all ages build empathy for others by being able to name their own feelings: anger, fear, boredom, jealousy, embarrassment, nervousness, loneliness or disappointment, and the entire range of emotions they experience. When they're angry, gently and honestly call it without judgement: "I see you're feeling angry." When they hear their feeling named, they start to gain control over it. Finding words is a progressive skill. The goal is to help every individual to say how they feel, why they feel this way and what they want to happen. A simple start is to teach your child to say, "I feel (name the feeling) because (state what happened)."

Name other people's feelings

When you see someone experience a strong feeling, and it's appropriate, you can quietly comment to your child or to students, "He seems frustrated. I wonder what happened?" or "She seems so sad. What do you think caused that?" or "How do you think he was feeling?" These kinds of comments draw children's attention to other people's experiences, and at the same time builds their emotional vocabulary through observation and empathy.

Educators and parents who use inductive discipline build empathy and prosocial behaviours

First, you could be forgiven if you need to ask, "What is inductive discipline?" It is a disciplining strategy that many use instinctively, and one that's lost on quite a few.

It's a technique where parents and educators alike, very briefly, explain to children and students why a behaviour was inappropriate or risky. By dispassionately explaining why a behaviour is inapt, and how it impacts negatively on others, the adult helps the child to come to a far more reasonable conclusion about this behaviour, and how it can be modified in the future. Inductive discipline gradually helps children develop self-control. The opposite to this is reflected in Ian Lillico's eloquent statement:

> Students who are punished often have revenge fantasies that interrupt true remorse for what they have done. They are not given the opportunity to make amends. Punishment clears the ledger and allows re-offending in the future without attendant feelings of guilt.
>
> (Lillico, 2004: 23)

Children of parents using an inductive style of discipline are more empathic, and empathic children are more prosocial (Krevans and Gibbs, 1996). So, the next time your son, daughter or student 'mis'behaves, gently point out the consequence it had on the people involved, and how it affected their feelings. Keep it brief. Don't go on and on, and refrain from getting steamed up. Children need to be held accountable for wrongdoing, and if a negative consequence needs to be applied, do it with poise and without feelings of spite or payback. Being held accountable, simply and logically, helps them grow into more responsible and empathetic people.

Have dinner together and share each other's experiences from the day

Years of research gives evidence that sitting down for an evening meal is good for the brain, body and soul. Dinnertime conversations can provide children with insights into other people's lives, which is essential for the growth of empathy. Also, it is well documented that dinnertime conversation improves both the vocabulary and literacy development of younger and older children (Snow and Beals, 2006). Older children also gain benefits from good-natured dinnertime interactions. This event becomes a powerful predictor of sound academic achievement, and is measured as more powerful than time spent in school, than homework, than playing sport or doing art (Hofferth and Sandberg, 2004). Finally, there are strong links between regular family dinners, better behaviours and better mental health. In one New Zealand study, a higher frequency of family meals together was strongly associated with positive moods in adolescents.

After the Buzz . . . Lesson 5

Similarly, other researchers have shown that teens who eat regularly with their families also have a more positive view of the future compared to their peers who don't (Utter et al., 2013).

Reading can build empathy

An emerging body of evidence highlights that reading to young people offers more than an opportunity to appreciate literature. Stories are a springboard into the feelings of others and how they handle them. In fact, a University of Cambridge study proved that reading fiction provides excellent training for young people in developing and practicing empathy (Nikolajeva, 2013). As common sense suggests, texts exploring everyday life situations do best to help young people understand what others might be experiencing. Rely on texts with well-rounded, believable characters, even if they are doing regrettable things.

Watch a movie together

Films also rouse emotions, spark our curiosity, create memories and become windows into other worlds. In some instances, a movie can nudge our conscience, shift our viewpoint or trigger feelings. The right kind of movie at the right time can stimulate empathy as well as any lesson or lecture could. Once you've finished watching the movie, ask:

- Why was this character loved so much?

- Why is another so disliked?

- Did you dislike them?

- What could have they done to help others like them more?

- Was there a reason for them to behave like this?

- Who was your favourite character? Why? What qualities did they show that you liked?

- Who was your least favourite character? Why?

- Who was the hero? What made them a hero?

- Who was the victim? How could you tell? Was it their fault? Was it anyone's fault?

- What reasons do you have to make this judgement?

- If you had been 'so and so', what would you have done to make things better?

Observing behaviour and emotion in this way guides children to see the complexities behind human interactions (Zumski Finke, 2015). Movies for young people of all ages that highlight empathy can be found at http://micheleborba.com/100-movies-for-kids-5-to-17-that-teach-9-crucial-empathy-habits/.

Go to a café, observe others and imagine their lives

To help your child interpret the feelings and thoughts behind the faces, words, voice tones and body language of others, go to a café with your teen and do a little 'top secret' people watching. We all do it! We wonder why someone is sitting alone in the café and what their life is like. Then our eyes detect a couple, close, leaning towards one another and holding hands. "What's this about?" we think. Are they beginning a relationship or ending one? What are their lives like? What work do they do? What clues are there to discover? Discussions that centre around people, their apparent feelings and hypothesising what their lives are like sharpen our empathic superpowers.

Helping others

At home, a practical way for your child to give to others, and see gratitude returned, is to arrange for them to prepare a meal for the family each week or fortnight. Nudging children to do more for others helps children to stretch their independence and empathy.

Without wishing to upset any parents, a good number of children have their very loving mothers and fathers squarely in their service. Why not consider steering your children to help others outside of the family. The idea of doing thoughtful things for others instantly immerses them in an emotionally richer world. As they absorb the thoughts and feelings of others, a more empathic view of life is promoted. Ask yourself, how long is it since your child sent a thank-you card, a small present, a warm email, a friendly note, a handmade card, or made a phone call to someone who has been helpful or needs their spirits raised? Start by setting them up to deliver kindnesses. Teaching children how to care underpins that they themselves are cared for.

References

Carnicer, J. and Calderón, C. (2013) Empathy and coping strategies as predictors of well-being in Spanish university students. *Electronic Journal of Research in Educational Psychology*, 12(1): 129–146. Available at: www.researchgate.net/publication/262635611_ (accessed July 2018).

Grühn, D., Rebucall, K., Diehl, M., Lumley, M. and Labouvie-Vief, G. (2008) Empathy across the adult lifespan: longitudinal and experience-sampling findings. *Emotion*, 8(6):

After the Buzz . . . Lesson 5

753–765. Available at: www.ncbi.nlm.nih.gov/pmc/articles/PMC2669929/ (accessed July 2018).

Hofferth, S. and Sandberg, L. (2004) *How American Children Spend Their Time*. Available at: http://onlinelibrary.wiley.com/doi/10.1111/j.1741-3737.2001.00295.x/abstract (accessed July 2018).

Krevans, J. and Gibbs, J. (1996) Parents' use of inductive discipline: relations to children's empathy and prosocial behavior. *Child Development*, 67(6): 3263–3277. Available at: www.ncbi.nlm.nih.gov/pubmed/9071781 (accessed July 2018).

Lillico, I. (2004) *Homework and the Homework Grid*. Western Australia: Tranton Enterprises.

Nikolajeva, M. (2013) 'Did you feel as if you hated people?' Emotional literacy through fiction. *New Review of Children's Literature and Librarianship*, 19(2): 95–107. Available at: www.tandfonline.com/doi/abs/10.1080/13614541.2013.813334?journalCode=r-cll20#.UihO1z_3OJY (accessed July 2018).

Ponischil, K. (2014) *Cultivating Kindness and Compassion in Children*. Available at: https://depts.washington.edu/ccfwb/content/cultivating-kindness-and-compassion-children-0 (accessed July 2018).

Snow, C.E. and Beals, D.E. (2006) Mealtime talk that supports literacy development. *New Directions for Child and Adolescent Development*, 111: 51–66.

Stafford, M., Kuh, D., Gale, D., Mishra, G. and Richards, M. (2016) Parent–child relationships and offspring's positive mental wellbeing from adolescence to early older age. *Journal of Positive Psychology*, 11(3): 326–337. Available at: www.ncbi.nlm.nih.gov/pmc/articles/PMC4784487/ (accessed July 2018).

Utter, J., Denny, S., Robinson, E., Fleming, T., Ameratunga, S. and Grant, S. (2013) Family meals and the well-being of adolescents. *Journal of Paediatrics and Child Health*, 49(11): 909–911. Available at: http://onlinelibrary.wiley.com/doi/10.1111/jpc.12428/abstract (accessed July 2018).

Van der Graaff, J. (2014) *Empathy in Adolescence*. Available at: https://dspace.library.uu.nl/handle/1874/294441 (accessed July 2018).

Zumski Finke, C. (2015) *Watching Movies May Help You Build Empathy*. Available at: www.pri.org/stories/2015-10-21/watching-movies-may-help-you-build-empathy (accessed July 2018).

After the Buzz . . . Lesson 5

What's the Buzz with Teenagers?

22 Role-play cards: Empathy

Role play 1

You are eager to see a new movie. On the morning you plan to see it, you get sick and can't go. Instead, you must stay home and rest. Your friends still go to see it. In this role play, your friends drop by your house after the movie. They are excited and enjoyed it! Show an empathic conversation where they understand how disappointed you are, and you respectfully express your disappointment. What might your friends say or do to give you some happiness and hope? (A group of three – you and your two friends)

Role play 2

You return a friend's iPad but have accidentally cracked the screen. You immediately apologise, take responsibility and offer to pay for it to be repaired. They are shocked, lose control and get upset about it. They tell you off in front of your friends and it's an embarrassing scene. Show how you could best handle this difficult situation by keeping control and remain empathic about your friend's upset. This role play highlights that we can't control the behaviour of others, but we can take charge of our own. (A group of four – you, your friend and two others)

Role play 3

Your teacher is annoyed with you for not handing in your assignment. You do, however, have a very good reason for this, but you haven't said a word to your teacher about the trouble that's been happening at home. Show how you might speak to the teacher, make an apology and explain your position in a way that helps them feel empathy for you. (A pair – you and the teacher)

What's the Buzz with Teenagers?

22 Role-play cards:
Empathy *continued . . .*

Role play 4

You've almost finished a big project that's taken all term. Even though it's a partner project, you've done most of it alone. Your partner is having a tough time at home and you're happy to support them. Your teacher sits you both down for an interview. They want to review your progress and check that the workload has been shared. Show how you might handle the interview showing understanding and compassion for your partner while keeping their dignity. This is tricky because you don't want to lie to your teacher either. (A group of three – you, your project partner and the teacher)

Role play 5

Your friend is often upset because they never get invited to parties. You've always said that you'd invite them when you have a party. The time has come for you to have a big family party and you realise your friend won't know anyone. What should you do? You could break your promise, not invite them and hope they never find out. Instead, you choose to catch up with them, make them feel welcome to come, talk to them about who'll be there and give them some ideas about how to connect to a few of your cousins. (A pair – you and your friend)

Role play 6

There's a boy/girl in your class who is a pleasant person, but you don't share their interests. Strangely, they've invited you over for an afternoon at their house on Saturday, and you've agreed to go. Let's pick up the role play with this person overhearing you say to a friend that you're a little nervous about going. Very calmly, this person sits down with you and your friend and says, "Hey, I'm really sorry you feel like that. You don't have to come if you don't want to. What can I do to make you feel better about it?" You can choose whether you go or not. What is most important is to treat this person with respect and kindness in this very awkward situation. (A group of three – you and two others)

---

22 Role-play cards: Empathy *continued . . .*

Role play 7

Your friend is often late for school. You know the reason for this: they carry a lot of responsibility getting their younger brothers and sisters ready each morning. For them, life at home is hard. One morning as they walk in late, the class cheers when they arrive on time. It's embarrassing for this person. How can you show empathy and help to your friend, and at the same time keep things calm and respectful with the others? (A group of five – you, the friend that walks in late and three others that represent the class)

Role play 8

Your friend tells you their mother has lost her job. They are a great friend and you know they have a complicated family life too. Your friend is very upset because they'll have to move to another part of the city and start at a new school. Show how you can use your empathy to support your friend and give them realistic hope for the future. (A pair – you and your friend)

Role play 9

There's a student in your class who has autism. He spends part of the week at your school and the other part at an autism school. You and your friends understand what autism means and are usually thoughtful towards him. In this role play, he walks up to you and asks if you'd like to come as his guest to a special morning at his autism school. You can choose whether you go or not. What is most important is to treat this person with respect and kindness in this tricky situation. (A pair – you and the student)

Resilience

"Going with the flow"

Key social and emotional principles (learning intention)

To reveal that resilience, also known as emotional and cognitive flexibility, is to be able to 'go with the flow', to adapt and find alternative solutions on the run. The alternative is to be consumed by the problem, stay stuck in it, acquiesce to power-lessness, and feel anxious or angry. A flexible thinker can take small and calculated choices to make changes that are more likely to find joy, success, or make sense of new or challenging situations. Teaching young people to understand and value this flexible mental set is the basis of a treasured lifelong skill termed resilience.

Materials required for this lesson

- Name tags.

- Chairs in a social circle for students to sit on.

- Whiteboard/butcher's paper/screen and markers.

- Create a simple outline of the lesson on the whiteboard/butcher's paper/ screen for students to follow.

- Display the *What's the Buzz?* group values (located in the introduction or at www.whatsthebuzz.net.au/main-menu/content-whats-the-buzz-with-teenagers).

- Organise feedback and reminder cards, or similar, to strengthen responsive behaviours (located in the introduction or at www.whatsthebuzz.net.au/main-menu/content-whats-the-buzz-with-teenagers, ready to print).

- Have Archie's story ready to read to students. This can be done directly from this lesson. Or, for a small registration fee, you can download the 16 Archie stories as you want them. Each story contains text, audio in the form of the authors reading to your students, and two large illustrations in full colour that will fill your screen. Access is available at www.whatsthebuzz.net.au/main-menu/content-whats-the-buzz-with-teenagers

- Pencils, pens and paper for students to do Part 1 of *Show me the Buzz*.

- Preview the film clips for 'What about Nolan and others?' in Part 1 of *Show me the Buzz*.

- Two small pieces of plasticine for each student and several large shallow containers to hold water for 'Resilience: good for you and for others' in Part 1 of *Show me the Buzz*.

- A tablet or laptop for each student to complete an online resilience survey in the activity 'How emotionally and cognitively flexible are you?' in Part 1 of *Show me the Buzz*.

- Print the role-play cards for 'Finding emotional flexibility' in Part 2 of *Show me the Buzz* (located at the end of the lesson or at www.whatsthebuzz.net.au/main-menu/content-whats-the-buzz-with-teenagers, ready to print).

- A few sheets of A4 paper, a texta and fastening tape to play the game 'Who am I?' in *The Buzz*.

- A collection of common household/classroom items to play the game 'More than you think!' in *The Buzz*.

- Several packs of Uno cards to play the game 'Killer Uno' in *The Buzz*.

- Prepare handouts for parents(s):

  One copy of this lesson for each parent to read.

  One copy of *After the Buzz: Social thinking ideas for parents and caregivers* to send home (located at the end of the lesson, ready to photocopy, or at www.whatsthebuzz.net.au/main-menu/content-whats-the-buzz-with-teenagers).

Lesson 6

Explanation

Question: What was Forrest Gump implying when he said, "Life is like a box of chocolates?"

Answer: "You never know what you're going to get!"

Life is not predictable. It's as rich and variable as the assortment of chocolates in Forrest's box. Yet some of us desperately seek order, routine and predictability so we feel safe. We like to know what's happening, how it will unfold and what will happen afterwards, and respond better when an event or day is carefully planned. As an example, many who are identified with autism spectrum disorder, anxiety or have suffered from trauma have an urge to control what's happening around them so they feel more secure. They do not cope well with the unexpected, and can quickly feel overwhelmed and out of sorts. These individuals tend to get caught up in the fight: "Why?" "Why me?" "That's not fair," "It's not what you said," "It's not what I want," and "I'm not doing it," wasting a lot of time and emotion fighting the inevitable. Meanwhile, many of their peers can 'go with the flow', adapt and find alternative solutions on the run, and with apparent ease.

Expressions such as 'going with the flow' and 'rolling with the punches' refer to cognitive flexibility or resilience. Resilience includes two primary skills – flexible thinking and set-shifting. Those who openly embrace differing responses and approaches to deal with challenges show flexible thinking, while those who get stuck are rigid thinkers. Set-shifting refers to an aptitude to move from an old way to a new way of going about things. Those of us who have developed flexible thinking cope better with change and new information on the go. The research points out very clearly that young people who can adapt to unexpected circumstances are more likely to engage in positive peer interactions, participate in class, enjoy school, enjoy life, persist and work through change with far more success (Dishion and Tipsord, 2011).

In recent years, the global catchphrases growth mindset and fixed mindset have been very heavily promoted by educators in schools (Dweck, 2007). Growth mindset is a way to help students understand that intelligences, skills and talents grow through planning, practice and an attitude that allows us to flexibly 'give things a go' and stick with it (Duckworth, 2016). The alternative is a fixed mindset, which is described as a faulty logic that tells us we are deficient as we face a challenge. Very quickly, our confidence and motivation vanish, and we give in to feelings of inadequacy. Carol Dweck and Angela Lee Duckworth's work prove that mindsets can be changed (see Carol Dweck's 'Developing a growth mindset' – www.youtube. com/watch?v=hiiEeMN7vbQ). Their contribution has been groundbreaking, and today we all celebrate and embrace their research. The one concern surrounding the terms growth mindset and fixed mindset is that teachers have inadvertently overplayed these terms. It has saturated students to a point where many today will roll their eyes and withdraw their effort because they've become averse to the terminology. Teaching students how to constructively adapt their thinking and behaviour in the face of change or challenge is a valuable lifelong skill, and we need to be shrewd in selecting a myriad of methods to present resilience-building. Like all new skills, acquisition takes time to master, and is dependent on one's temperament, personality and developmental capabilities, as well as environmental factors they have – or have not – been exposed to. Once they do learn how to handle change more flexibly, the twists and turns in life become easier to navigate, assisting kids to thrive for years to come.

The ancient Chinese philosopher Lao-Tzu, who was the founder of Taoism and lived during the Zhou dynasty, apparently wrote, "Life is a series of natural and spontaneous changes. Don't resist them – that only creates sorrow. Let reality be reality. Let things flow naturally forward in whatever way they like."

More recently, Andrew Fuller, Australia's favourite psychologist, stated, 'Resilience is the happy knack of being able to bungee jump through the pitfalls of life' (Fuller, 2014).

1. *What's the Buzz?*

Actively greet students as they enter. Provide chairs in a social circle for them to sit on and have a brief lesson plan on the screen, whiteboard or butcher's paper for students to see. As students are settling, hand each of them a 'Thumbs up feedback card' to highlight their thoughtful behaviour and using the group values.

Let's begin

Frame the lesson by introducing the learning intention. To do this, ask your group these questions:

Have you ever noticed that some people don't fuss much when things don't go their way? Instead, they work out how best to deal with it and get on with it?

This is what it means to 'go with the flow' or to show 'resilience'.

I have five statements about resilience. Some are *facts* and others are *myths*. Stand up if you believe the statement is a *fact*. Stay seated if you believe it is a *myth*.

1. Resilience is all about thinking positively

Those of you sitting down have it because this is a *myth*. There's plenty of research that resilience is more than thinking positively. It also includes personal optimism, humour, good relationships, cognitive flexibility and hope.

2. You are either born with it or not

This is a *myth*. The largest part of resilience is gained by learning. It is not a gene that people are born with. People may have natural dispositions to be pessimistic or optimistic, but the development of resilience involves behaviours, thoughts and actions that are learned and developed.

3. Resilience is like following a recipe – if you follow it, you'll be resilient

Hope you're sitting down because this is a *myth* too. Resilience isn't a single skill or a single recipe. Rather, it's a quality supported by attitudes around positive problem-solving, being able to regulate our emotions and socially reference, a drive to become more self-aware, having quality support networks/role models around us, being willing to take responsibility for our own actions, seeking opportunities to grow, and finding a sense of what's important about life.

4. Resilience is all about preparing for what might happen

Those of you who are sitting know it's a *myth* because it's impossible to prepare for every event that may suddenly become a challenge. Resilient attitudes and behaviours grow over time and are reflected in the way we respond to unforeseen situations with increasing confidence.

5. What doesn't kill you will make you stronger

What rubbish. It's a *myth*, so I hope you're sitting. People love to hear stories about others who've overcome hardship and thrived because of the tough experience. Too much hardship, too early or too quickly, can disable people, and that's a *fact*. It's true that a few people feel a sense of personal growth following a terrible event, but this growth happens because of the way in which this person chose to respond. In the words of Epictetus (AD 50–135), "It's not what happens to you, but how you react to it, that matters."

Today, Archie has big ideas about how his day should turn out. Will he be ready to 'go with the flow' and be resilient? Let's find out.

Archie's story: "Going with the flow"

Archie felt moody and edgy. Things weren't right. He knew he was escaping into gaming and YouTube too often, and his mother and father kept nagging him about it too. He was taking ages to fall asleep because he kept thinking about things that weren't worth thinking about. The extra work in middle school seemed endless, and just as challenging were his friendships because they continued to change as well. It felt like he'd stepped on to a roller coaster that he didn't want to be on.

23 Archie's story: "Going with the flow" – first image

Lauren Eldridge Murray

This image can be downloaded from http://whatsthebuzz.net.au/main-menu/content-whats-the-buzz-with-teenagers and will fill your screen in colour. There is also the option to have the authors read the story to students.

He was even annoyed by Kelvin, his family's third whippet. Kelvin was the nephew to Maxi and Luca, his two older dogs. At the moment, Kelvin felt too energetic, too annoying and was too much for Archie to deal with. He felt irritated by Kelvin's peppy puppy behaviour, especially the way he slipped under Archie's quilt at night and twisted himself, grabbing all the quilt and leaving Archie freezing. In this mindset, Archie couldn't see that all Kelvin was trying to do was be close to him.

Today, Archie wanted to shake off his darkness. He made a promise to himself to be more positive and readier to roll with things. Mr Messma, their home group teacher, had planned a different day of learning. It was going to be a day of activity and surprises. In the weeks leading up to today, the class had brainstormed ideas on possible activities. No one knew which ideas would be chosen, but all the ideas had been placed into a jar ready to be drawn out. There were loads of great activities and Archie liked most of them. He had a good feeling about how things might unfold. His eyes were glued to the jar as the class sat down ready to start.

Archie tried to remember some of the most appealing activities. There was bungee jumping eggs, making a potato cannon, rainbow foam, colour hunt, building an edible ancient temple, launching a water-powered rocket, pizza-making, a ninja warrior course, and best of all Archie's idea – coding – using CodeMonkey and some other apps the technician at school agreed to set up.

Mr Messma was wearing his usual big smile. He was as enthusiastic as his students! Eager, Archie, Joanna, Tobias and Ayman sat together and waited for the announcement of the first activity. There would be time for the class to do four activities across the day. Mr Messma called Archie up to draw the first activity from the jar. Archie's heart was beating like a conga drum. He was loaded with excitement. "Please let it be coding, please let it be coding, please let it be coding," Archie wished to himself as he reached into the jar. His fingers fumbled about for a few seconds and he pulled out a small folded piece of paper. He quickly unfolded it and read it out: "Class debate. The topic is: 'Cats are better than dogs'."

Archie scowled. He felt irritable straight away. He couldn't stand debating. It was boring, he always ended up on the opposite side of what he believed in, and hated speaking in front of people anyway. This supposedly fun day had just taken a giant nosedive. Forget being positive, having a good day or anything to do with 'smart thinking'. He was already over it. His body felt tight and his heart was thumping. Archie could sense everyone's eyes on him. What also annoyed him was the whole class seemed excited over such a

24 Archie's story: "Going with the flow" – second image

Lauren Eldridge Murray

This image can be downloaded from http://whatsthebuzz.net.au/main-menu/content-whats-the-buzz-with-teenagers and will fill your screen in colour. There is also the option to have the authors read the story to students.

boring idea. Even Joanna seemed happy as she chatted with Tobias and Ayman. Yet earlier on, she'd said that debating was ordinary. Why is she suddenly so happy? Is she faking it?

Before Archie could blink, Mr Messma started handing number cards to each person. Having an odd number meant you had to take the cats' side and even numbers put you on the dogs' side. Archie begged the universe and every superpower known to put him on the dogs' side! He loved Maxi, Luca and even Kelvin, who was just too big for his boots. He couldn't pretend that cats are better than dogs. It would be disloyal to his dogs.

Archie turned his number card over to see number 17. "Typical," he thought to himself, "I've got the very thing I didn't want." Feelings of dislike, disappointment and injustice surged through his mind. "Errrgh! How am I going to handle this? Do I even want to?" he thought to himself. Joanna, who also adored dogs, had to argue for cats too. She could see Archie wasn't handling this well, so leant closer to him and whispered, "Hey Arch, just go with the flow and find a way to have fun with it. It's not all bad, and we're both on the same side."

This didn't help. It made Archie feel more stuck in his negative thoughts: "Seriously? This isn't fun, it's stupid." In his head, he wanted to prove the activity was bad. He could make his point by refusing to do it, or he could do it badly to prove how boring it was. What he couldn't see was that everyone else in the class had switched their focus. Their goal was to have fun together, and the debate itself was less important. Archie felt out of step, irritable and alone.

Discussion based on the questions and statements below will occur later in *Do you know the Buzz?* For now, simply read them to get students thinking. Encourage them to listen and respond to each question by putting their thumb up if they 'agree' or think 'yes', thumb down if they think 'no', and thumb to the side if they think 'maybe'. Move very quickly through them. No verbal responses are required.

Your thoughts on these statements and questions?

- It's normal to feel moody, irritated or angry sometimes.

- Are stress and lack of sleep likely to make us less resilient?

- Archie's stress warning signs were playing too many video games, not being able to get to sleep and feeling irritable. Do you know your own stress warning signs?

- Do you agree with this statement? "Some people must work harder than others to be emotionally flexible and 'give things a go'."

- Archie was irritated and scowled when he drew out the class debate activity. Do you think it would have been better if he'd put on a 'brave face' instead?

- Can you think of a reason why Archie's disappointment about debating hit him so hard? How may he have been really feeling?

- Who agrees with what Joanna said to Archie? It was, "Hey Arch, just go with the flow."

- Is it okay to look unhappy sometimes when things don't go your way?

- Is it okay to act out your unhappiness to an extent that spoils or harms what others are doing?

- Do you agree with this statement? "There is a big difference between 'going with the flow' and 'faking it a bit to get over a hump'." Can you explain?

- Do you think Joanna handled the situation well?

- Can you think of a way that Archie could have shown a little more flexibility and 'gone with the flow'?

- Has there been a time when you faced a challenge, and became pessimistic and negative?

- Has there been a time when you faced a challenge, and dug deep, found some resilience and felt pleased with yourself?

- How important is 'emotional flexibility' on a scale of 1 to 5, with 5 being very important? Hold up your fingers to show your rating.

2. *Show me the Buzz*

Show me the Buzz provides students with the opportunity to discuss a variety of social and emotional ideas, absorb the thoughts of others, debate them, create role plays and receive feedback from the group. We have learned that this approach heightens understandings and the transference of skills. There is always a Part 1 and a Part 2. Choose one activity from either Part 1 or Part 2, depending on what appeals to you, the time you have and your group's likely preferences. There's plenty of content in *Show me the Buzz*, so the lesson can be revisited time and time again while continuing with this same topic.

Part 1

1. Group discussion

Archie's reaction to the class debate was big. Why did he react so strongly? What's really going on for him? Is it all about the debate, or is there something more driving his inflexibility? Share your hypothesis.

2. Write, role-play and film

Continue writing Archie's story. Develop one of two options. Option 1: take it in a direction where Archie composes himself, finds some emotional flexibility and 'goes with the flow' just as his friends are. Show how his friends support his effort to gain flexibility. Option 2: continue writing Archie's story, showing him becoming more hostile, refusing to show emotional flexibility, protesting and spoiling the activity for others. Highlight the multiple consequences Archie faces from teachers, students and friends.

3. Identify situations when you need to call on your resilience

Break students into groups of three or four. Provide each group with a blank A4 sheet of paper and a pen or pencil for a recorder to write with. Ask the recorder to draw a vertical line down the centre of the sheet to make two columns. In the left-hand column, the group is to help the recorder make a list of typically challenging things at school that often require a positive and flexible approach. In the right-hand column, list tricky situations at home where 'resiliency' is helpful. Afterwards, share with the larger group. If time permits, encourage students to recall and share a time when they were not able to 'go with the flow'. What happened? Did they melt down, get huffy, go quiet, get angry or storm off? Ask each student, "Do you have a typical style you use when you become overwhelmed? Would you categorise it as fight, flight or freeze?"

4. What about Nolan and others?

Nolan awakens the spirit of emotional flexibility, or resiliency, through humour. He will leave you, and your students, smiling. Play the 'Nolan's cheddar' film clip – www.youtube.com/watch?v=ipEP9YOFLHk. Afterwards ask, "How does Nolan's thinking and actions help to explain resilience?"

Next watch these series of short clips:

- 'What is resilience?' – www.youtube.com/watch?v=gcbTmw1Y48I

- 'What is resiliency?' – www.youtube.com/watch?v=c-cQPF8Qk04

- 'Definition of resilience: a light-hearted animation' – www.youtube.com/watch?v=WnH45nKEEgU

- 'Elon Musk: motivation – do it in spite of fear' – www.youtube.com/watch?v=0UnmpQQXOzg

Once finished, ask:

- What is resilience?

- Can you give five other words or phrases that describe resilience?

Lesson 6

- Name some of the most basic things we need to take care of to develop resilient thinking.

- Why do we need to be cognitively and emotionally flexible?

- What's the idea of a resilient person having plans A, B and C? What does this mean?

- Why is learning how to regulate our emotions vital when it comes to becoming more resilient?

- What does Elon Musk teach us about the relationship between success, failure and being flexibly open to new experiences?

5. Collect pictures and images that show resilience in action

Sharpen your students' imagination by showing them a few images you've collected to highlight how you see 'resilience'. This is easy – use Google and search for 'images that show resilience'. There are hundreds to choose from. The students' task, individually or in pairs, is to take their own photos, or collect photos from Google images or magazines, to present the many facets of 'resilience'. In this activity, nothing written is required. It is an enjoyable task that delivers great conversations and big results as students share the images they've collected. In a similar vein, support students to collect their three most favourite resilience-style sayings from Google images, with a view of sharing these with the group. You could take this a step further and get them to make their own 'resilience', 'emotional flexibility', 'cognitive flexibility' or 'go with flow' posters or a collage.

6. Negative self-talk

Did you notice Archie's negative self-talk? He said, "Seriously? This isn't fun, it's stupid." It's not unusual for us to create a negative conversation in our minds when confronted with a challenging situation. This is because human beings' brains are wired with a negative bias, a greater rush and sensitivity to stir up negative feelings. The reason for this is to keep us safe. From the very beginning, our very survival depended on our skill at identifying possible dangers and evading them. So, we developed systems that notice danger, differences and risk, and our negative self-talk chatter is a part of this. Students need to know that negative self-talk holds a secret meaning, and it's their job to spot it. The first step is to work out how they might be feeling as the negative comment presents itself. Next, try to imagine what is really driving the negative self-talk. That's right, there's something deeper that's causing this feeling. What is it? Our job is to be a detective, to translate this and put a resilient approach on it with a positive statement. Here are some examples. Write them on to the whiteboard or screen. Teach students how to think from left to right.

Negative self-talk	I feel	The translation	A positive replacement statement
"I'm an idiot."	Embarrassed	"I don't want to look stupid."	"I can wait, listen or ask a friend."
"That's stupid anyway."	Annoyed	"Oh no, there's more work to do!"	"I can team up with a friend."
"This is boring."	Worried	"Where do I start? Can I even do it?"	"I'll tackle one thing at a time."
"I hate them."	Hurt	"Why do they ignore me?"	"I can't control them – just me!"

Now you have these examples as a model, invite students to say the negative self-talk statements that often spring forth in their minds. List these under the 'Negative self-talk' heading, and then work across the columns completing the 'I feel', 'The translation' and a 'A positive replacement statement' columns.

7. Resilience – good for you and for others

Here's an activity to examine cognitive flexibility, what it looks like and how it can influence others. This transforms an abstract concept into a thoroughly practical and real-world understanding! To begin, break the class into groups of three or four and provide each student with two pieces of plasticine (do not use Play-Doh) and a large shallow container filled with water to share. Direct students to make two plasticine balls, each with a diameter of about 4–5 cm, just like the ones you are holding.

Once they've done this, take your plasticine ball and hold it above the water in your container. Ask, "What do you think will happen if I place my ball on the surface of the water?"

They will, of course, respond by saying, "It will sink."

You reply, "Well, I want it to float!"

Immediately place the ball on to the water, and – as predicted by students – it will sink. Take it out and try again. Repeat this several more times. Stop, then explain that what you've been doing represents a person who chooses not to think flexibly, and does the same action repeatedly, even though it is not working for them. As Albert Einstein once famously said, "The definition of insanity is doing the same thing over and over and expecting different results."

Next, ask, "I want you to shift your thinking from my thinking. I want you to think flexibly. What can you do to make your piece of plasticine float?"

Provide students time to experiment. Your hope is that one of them may hit on the idea to shape one of their plasticine balls into a boat shape that is able to float, and the others will follow. When the time is right, capture the attention of your students and shape one of your balls into a boat. As you do this, state that what you're doing is a resilient action, based on being cognitively flexible. In this moment, you might say, "I'm choosing a positive way to solve the problem."

Gently place the boat on the water and watch it float. Once it's floating, state, "But there's more. Watch carefully."

Gently reach into your container and take out the first plasticine ball that sank to the bottom. Gently place it inside the floating boat.

Ask, "You've seen what I did. What does this represent?" The answer is it shows what happens when a person chooses to reshape their attitude. Not only is it better for that person, but their new thinking can also help to carry the thinking of others along the way. And quite often we carry others, even without knowing it. Encourage students to carefully place their second plasticine ball in their floating boat.

8. How emotionally and cognitively flexible are you?

Here are a few questions for you and your students to discuss. As a facilitator, be brave, and answer each question about yourself first, then invite students to answer the same question about themselves. Allow plenty of time because the questions will prompt perceptive insights. Rate yourself out of five for each question and then answer it (5/5 = very resilient, 3/5 = mostly resilient, 1/5 = not resilient yet).

- How resilient are you?

- Are you naturally an optimist (glass half full) or a pessimist (glass half empty)?

- Explain your optimism or pessimism by explaining how you naturally think and deal with problems.

- When or where are you more likely to think and behave inflexibly and pessimistically?

- When or where are you more likely to think and behave flexibly and optimistically?

- How might resilience and optimism partner each other?

- How emotionally and cognitively flexible are your mother and father? Rate them.

- Has their flexibility or inflexibility helped or hindered you?

- Are you more resilient now than when you were younger?

- Are you choosing friends who encourage your wellbeing and your flexibility? Why is this important?

As we do a little exploration, we begin to see that resilience is a complicated and fickle quality that hinges on many variables that can be practised and developed. To finish up, consider encouraging students to complete one or several of these online resilience surveys. Always work through them prior to the lesson so you are certain which survey best suits your group:

- 'How resilient are you?' – www.verywellmind.com/quiz-how-resilient-are-you-4008851

- 'Resiliency test' – https://testyourself.psychtests.com/testid/2121

- 'How resilient are you?' – www.mindtools.com/pages/article/resilience-quiz.htm

- 'Resiliency quiz: how resilient are you?' – www.resiliencyquiz.com/index.shtml

- 'How resilient are you? Take the test!' – www.lifehack.org/articles/lifestyle/how-resilient-are-you-take-the-test.html

Part 2: Role plays – resilience

The role plays are in the photocopiable section at the end of this lesson. They are also available online at www.whatsthebuzz.net.au/main-menu/content-whats-the-buzz-with-teenagers. You may either read them to students, or print them and hand each group a role play. Help students to form small groups. Each role-play card states the number of students required. It does not matter if the same role play is given to several groups. Give students a few minutes to rehearse, and move between groups to provide plenty of coaching and enthusiasm.

Next, ask each group to perform their role play. If a student does not wish to perform, allow them to pass. So much can be learned through observing. Always perform role plays in the middle of the social circle. Consider capturing the action on video or photo by using your iPad, camera or smartphone. Encourage others to give constructive feedback after each role play.

3. *Do you know the Buzz?*

Do you know the Buzz? is a lively group 'discussion time' where students briefly respond to a series of questions and statements highlighted by Archie's story. The goal is for them to exchange ideas, and in the process 'mind map' their way more empathically through the complexities of social and emotional situations. This should also provide facilitators with an insight into the depth of student understandings. To do this, have students sitting on chairs in a social circle.

Your thoughts on these statements and questions?

- It's normal to feel moody, irritated or angry sometimes.

- Are stress and lack of sleep likely to make us less resilient?

- Archie's stress warning signs were playing too many video games, not being able to get to sleep and feeling irritable. Do you know your own stress warning signs?

- Do you agree with this statement? "Some people must work harder than others to be emotionally flexible and 'give things a go'."

- Archie was irritated and scowled when he drew out the class debate activity. Do you think it would have been better if he'd put on a 'brave face' instead?

- Can you think of a reason why Archie's disappointment about debating hit him so hard? How may he have been really feeling?

- Who agrees with what Joanna said to Archie? It was, "Hey Arch, just go with the flow."

- Is it okay to look unhappy sometimes when things don't go your way?

- Is it okay to act out your unhappiness to an extent that spoils or harms what others are doing?

- Do you agree with this statement? "There is a big difference between 'going with the flow' and 'faking it a bit to get over a hump'." Can you explain?

- Do you think Joanna handled the situation well? Why or why not?

- Can you think of a way that Archie could have shown a little more flexibility and 'gone with the flow'?

- Has there been a time when you faced a challenge, and became pessimistic and negative?

- Has there been a time when you faced a challenge, and dug deep, found some resilience and felt pleased with yourself?

- How important is 'emotional flexibility'? Please comment.

4. The Buzz

The Buzz is an opportunity for the group to play games that strengthen their relationships and the skills central to the lesson.

Game: Master and servant (passive)

To start, arrange the group into pairs. Allow each pair to perform to the group. They must decide on who will be the master and who will be the servant. The master begins by asking the servant for something. The servant responds ever so politely with an excuse about why this can't happen. This is wonderful practice for 'thinking on the fly' and coming up with alternate ideas. The goal is for each pair to act out their parts in front of the group for a minute. To help, here is a typical conversation between master and servant that you might like to share with the group first:

Master: Get me some warm socks.
Servant: Of course, sir. Oh, except there aren't any clean socks.

Master:	Then get me a blanket!
Servant:	I would, sir, but we wrapped the dogs up in them.
Master:	Then take me somewhere warmer.
Servant:	Oh, what a dreadful thing, dear sir, there are no warm places left in the palace.
Master:	Then take me somewhere else.
Servant:	I can't take you anywhere today, sir, as all the carriages are out.
Master:	Why can't you get me anything I'm asking for today?
Servant:	Because everything you're asking for is already being used.
Master:	By whom?
Servant:	There was terrible weather last night and we took in everyone in the district.
Master:	Well, get rid of them!
Servant:	So sorry, sir, I can't. That would be unkind, and you'd hate that!

Game: What's this? (passive)

You begin this game by standing up and moving from the social circle to touch any object in the room. As you do, ask the group, "What's this?" Give each person in the group a turn at offering a new creative name and a new bizarre explanation of what this thing does as quickly as they can. For example, you might touch a fire extinguisher and say, "What's this?" A response may be, "It's a smell remover. You pull the trigger and any smells in the room are extinguished!"

Game: More than you think! (moderately exciting)

For this game, gather enough basic household/classroom items for each person in the group. Such items might include a wooden spoon, an egg beater, a small vase, a chopping board, a remote control, a drink bottle, a saucepan, a toothbrush, a small pot plant, a lunchbox, a plastic bowl and so on. Participants sit in a social circle and are each handed one of the items. The aim is for them to switch on their flexible thinking because when it's their turn, they must introduce the item in a completely novel way. The objective is to creatively explain an alternative use, purpose or context for the item they're holding. Begin the game by modelling it yourself. Start by saying, "Surprise, surprise, this isn't a . . ." This activity is a lot of fun when students team up in pairs. Give the pairs a little rehearsal time first.

Game: Who am I? (passive for all ages)

This game demands flexible thinking! To begin, arrange the group into a social circle. Clip a piece of paper with a name on it to a player's back. This player must not see or hear the name attached to their back. Popular names include Homer, Marge or Bart Simpson, SpongeBob SquarePants, Batman, Superman, Barbie, Porky Pig, Dora, Harry Potter, Winnie the Pooh, Cinderella, Santa, Bugs Bunny, Easter Bunny, Scooby-Doo, Marvin, Daffy Duck, Tweety, Sylvester, Road Runner and so on. The aim of the game is for this player to find out who they are. Choose a group member to start. Ask them to swing around in their chair and turn their back towards the centre of the circle. Clip the name of their character on to their back. At this point, all the other players can see the name. Next, invite the player to ask questions about who they might be, but the group can only answer with "Yes" or "No." Players are successful when they finally ask, "Am I . . .?" and receive a "Yes!" It is best to let your group know that only two or three players will get turns, and you will follow up in subsequent weeks.

Game: Killer Uno (exciting)

This old favourite is always enjoyed, but it will take some time to play. First, establish the rules (https://hubpages.com/games-hobbies/killer-uno-rules). To play 'Killer Uno', all you'll need is a regular deck, or decks, of Uno cards. The basic rules of Uno apply, with the addition of two extra rules to give the game a faster pace and unexpected twists. This requires the capacity to 'go with the flow'. Here are the two additional rules:

- *Passing zero*: When a player receives a zero card, they call, "Stop and hand over your cards!" Every player passes their hand to the player next to them. If play is moving to the right, pass to the right; if play is moving to the left, pass to the left.

- *Slap six*: When a player plays a six, they must immediately slap the table hard. All players do the same as fast as they can. The last player to slap the table must draw two cards.

After the Buzz: Social thinking ideas for parents and caregivers

Lesson 6: Resilience

Key social and emotional principles (learning intention)

To reveal that resilience, also known as emotional and cognitive flexibility, is to be able to 'go with the flow', to adapt and find alternative solutions on the run. The alternative is to be consumed by the problem, stay stuck in it, acquiesce to power-lessness, and feel anxious or angry. A flexible thinker can take small and calculated choices to make changes that are more likely to find joy, success, or make sense of new or challenging situations. Teaching young people to understand and value this flexible mental set is the basis of a treasured lifelong skill termed resilience.

After the Buzz presents further ideas for parents, guardians and educators to encourage the social and emotional thinking students have touched on during the lesson. Our children rely on us to consolidate these skills by positively modelling them, and emphasising the language and ideas contained within the lesson. As always, here are a few practical ideas to help your children move away from rigid thinking and towards a more resilient style.

Drill down below the behaviour: Do you know what your child's rigid thinking is really about?

As frustrating as it can be, there are usually reasons behind rigid thinking patterns in children and teens. It may be your child's temperament, where they are developmentally younger, or part of a disability, anxiety, perfectionism or an emotional response to trauma in the past. The good news is that most get there in their own time – and do it better with a little well-placed coaching. When you see them struggling offer clear, succinct guidance, you might say, "I can see you're finding it tricky to do it this way. How about trying . . .?" If they begin to take their frustration out on you, then gently withdraw. Later, when everyone is calm again, briefly revisit the situation to underpin a more resilient and flexible attitude. Always work on modelling this pliable behaviour yourself!

Invent family sayings that add to resiliency

Encourage everyone to use flexibility mantras – out loud – when things don't go as planned, such as:

- "Just go with the flow."

- "Epic FAIL = epic first attempt in learning."

- "I can handle this."

- "Just one thing at a time."

- "This doesn't have to get me down."

- "It's not the end of the world."

- "I'm smart enough to get through this."

- "There's another way to do this."

The more they hear it, the more they'll use it themselves.

Build opportunities to build emotional flexibility

First, create a safe home environment where 'having a go' is a big part of your philosophy. Sometimes at dinner run 'FAIL sessions'. Together, share times you've tried, FAIL(ed) and what you learned from it. Constantly share your own mistakes, FAILS and successes. These three go together! They are in the same family. For too long, we've favoured one child in this family called 'success'. Set small goals with your kids where they risk FAIL(ure) and success. Encourage, monitor and coach them as they 'give it a go'! Sometimes deliberately set them up so they are likely to FAIL in the first instance, but the learning from the first FAIL will provide a brilliant springboard into ultimate success.

Teach positive, flexible self-talk

When your kids say, "I'm no good at this" or "This is too hard" or "It's not worth trying," remind them that they would never let a friend say such negative things and get away with it. Once kids begin to spot their negative self-talk, help them to reframe it into more positive statements, such as:

- "I'm not good at this yet!"

- "This is hard, but I'll get it."

- "I'm behind now, but I can catch up."

After the Buzz . . . Lesson 6

Explain that it takes practice to switch negative self-talk off and positive self-talk on. The best idea is to teach your child to stop, take a few deep breaths, state the problem to themselves, think of two solutions and choose one. As kids learn to talk themselves through problems, they experience less emotional blocking and are better able to cope.

Rock the boat

Yes, from time to time, deliberately rock the boat, bend the rules and throw in a bit of chaos. While rules are crucial, rigid thinkers are often too preoccupied by them, with a terrible focus on telling others how to stick to them! So, arrange ways for your kids to cope with change. Instead of doing everything in the same way each day, tweak small changes to the routine every so often. Seemingly small changes, such as where to sit in the car or showering before dinner instead of after, teach flexibility.

What about changing the rules to your favourite games? Introduce 'Killer Uno', where two new rules are added. First, there's 'passing zero'. When a player receives a zero card, they call, "Stop and hand over your cards!" Every player passes their hand to the player next to them. If play is moving to the right, pass to the right; if play is moving to the left, pass to the left. Second, there's 'slap six'. When a player plays a six, they must immediately slap the table hard. All players do the same as fast as they can. The last player to slap the table must draw two cards.

Praise flexibility

Make a point of praising your child when they display emotional flexibility. You might say:

- "I am so proud of how you just handled that."

- "That was tricky. I loved the way you went with the flow to make it work."

- "Good on you, you didn't give up. You just found a different way to do it."

This kind of praise leads a child to see they hold the power to success. Always try to link effort, cognitive flexibility and accomplishment together.

What about trading disappointment for a treat?

Disappointments, upsets and even being at a loose end are a part of the emotional ebb and flow of life. They happen, and we need to embrace these emotions so we can learn to deal with them. So, if your child was planning to catch up with a friend one afternoon and the friend suddenly cancels, it's not helpful to say, "Oh, don't worry. I'll make it up to you by taking you shopping."

The sobering reality is that every young person needs to feel their emotions and work on ways to cope with disappointment and distress. If you like, you can ask them if they have any ideas about what they can do to move on from the disappointment. Remind them that spending too much time in the thick of the emotion can spoil the time that could be spent doing something else instead. To respond empathetically you might say, "I know you're disappointed. I would be too, but I'm sure there's a good reason."

Place this quote on your fridge: "Smile, breathe easy and go slowly"

Model it as much as you can. Little of the drama that goes on in families is necessary or helpful. Yes, we need to be available to our children, but let's meet them more resiliently ourselves. Make a pledge to yourself to be connected and poised. Also, remember that very little of the hubbub in families must be resolved immediately. Smiling, pausing and breathing can help clear the air and buy a little time to come up with better solutions. It's so simple: slow, diaphragmatic breathing oxygenates your brain so you can think straight. Teach your children to breathe slowly and deeply whenever things don't go as planned. It clears their perspective and helps them cope.

Life, chaos and hope

Frequently discuss that things often won't work out the way we want them to, and that's just how life is – unpredictable and chaotic. We are not able to control other people's thoughts or behaviour. All we have is a willingness to control our own feelings, actions and perspectives. You can encourage your children to adapt, be flexible and find solutions, but even then this may not guarantee things will turn out the way they want. The greatest hope we have is the trust we share in each other, and conversations with loved ones, which helps make sense out of the senseless. Playfully discuss the meaning behind these:

> It's a cruel and random world, but the chaos is all so beautiful.
>
> Hiromu Arakawa

> Life is nothing without a little chaos to make it interesting.
> Amelia Atwater-Rhodes, *Demon in My View*

> Chaos was the law of nature; Order was the dream of man.
> Henry Adams, *The Education of Henry Adams*

> I finally figured out that not every crisis can be managed. As much as we want to keep ourselves safe, we can't protect ourselves from everything. If we want to embrace life, we also have to embrace chaos.
> Susan Elizabeth Phillips, *Breathing Room*

After the Buzz . . . Lesson 6

Plan times to smile and laugh together

We know that a little humour and laughing releases dopamine, a happy hormone, which is good medicine for us. They lift our spirit and reduce tension. Laughing spreads happiness, goodwill and tolerance, and is often compared to a mild internal physical workout. As we laugh, the muscles in our face, neck, chest and diaphragm all work hard. Then when we stop laughing, these muscles relax, and we are more relaxed than we were previously. So, find a way to lighten up and laugh with each other. Why not get a cheap second-rate joke book and read a few jokes to your kids? Inflexible, rigid thinkers often struggle to understand jokes. Jokes can be a great way to talk about wordplay and how changing the meaning suddenly makes it funny. Taking life too seriously can drain our resiliency.

References

Dishion, T. and Tipsord, J. (2011) Peer contagion in child and adolescent social and emotional development. *Annual Review of Psychology*, 62: 189–214. Available at: https://www.ncbi.nlm.nih.gov/pmc/articles/PMC3523739/ (accessed July 2018).

Duckworth, A. (2016) *Grit: The Power of Passion and Perseverance*. New York: Simon & Schuster.

Dweck, C. (2007) *Mindset: The New Psychology of Success*. New York: Ballantine Books.

Fuller, A. (2014) *Ten Hints for Creating Resilient Families*. Available at: http://andrewfuller.com.au/wp-content/uploads/2014/08/Ten-Resilience-Hints.pdf (accessed July 2018).

After the Buzz . . . Lesson 6

What's the Buzz with Teenagers?

25 Role-play cards: Resilience

Role play 1

You've left your costume and props needed for a drama rehearsal today at home. You know your lines, but you wish you had the props, plus you spent ages making them. This role play begins as you're discussing the problem with your teacher. Take the lead and show us the emotional flexibility required to deal resiliently with this situation. If time permits, do a 'take two'. This time, perform the role play showing no resilience about the situation. (A pair – you and the teacher)

Role play 2

Every so often, your family goes out for a pizza night together and it's great. You're all set to leave when there's a knock on the front door. A family friend has unexpectedly dropped by with roast chicken and chips for dinner – not your favourite! Your plans must change. Show how you and your mum/dad respond using emotional flexibility and courtesy, while your younger brother/sister can't get past themselves and 'go with the flow'. (A group of four – you, the visitor, your mum/dad and your brother/sister)

Role play 3

You must play a sport at your school. Sport is not your thing, and you're not the best at ball sports, so you decide to give gymnastics a try. When you go to register at the office, you find out that gymnastics is booked out. The only option is basketball. Show a resilient way of dealing with it. Then replay the role play and show yourself refusing to 'go with the flow' and becoming emotional about not getting your own way. (A pair – you and the person who is registering you)

What's the Buzz with Teenagers?

25 Role-play cards: Resilience *continued . . .*

Role play 4

You go shopping for new sneakers. You know exactly what you want – the brand, colour, size – and you have your money ready to spend. The shop assistant goes to look for your size, and when they return they tell you that your size is not available. And worse still, there are no others left in the city! The shop assistant shows you two other pairs in good brands, great colour and in your size. These are not what you planned to buy! In your discussion with the sales assistant, show how you arrive at a creative and flexible solution. (A pair – you and the shop assistant)

Role play 5

As you're waiting at the bus stop, a person you vaguely know runs towards you, waving and calling out, "Hi! Great to see you. Let's sit together on the bus!" This person isn't really a friend. You get along with them but they can be mildly annoying. Show how you could 'go with the flow', be kind enough and make an awkward situation work. (A pair – you and the annoying person)

Role play 6

It's after school and you're about to begin district sports training. The problem is that you're starving! You left your lunch at home, so had no lunch, and you don't have any money either. Role-play one way to flexibly think your way through this so you receive some food and drink before training. Let's see you having to persist! (A pair – you and one or two others)

---

25 Role-play cards: Resilience *continued . . .*

Role play 7

You're in class and have just been accused by someone of pushing their pencil case on to the floor from their desk. You didn't do it. The teacher moves towards you and says, "Just pick it up and put it back!" Take the challenge and show us the emotional flexibility required to resiliently deal with this situation. (A group of three – you, the complaining student and the teacher)

Role play 8

You've been working with a group of friends to complete a group project. It has been disastrous as none of them have done any work. You've done it all and you've done enough for the project to get a pass. You promise yourself that you'll never work with them again. As you hand the project in to your teacher, they ask, "So, how did you go working together?" Show us a resilient response. Role-play what you could say that shows your frustration but at the same time is respectful towards your friends. (A pair – you and the teacher)

Dealing with disappointment (loss and grief)

"They loved each other"

Key social and emotional principles (learning intention)

The purpose of this lesson is to teach the essential facts about disappointment, loss and grief because they are tricky feelings to cope with, yet are unavoidable. The lesson also embraces how to support others who've been affected by disappointment, loss and grief.

Materials required for this lesson

- Name tags.

- Chairs in a social circle for students to sit on.

- Whiteboard/butcher's paper/screen and markers.

- Create a simple outline of the lesson on the whiteboard/butcher's paper/screen for students to follow.

- Display the *What's the Buzz?* group values (located in the introduction or at www.whatsthebuzz.net.au/main-menu/content-whats-the-buzz-with-teenagers).

- Organise feedback and reminder cards, or similar, to strengthen responsive behaviours (located in the introduction or at www.whatsthebuzz.net.au/main-menu/content-whats-the-buzz-with-teenagers).

- Have Archie's story ready to read to students. This can be done directly from this lesson. Or, for a small registration fee, you can download the 16 Archie stories as you want them. Each story contains text, audio in the form of the authors reading to your students, and two large illustrations in full colour that will fill your screen. Access is available at www.whatsthebuzz.net.au/main-menu/content-whats-the-buzz-with-teenagers

- Whiteboard, markers and plenty of pencils, pens and paper for students to do activities from Part 1 of *Show me the Buzz*.

- Print 'The ball of disappointment' in Part 1 of *Show me the Buzz* (located at the end of the lesson or at www.whatsthebuzz.net.au/main-menu/content-whats-the-buzz-with-teenagers) plus coloured pencils for students to complete the activity.

- Print the role-play cards for 'Dealing with disappointment' in Part 2 of *Show me the Buzz*.

- Slips of paper, pencils and two dice to play the game 'Dealing with disappointment' in *The Buzz*.

- Print numbers 1 to 5, the scenarios and 'Disappointment: Catastrophe scale' ready to play 'Let's catastrophise!' in *The Buzz*. These are in photocopiable section at the end of the lesson or at www.whatsthebuzz.net.au/main-menu/content-whats-the-buzz-with-teenagers

- Organise a bowling ball and bowling pins to play 'Disappointment 10-pin bowling' in *The Buzz*. Have ready an assortment of inexpensive giveaways!

- Use a basketball, or similar, and one bowling pin to play the game 'Guard the pin' in *The Buzz*.

- Prepare handouts for parents(s):

  One copy of this lesson for each parent to read.

  One copy of *After the Buzz: Social thinking ideas for parents and caregivers* to send home (located at the end of the lesson, ready to photocopy, or at www.whatsthebuzz.net.au/main-menu/content-whats-the-buzz-with-teenagers).

Lesson 7

Explanation

We're compelled to build a lesson based around disappointment because it affects us all, quite regularly. Early in childhood, disappointment occurs because someone might not get their way, is not first, has been left out, or may have lost a game. Disappointment does, however, become more complex as children grow into adolescents. Around this time, a painful understanding emerges – that is, disappointment also contains threads of other emotions that can feel incredibly intense to wrestle with. In isolation, feelings such as sadness, hurt, embarrassment, contempt, fear, regret and so on are often tough to deal with, but when disappointment is added to the mix it's so much more challenging.

Loss and grief are a big part of the disappointment experience. Almost any loss causes grief: the death of a loved one or a cherished pet, the ending of a close friendship, the breakdown of a parent's marriage, the loss of good health, a family member's serious illness, the loss of feeling safe, moving from the family home, and so much more. Even subtle losses and disappointments can trigger a momentary but deep sense of grief.

We coach young people to consider a few key ideas when they're confronted with disappointment, loss and grief. First, we motivate them to recognise the feelings they are experiencing. This can be tough because many other feelings can be entwined. Having friends or family to share with helps to offer a broader perspective so feelings can be more accurately identified and processed. Next, we encourage young people to be emotional and experience the feeling – to cry, scream, grieve; to feel miserable or broken-hearted and talk about it; to take time to be with their emotion without trying to fix or change it. By being present with them, they sense they do not have to do this alone. We also reassure them to take their time. The goal is to work through the experience, but we also help them from becoming stuck in anger, bitterness or despondency. We actively support them so they can grow from this setback.

As friends and family, we must also be aware about their resilience, or their capacity to bounce back from hardship. Some of us can take a knock-back and rise up again, while others quickly acquiesce to negative feelings. Our role here, as friends, parents and educators, is not to take responsibility for them, but to walk with them so it feels easier for them to face it with a better attitude and improved energy. The skills required to deal effectively with disappointment, grief and loss take a long time to be learned. Most of us have battled for years to master the art of composure in the face of these feelings, but admit it's never textbook straightforward.

1. *What's the Buzz?*

Actively greet students as they enter. Provide chairs in a social circle for them to sit on and have a brief lesson plan on the whiteboard or butcher's paper for students to see. As students are settling, hand each of them a 'Thumbs up feedback card' to highlight their thoughtful behaviour and using the group values.

Let's begin

Explain that the lesson is about disappointment, loss and grief. The lesson also touches on how best to support someone who has been affected by these challenging emotions.

Ask students to:

- define disappointment;

- explain what grief and grieving are; and

- describe various losses.

Next, ask students:

- What sort of loss would disappoint you?

- What is the difference between a mild and shocking disappointment?

- What kind of disappointment would cause you to grieve?

- What is a serious loss you have suffered?

Next is a super quick quiz.

Quiz: Myth or fact?

Students call out 'myth' if they think the statement is a myth, and 'fact' if they believe the statement is a fact:

- Disappointment happens to everyone. (fact)

- You can only grieve over the death of a person. (myth)

- You cannot grieve intensely over the loss of a pet. (myth)

- To grieve properly, you must go through the five stages of grief – denial, anger, bargaining, depression and acceptance. (myth)

- We can be disappointed in ourselves, disappointed in another, disappointed for another or disappointed about a situation. (fact)

- Try to 'get over' your grief as fast as you can. (myth)

- You should be over your grief within four months. (myth)

- Time fixes all disappointments and losses. (myth)

- When you look happy after a friend or family member dies, you are disrespecting them. (myth)

- It is better to lock disappointments, losses and grief out of your mind. (myth)

- Deal with disappointment, loss and grief by sharing your thoughts and feelings with friends and family. (fact)

- Funerals are important to help us deal with life-and-death issues. Kids should usually go. (fact)

- If you're grieving and you don't cry much, that's okay. (fact)

While these questions and statements have been designed as a quick exercise, consider coming back to them later. As hard as it is to talk about sadder emotions and events, we must sensitively work with students to do this together, to listen to each other, and to compare thoughts in a setting that provides safety and healthy exchanges.

Archie's story: "They loved each other"

A few months ago, Archie, Joanna, Tobias and Prisha helped Ayman and his father organise Ayman's brother Tarik's sixth birthday party. You might remember that Oliver had complained he didn't want to be at a 6-year-old's birthday party because he had better things to do. Then Joanna, gave him a piece of her mind by telling him not to take himself so seriously and stop being Mr Grumpy Sour Pants. Tobias took a softer approach and saved the day by cleverly getting Oliver involved!

Since the party, Ayman had promised Archie, Joanna, Tobias and Prisha they could come back to his house and see the pair of rabbits Tarik had bought with his birthday money. Ayman and his dad had bought the rabbit hutch Tarik really wanted, even though it was too big, too fancy and too expensive. As Ayman's dad said, "You're only 6 once!" To be honest, it was worth every cent as Tarik adored his bunnies and attended to their every need – cuddles, water, carrots, greens, pellets, hay and always more cuddles.

The day had finally come to meet the rabbits. The boys danced with excitement along the low brick fences as the girls walked beside them on the footpath telling them to get down. Everyone laughed. The boys had no intention of getting off the fences and the girls were happy watching them pretend to be very bad acrobats.

"So what kind of rabbits are they, Ayman?" asked Joanna.

Lesson 7

26 Archie's story: "They loved each other" – first image

Lauren Eldridge Murray

This image can be downloaded from http://whatsthebuzz.net.au/main-menu/content-whats-the-buzz-with-teenagers and will fill your screen in colour. There is also the option to have the authors read the story to students.

"Cashmere Lop," replied Ayman.

"Never heard of Lop rabbits before. What do they look like?" called Tobias as he tried a cartwheel on the narrow brick wall. The cartwheel didn't work and Tobias landed awkwardly on the footpath. He was as agile as a cat and always had more lives left.

"They're small and have silky grey fur. But they've got long, wide ears that hang down to the ground and are too big for them," answered Ayman.

"What did Tarik name them?" asked Archie.

"Big ears 1 and 2," joked Tobias.

"He called them Lily and Lola," replied Ayman, ignoring Tobias.

"I bags first hold – please?" called Prisha.

"Sure," laughed Ayman as they reached his house.

"Not if I get there first," shouted Joanna, as she sprinted down the side of Ayman's house and into the backyard. Everyone ran fast and arrived at the amazing rabbit hutch together. They waited for Ayman to open the lid and take the rabbits out.

As the lid opened, the five friends were devastated by what they saw. Lily, with her beautiful blue eyes, looked up at them. But Lola lay limp. A ghastly silence fell over the group because Lola's death was painfully clear to see.

Ayman reached into the hutch. First, he picked up Lily and without a word handed her to Prisha as he'd promised to do. Then he drew a deep breath and reached down for Lola. He lovingly wrapped his large fingers around her small motionless body, lifted her up and cradled her close to his chest.

Joanna sensed Ayman needed help, so she reached out and took Lola's lifeless little body from him. As she did so, Ayman burst into tears; his tears ran fast and reached the hearts of his friends. Everyone teared up. There was no stopping those feelings.

Ayman was first to find his words and said, "I'm sorry you had to see Lola like this."

"Ayman, you don't need to say sorry to us. We're your friends. We want to be here for you," Tobias stated.

"How's Tarik going to handle this?" grieved Ayman as he realised someone had to break the news to him. "It was horrible watching how hard it's been for him since Mum died, and now he's got to say goodbye to Lola," grieved Ayman.

Prisha was emotional but calm. She held Lily against her chest in one hand, and with the other she grasped Ayman's arm and said, "Death is part of life. Let's not

27 Archie's story: "They loved each other" – second image

Lauren Eldridge Murray

This image can be downloaded from http://whatsthebuzz.net.au/main-menu/content-whats-the-buzz-with-teenagers and will fill your screen in colour. There is also the option to have the authors read the story to students.

forget to share all the goodness Lola's life brought." Her words were needed. Quickly, Tobias added, "There are two goodnesses we'll tell Tarik about. The first is the joy Lola gave to him, and the second is the best life he gave to her. They loved each other!" He smiled while talking about death.

Archie never said a word. He was shocked by Prisha and Tobias' attitude about death. It was reasonable, sensible, respectful and gave death a proper place. In his family, death had no place. No one talked about it unless it happened, and then it was dealt with quickly, so it didn't have to be talked about for too long.

Always practical, Joanna added, "And, we need to be sure Tarik doesn't blame himself. It wasn't his fault. Nor was it yours, Ayman. Stuff happens."

Discussion based on the questions and statements below will occur later in *Do you know the Buzz?* For now, simply read them to get students thinking. Encourage them to listen and respond to each question by putting their thumb up if they 'agree' or think 'yes', thumb down if they think 'no', and thumb to the side if they think 'maybe'. Move very quickly through them. No verbal responses are required.

Your thoughts on these statements and questions?

- Have you ever experienced the death of a pet?

- Was it a big loss?

- Have you ever experienced the death of someone close to you?

- Have you had other disappointments and losses in your life?

- Have you experienced what it feels like to grieve?

- Did the feeling of grief become easier to live with as time went by?

- Would you agree that disappointment, loss and grief are closely linked?

- Ayman burst into tears. Does this show that he's a weak person?

- Do you agree with this statement? "You must cry when a pet or someone dies, otherwise you are not being respectful."

- Do you know why Ayman said, "I'm sorry you had to see this" to his friends?

- Who agrees with Prisha's statement? "Death is part of life. Let's not forget to share all the goodness Lola's life brought."

- Whose family is more like Archie's – in that death isn't talked about unless it happens, and then it's dealt with quickly?

- Is Prisha's family's attitude about life, death and grieving a healthy one?

2. *Show me the Buzz*

Show me the Buzz provides students with the opportunity to discuss a variety of social and emotional ideas, absorb the thoughts of others, debate them, create role plays and receive feedback from the group. We have learned that this approach heightens understandings and the transference of skills. There is always a Part 1 and a Part 2. Choose one activity from either Part 1 or Part 2, depending on what appeals to you, the time you have and your group's likely preferences. There's plenty of content in *Show me the Buzz*, so the lesson can be revisited time and time again while continuing with this same topic.

Part 1

1. Develop an ending to Archie's story

Take this story further. Imagine Tarik suddenly walks into the backyard. What might Ayman say to his younger brother? What style is Ayman likely to use? Show Tarik's reaction to this devastating loss. What might he say? Would it be best for the friends to leave or to remain? If they were to stay, show how they could be most helpful. Give groups the opportunity to adapt their writing into a short play with the additional option of videoing it.

2. Group discussion

Make three columns on the screen or whiteboard for students to see. From left to right across the top of the columns, write 'disappointment', 'loss' and 'grief'. Ask students to share the things that have made them feel disappointed. Record these situations on the screen or whiteboard. Do the same for the 'loss' and 'grief' columns too. Allow plenty of exchange, and stress that any loss can cause disappointment and grief. The most frequent losses include parents divorcing, friendship break-ups, loneliness, sickness, achieving poorly at school, difficulty seeing a future, family money worries, death of a pet or a loved one, a serious illness in the family, having to move to a new house, a break-in at home, a frightening incident, and the loss of a long-held dream or expectation.

3. Group synonym brainstorm

Once again, make three columns on the screen or whiteboard for students to see. From left to right across the top of the columns, write 'disappointment', 'loss' and 'grief'. The challenge is to work together to find eight alternative words for each of the words. Here's some secret help:

- 'Disappointment' – displeasure, sadness, regret, dismay, sorrow, despondency, heavy-heartedness, depression, disenchantment, disillusionment, dissatisfaction, disgruntlement.

- 'Loss' – mislaying, misplacement, reducing, forgetting, overlooking, denied or left without, disappearance, losing, penalty, waste, squandering, forfeit.

- 'Grief' – sorrow, misery, sadness, anguish, pain, distress, agony, torment, suffering, heartache, heartbreak, woe, desolation, despondency, dejection, despair, angst, mourning remorse, regret.

An alternative approach is for you to list eight words under each heading but leave several letters out of each word and ask students to discover the word.

4. Break free of the 'man box' and the 'pretty pink girl box' so you can express your emotions

To begin, what's the 'man box'? To learn more, view https://rc.richmond.edu/masculinity/manbox.html.

It represents the old stereotype about men that limits young males from becoming their best emotional selves. Once boys were taught that to be a 'real man', you should be tough, risky, suck it up, drink big, show no emotions and never share them, except for anger, because aggression and violence was manly! Even today too, many boys are hanging on to the old man box stereotype. They believe that men are strong and girls are weak, that men are superior and women are inferior, and this thinking continues to cripple the way men share feelings, form friendships and behave.

- 'A call to men by Tony Porter' – www.youtube.com/watch?v=td1PbsV6B80?

- 'Tim Winton laments the power of toxic masculinity on young men' – www.youtube.com/watch?v=zEiPlprMUGo

- 'Masculine man: how weak men deal with emotions' – www.youtube.com/watch?v=dfZ-YkVkirY

- 'Australia is gripped by misogyny, says author Tim Winton' – www.youtube.com/watch?v=ary3sBesDpU

Sadly, the 'pretty pink girl box' has been just as limiting for girls and women. Girls were once taught to be only 'girly', to crave frilly dresses and to only play house and dolls. Their bedrooms were filled with butterflies, rainbows, unicorns and flowers. In doing this, we told girls they were to look pretty for men, serve food, take care of babies and their man, while the man did the important work. This limiting stereotyping has delivered discrimination and injustice to women in the domestic and commercial worlds.

- 'Always #LikeAGirl – unstoppable' – www.youtube.com/watch?v=VhB3l1gCz2E

- 'Boys and girls on stereotypes' – www.youtube.com/watch?v=aTvGSstKd5Y

These stereotypes are not okay and have not yet been left in the past. Only recently have enough of us started to say that we want young men and women to grow into real people who follow their hearts and minds. One of the nuttiest ideas from the past was for men and boys not to share their feelings and never cry. Let's encourage everyone to share their feelings, cry when they need to, share problems, and discuss worries and fears. Why? The answer is simple: it will build much better emotional health in men, women and within families.

Lesson 7

To finish up, ask each student to write a few sentences on a slip of paper about a time when they felt disappointed or experienced loss or grief. Collect the slips of paper and read one out at a time, without mentioning who wrote it. Consider adding several yourself that you know will be pertinent to your group. The group's task is to sensitively offer suggestions on how to deal with each situation. Our aim is to get our young people talking, and for them to see that by talking and sharing ideas there's multiple ways to find support and solve problems.

5. 'The ball of disappointment'

This is an idea that helps us understand the range of emotions we can also experience when we're feeling disappointed. At first glance, the image is hard to interpret because there are so many emotions intertwined together. Yet this mirrors what happens in the real emotional world because while we may be disappointed, there are likely to be many other emotions tangled up as well! Knowing this is an incredibly helpful start. Relief comes fast when we're able to identify which other emotions are at play besides disappointment. To give students practice at identifying some of the emotions that accompany disappointment, give each student a copy of 'The ball of disappointment' (available in the photocopiable section following this lesson). Ask them to think about a time that was very disappointing for them, and keep it in mind. As they revisit this memory, ask them to use their coloured pencils to colour each of the feelings they felt during this disappointing time. Give students 10 minutes to do this. Suggest that they share the disappointment they had in mind with another person. If time permits, encourage a few students to share.

6. How do you deal with disappointment, frustration, loss or grief?

Sit students on chairs in a social circle. Explain that the aim of the activity is for each of them – one after the other – to suggest a way to deal with disappointment, frustration, loss or grief. Tell them that you will continue to go around the social circle seeking ideas until they have nothing left. When each student runs out of ideas, they slide off their chair and sit on the floor in front of it. The last two players remaining seated win! Here are some ideas to ease disappointment, frustration, loss and grief. You may wish to share some with students before you begin:

- "Stop, take a few deep breaths and calm myself."

- "I colour in mandalas. That calms me."

- "Stop and walk away to give myself time to think."

- "Ask myself if this is worth getting too upset about."

- "Ask myself if having a good cry might help."

- "Allow myself to feel sad."

- "I do a dot-to-dot."

- "I draw my disappointment."

- "Make a positive statement to put things in perspective."

- "I use my hand massager on myself."

- "Talk about it with my parents or friends. A worry shared is a worry halved!"

- "Think about what I can learn from this, and how to cope better next time."

- "It helps when I listen to meditations."

- "I play with stretchy fidgets and just think."

- "Be kind and forgive myself".

- "Move away from the person or whatever made me disappointed."

- "Tell yourself exactly what problem is – name it."

- "I think of the catastrophe scale and remind myself just how big this loss or disappointment should be."

- "I switch to my happiest thoughts for a while."

- "I write about it in my journal, so it becomes the keeper of badness and sadness."

- "I put in my earphones and listen to music."

- "I watch YouTube to calm down."

- "I go do my hobby thing!"

- "Take a long walk with a friend."

7. Three questions about disappointment, loss and grief

1 We all need to be happy, so is experiencing disappointment, loss and grief a bad thing?

2 Are these feelings likely to bring any benefit to a person's life in the longer run?

3 What about this quote: "That which does not kill us makes us stronger." Do you agree?

It's a good idea to write the three questions on the whiteboard or screen so students can refer to them. Next, split your group into smaller groups of three or four and give students the opportunity to share their opinions more intimately. When you feel the time is right, bring the entire group back together for a general discussion. Here are several themes to add to the discussion:

- It is impossible to live a perfectly happy life all the time. Feeling sad, disappointed, despondent, bored or distressed by grief – for a while – gives us time to slow down and think more deeply. There is a place for these feelings in each of our lives, as they provide a space for us to reflect and resolve to be better people. These trickier feelings are part of living, and we shouldn't avoid or be afraid of them. Importantly, these tricky feelings pass. And without them, we lose a critical reference point about appreciating the balance of a healthy emotional life.

- As for the quote by Friedrich Nietzsche, "That which does not kill us makes us stronger," don't read too much into it. All it's meant to do is inspire resilience and determination. The idea is that we can stand up to more than we think we can. However, confusion, hardship and chaos do not toughen people up or prepare them to deal with difficulties. It is friendship, love, care, belonging and feeling valued that strengthen our capacity.

- A few studies have shown that some survivors of traumatic situations believe the hardship stimulated positive changes for them. This is called post-traumatic growth. These people will say they have a renewed appreciation for life, are more inclined to adopt a world view rather than being focused on themselves, feel more satisfied spiritually, and report their relationships improve. On the flip side, many others who've experienced a traumatic situation are beset by a collection of post-traumatic stresses: nightmares, flashbacks, avoidance, anxiety, depression and more.

8. Find a 'positive perspective buddy'

Encourage students to find a school friend, a friend outside of school or family member to be their 'positive perspective buddy'. This is someone who promises to be there for them, to be a great listener, to help them find the positive side of things and never let them take things more seriously than they are. A perfect place to start is to explain who you have in your life as a 'positive perspective buddy' and how you have used them in the past.

Part 2: Role plays – dealing with disappointment

The role plays are in the photocopiable section at the end of this lesson. They are also available online at www.whatsthebuzz.net.au/main-menu/content-whats-the-buzz-with-teenagers. You may either read them to students, or print them and hand each group a role play. Help students to form small groups. Each role-play card states the number of students required. It does not matter if the same role play is given to several groups. Give students a few minutes to rehearse, and move between groups to provide plenty of coaching and enthusiasm.

Next, ask each group to perform their role play. If a student does not wish to perform, allow them to pass. So much can be learned through observing. Always perform role plays in the middle of the social circle. Consider capturing the action on video or photo by using your iPad, camera or smartphone. Encourage others to give constructive feedback after each role play.

3. *Do you know the Buzz?*

Do you know the Buzz? is a lively group 'discussion time' where students briefly respond to a series of questions and statements highlighted by Archie's story. The goal is for them to exchange ideas, and in the process 'mind map' their way more empathically through the complexities of social and emotional situations. This should also provide facilitators with an insight into the depth of student understandings. To do this, have students sitting on chairs in a social circle.

Your thoughts on these statements and questions?

* Have you ever experienced the death of a pet? How disappointed were you? Did you cry? Was it a big loss?

* Have you ever experienced the death of someone close to you? Who was it? How hard was it? How did you cope?

* Have you had other disappointments and losses in your life? What are your biggest one or two?

* Have you experienced what it feels like to grieve? How would you describe that feeling?

* Did the feeling of grief become easier to live with as time went by?

* Would you agree that disappointment, loss and grief are closely linked?

* Ayman burst into tears. Does this show that he's a weak person? Explain.

* Do you agree with this statement? "You must cry when a pet or someone dies, otherwise you are not being respectful."

* Do you know why Ayman said, "I'm sorry you had to see this" to his friends?

* Who agrees with Prisha's statement? "Death is part of life. Let's not forget to share all the goodness Lola's life brought." Why do you agree or disagree?

* Whose family is more like Archie's – in that death isn't talked about unless it happens, and then it's dealt with quickly?

* Is Prisha's family's attitude about life, death and grieving a healthy one? Can you explain.

4. *The Buzz*

The Buzz is an opportunity for the group to play games that strengthen their relationships and the skills central to the lesson.

Game: Dealing with disappointment (passive)

This activity can be done with any size group. Organise the group to sit in a social circle. Supply them with a strip of paper and a pencil, and ask them to boldly write three numbers from 2 to 12 (inclusively) on the slip of paper. The numbers recorded remain in front of them on the floor, so they and others can see them during the game.

You'll need two dice. Once you have the attention of the group, roll both dice. The idea is to add the two numbers rolled together. Those players who have this number on their slip of paper win, and those who don't lose. It's very simple!

However, to increase intensity, hand the winners an inexpensive gift; stationery or small items purchased at a discount or dollar shop. As the winners receive their gift, the losers must take a deep breath and make an optimistic statement to the group that puts the loss into perspective:

- "Win some, lose some. It'll be okay."

- "Worse things could happen."

- "That's the way it is."

- "That's the way the cookie crumbles."

- "This wasn't my plan, but I can handle it."

- "Hey, glad you winners won this time!"

- "Let's play again!"

- "I can handle it."

- "I dare you to give me another go."

- "There's always next time."

- "I'm pleased someone is happy!"

- "Hey, it won't matter tomorrow."

This simple exercise gives students an opportunity to create and listen to phrases that can be used in times of disappointment, loss or frustration.

Game: Let's catastrophise! (exciting)

First, show students our 'catastrophe scale'. This is in the photocopiable section at the end of this lesson. Explain that a 'catastrophe scale' is a method to rate the intensity of disappointment, frustration or any emotion. Our 'catastrophe scale' is graded from 1 to 5, with 1 being a slight setback, 3 suggesting it's a problem that must be shared with a trusted friend or adult, and 5 is an awful disaster.

Catastrophe scales help to place the issue into perspective: "How big is this?" "Does it really matter?" "Will it really matter tomorrow?" "Is it so bad that it has to wreck my day?" "Who can I talk to about this?" "Is there a quick way to make this better?" Display it where students can see it throughout the game.

To play 'Let's catastrophise!', you'll need to print the scenarios. They are in the photocopiable section at the end of this lesson. Hand out a scenario to half of the students. To the remaining half, randomly hand out a number (1, 2, 3, 4 or 5) to each student. The numbers are also in the photocopiable section at the end of this lesson, ready to be printed.

The goal is for players to move about and find a match. In other words, a player holding the scenario and a player holding the number (which suggests the intensity of the scenario) must agree that they match. Players may have to approach several other players to get an agreed match. It is possible that some players will not be able to agree, so cannot find a match. This is okay as this is not a win or lose game. Rather, it's a chance for students to discuss why – or why not – an agreement can be made. Say 'go' and give the players a few minutes to find their matches, if they can! Allow time afterwards to check in with the pairs who've found each other. Listen to the reason why they believe the scenario and the number from the 'catastrophe scale' matched. It's also amusing listening to players who couldn't find a match.

Game: Disappointment 10-pin bowling (moderately exciting)

Bring out a bowling set to play 'Disappointment 10-pin bowling'. Prior to the lesson, write a message from below on slips. Arrange the pins and tape a slip of paper containing a message on the pins.

- Take one and keep for yourself.

- Take one and give it away.

- Take two. Keep one and give one away.

- Take two and give both away.

- Disappointing, but you miss out.

- Sorry, there's nothing for you.

- So sad, so sorry!

- Take one and give it to the facilitator.

- Take one, then put it back.

- Take two. Give one to someone taller than you and the other to someone shorter.

In this game, players take turns to bowl the ball and knock a pin down. The pin that counts is the first one that falls. Once a pin is knocked down, the bowler comes up to read the message and must do what it says with a positive attitude. Have a collection of inexpensive items that students can choose from. This game is good fun, but be alert because a few may struggle with their disappointment! Reinforce that we are playing for fun and friendship. The other thing players will soon twig to is that while they may miss out on a reward after they have bowled, there will be ample opportunity to receive gifts from others.

Game: Guard the pin (exciting)

This game requires a volleyball (or similar) and one 10-pin bowling skittle. Arrange players to stand in a large circle facing towards the centre. The bowling skittle is placed in the centre of the circle and a guard is chosen to protect it. The guard stands in the centre of the circle near the pin. The objective is for players to knock down the bowling skittle with the ball by bowling it over. All throws must be under-arm. The guard can use all parts of their body to stop or deflect the ball. No one is permitted to kick the ball, although the guard can stop the ball with their foot. The person who eventually knocks down the bowling skittle becomes the new guard. Players quickly learn that unless they cooperate and communicate by rolling the ball to one another, it is very difficult to get the ball past the guard.

After the Buzz: Social thinking ideas for parents and caregivers

Lesson 7: Dealing with disappointment (loss and grief)

Key social and emotional principles (learning intention)

The purpose of this lesson is to teach the essential facts about disappointment, loss and grief because they are tricky feelings to cope with, yet are unavoidable. The lesson also embraces how to support others who've been affected by disappointment, loss and grief.

After the Buzz presents additional ideas for parents, guardians and educators to encourage the social and emotional thinking students have touched on during the lesson. Here are a few everyday ideas to help your child, or students, deal with disappointment, loss and grief in the healthiest of contexts. In addition, there are tips on how to improve your child's ability to deal with disappointment, loss and grief, and guide them in positive directions.

Create a healthy context for death

The coping skills required to deal effectively with death and grieving take time to learn. They are a work in progress, and are significantly enhanced if children receive open and educated modelling from home. Parents who chat about the place of death in life, and use it as a time to celebrate the goodness that life brought to others, project an irresistible positive influence. These are the parents who cleverly insist their children have pets because they know the time will come when the inevitable happens. The opposite are parents who feel afraid of death, choose rarely to discuss it with their children and avoid it.

Dealing with death and grief

Grief is a normal response to a significant loss. Significant losses include the death of a loved one or the passing of a beloved pet, a relationship or friendship break-up,

After the Buzz . . . Lesson 7

and many other big life changes. During this time, we feel a variety of emotions, and we should reassure our children that it's normal to feel overwhelmed for a while. Everyone grieves differently, with and without tears, and at different speeds. Encourage the person grieving to:

- Accept these deep feelings of loss, and identify any other feelings as well.

- Understand that grieving is a process. It will take time.

- Spend time with friends and family.

- Talk, laugh and cry with friends and family about this loss. Keep talking.

- This is the time to take care of yourself. Exercise, eat properly, and get enough sleep to stay healthy.

- Return to your normal interests. It's important to do the things that bring you happiness.

- If necessary, talk to a professional – a school counsellor, psychologist or grief therapist.

For additional information about grief, begin with these websites:

- https://childhoodgrief.org.au/

- https://kidsaid.com/

- www.dougy.org/grief-resources/help-for-kids/

- www.grief.org.au/

Make yourself available to listen

These are tough feelings to work through, and initially many of us tend to over-react. However, as adults, it's our job to lend an ear and show empathy for what they are feeling. Work at remaining calm. Your calmness will help provide clarity.

Use a 'catastrophe scale' to put things into perspective

A 'catastrophe scale' is a rational way to rate the intensity of disappointment, frustration or any emotion. Our 'catastrophe scale' is in the photocopiable section at the end of this lesson and is graded from 1 to 5 – 1 being a slight setback, 3 suggesting it's a problem that must be shared with a trusted friend or adult, and 5 is an awful disaster. Print it and use it at home. Catastrophe scales help us keep the issue

After the Buzz . . . Lesson 7

in perspective: "How big is this?" "Does it really matter?" "Will it really matter tomorrow?" "Is it so bad that it has to wreck my day?" "Who can I talk to about this?" "Is there a quick way to make this better?" This is a sensible way to help each of us see the light at the end of the tunnel and get through the emotional pain.

Mothers, sons and disappointments

Too often, we work with children, usually boys, who at 4 or 14 years of age repeatedly yell, kick, hit and smack their mothers when they're disappointed, thwarted or sad. These are not bad young people, but this behaviour isn't acceptable, and gradually extinguishing it relies our wisdom and consistency. We coach parents to do a couple of things. First, after the event, when everyone is calmer, briefly chat about what happened and revisit your expectation of how they could have expressed their upset. Help the child learn from the incident. Avoid getting bogged down questioning them on "Why did you do it?" The truth is they may not know or may not be able to articulate this. Always matter-of-factly apply a sensible negative consequence after this kind of behaviour has occurred.

Second, return to one theme: "Your mother is the last person on earth you should ever hurt. She gave you life. She is the person you most need to treasure every single day." And remember, keep it brief. This is more empowering when it comes from fathers or male role models to boys. This is a reminder that boys don't emerge from the womb knowing how to treat women. It takes years of thoughtful and gentle modelling from dads and other males for them to see how it's truly done.

Teach children from the earliest of ages how to regulate their emotions and calm

Support them to find what works. Here are a few supportive ideas used to calm jangled feelings:

- Stop, take a few deep breaths.

- Stop and walk away to make time to think.

- Having a good cry can help.

- Allow the feeling of sadness.

- Do a dot-to-dot.

- Draw or journal the disappointment or loss.

- Make a positive statement out loud to help put things in perspective.

- Talk about it with parents or friends.

- Listen to an audio story or meditation.

- Play with a fidget and just think.

- Move away from the disappointment.

- Tell yourself exactly what disappointment is.

- Identify the other feelings accompanying the disappointment.

- Switch on your happiest thoughts for a while.

- Put in your earphones and listen to music.

- Watch YouTube to calm down.

- Go do your hobby.

- Take a long walk.

Coping with disappointment

Most of us have an innate urge to protect our children from negative emotions, especially disappointment. Yet a child's ability to cope with it is built through learning how to deal with it. Disappointment is essential for healthy emotional growth. It is through the pains of childhood, with balanced parental input, that children are prepared to deal with more complex disappointments later in life. Keep this in mind, and try to refrain from rushing in and fixing their problems for them or not allowing them to feel disappointed. Instead, help them work through their disappointed feelings by encouraging them to put the disappointment into words. Acknowledge your child's feelings, but also focus on creating a positive way forward. The truth is none of us can be happy all the time. So, prepare your son or daughter to be sad or disappointed sometimes. Teach them that there is a place for disappointed and sad feelings in their life, and that these feelings pass.

When rehearsal sidesteps disappointment

In situations where disappointment and upset is likely to happen, be sure to plan for it! Discuss the upcoming event and pinpoint the moments that are likely to cause stress. Explore supportive options. One way may be an inconspicuous touch or secret signal at the critical moment, so they are reminded that you care, the moment will pass and all will be well. Spending time discussing what is likely to happen helps children to find extra emotional resources needed later when it counts.

A final word on helping your child cope with disappointment and loss

Be realistic. Rather than wrapping them up in cotton wool, let your children know life is wonderful, but it's also full of setbacks and disappointments. This is the nature

After the Buzz ... Lesson 7

of life. Show them that you believe in them, and allow them to strive, fail and suc-ceed so they can build a real sense of 'hands-on' faith in themselves. Here are our last few suggestions on how to respond to your children's disappointments and losses:

- Support them and allow them to feel disappointment just as you encourage them to feel success.

- Never blame others or put a spin on a situation to make your children feel better.

- Never buy your kids off with gifts and sparkling distractions to ease their disappointment or loss. Instead, offer a healthy perspective that helps your child to grow emotionally.

- Allow them to absorb their rightful share of responsibility.

- Help your children use their disappointment to find new ways to do things, to become more adaptable and build resiliency.

- Finally, be sure they know you love them and that your goal is to help them live a whole, healthy life.

After the Buzz ... Lesson 7

What's the Buzz with Teenagers?

28 The ball of disappointment

Think of a time that was very disappointing. As you revisit this memory use your coloured pencils to colour each of the feelings you also felt during this disappointing time. This idea helps us to see that our emotions often become tangled together. It's a helpful start to identify which others are at play besides disappointment. Later, if you want to, share the disappointment and explain why the different feelings you've coloured in were also present.

29 Role-play cards: Dealing with disappointment

Role play 1

You're two days away from going to your first concert. You've put all your savings towards the ticket. You and your two best friends are counting down the hours. While you check out the latest updates on the band's website, the three of you come across an unexpected disappointment. The tour has been cancelled because the lead singer was in a serious accident. You and your friend feel like you've been hit by a lightning bolt. Show how you'd talk it through together to make sense of the disappointment and regroup your emotions. (A group of three – you and your two friends)

Role play 2

You love your new pet so much. And to think that your parents gave her to you as a surprise on Christmas morning! You name it Ally. A few weeks later, you notice Ally licking her leg a lot. Soon she begins to limp and won't let her paw touch the ground. Her leg is very swollen. You take her to the vet and find out she has deep-vein thrombosis and might not make it through the night. Show how you deal with this unforeseen setback while you wait for the vet to call. You can make up your own ending. (A group of three – you, the vet and your mum or dad)

Role play 3

Your grandpa is 93 years old. He's always been special to you, but now he's sick. You notice all the adults are talking seriously and secretly, and everyone looks sad. There are enough clues for you to know something is very wrong, but no one is saying anything to you. Show how you'd raise the subject with your mum or dad. Use an approach that convinces your parents you are mature enough to be completely involved in this tough time. (A group of three – you, your mum or dad, and a brother or sister)

29 Role-play cards: Dealing with disappointment *continued . . .*

Role play 4

Last night, there was a wild thunderstorm and this morning your dog is missing. You spend the day with dad looking all over the district, and place 'lost dog' notices everywhere. The next day, you want to keep looking, but your parents insist you go to school. The loss of your dog is almost too much to bear. Show what you'd do to cope with this situation as best you can, which may involve sharing what has happened with friends or a teacher. You may choose how the role play ends. Will your dog be found? (A group of three – you, friends or a teacher)

Role play 5

In this role play, your parents tell you they are separating. You had no idea anything was wrong between them. You're shocked, but they don't want to discuss it any further with you and your brother/sister. You have so many questions. In scene 1, you and your brother/sister spend some time talking about it. Show us what you'd say to each other. Develop a plan so your mum and dad understand this is a huge loss to you both, but you're smart enough to deal with this together. In scene 2, let's see you take this to your mum and dad the next day. Good luck; show us your combined best! (A group of four – you, your brother or sister, and your mum and dad)

Role play 6

Your best friend's mum has been sick for a long time. Everyone knows that she has a terminal illness. It's very sad, and even sadder because she's only 35 years old. Your best friend is over at your house when the phone rings. You overhear your parents talking to their father. You gather their mother has passed away and their dad is on the way. Your friend senses you know something. What should you say while they are waiting for dad to arrive? (A pair – you and your friend)

29 Role-play cards: Dealing with disappointment *continued . . .*

Role play 7

Your grandmother died in the early hours of this morning. She was 99 and had been in great health until recently. You thought she'd live forever. Your heart hurts and you can't stop tearing up. In this role play, show how your friend offers you a few kind words that make all the difference. (A pair – you and your friend)

Role play 8

Your family has spent the last year building a new house. The plan was to include a fabulous swimming pool, and you've mentioned this to a lot to friends. It's getting near the end of the build and your parents tell you they can't afford the pool. Given how much you've talked to friends about coming over to swim, this now feels embarrassing. Your parents don't seem to understand how big this loss is to you. In the role play, explain how you feel to your parents, show that you accept the decision, but are struggling to know what to say to your friends. (A group of three – you, Mum and Dad)

Role play 9

You and everyone in your group are invited to a friend's party on their llama farm. It promises to be a wonderful afternoon with friends and with the quirky llamas! On your way, your car breaks down. You spend most of the afternoon waiting for a mobile mechanic to come and help. Sadly, you arrive as it's finishing. In this role play, show your courage and poise. Show how you'll greet your friend, wish them happy birthday and meet your friends while you handle your disappointment as best you can. (A group of four – you, your friend and two others who were invited)

---

29 Role-play cards: Dealing with disappointment *continued . . .*

Role play 10

Two days ago, a bushfire destroyed your family's holiday house. It's basic, but it's been in your family for years and holds many precious memories. Now the fires are all out, your parents ask if you'd come with them to visit the ruins and face what has happened. This is tough. Show how you'll talk this through with your parents, express your sadness, support them and decide on what's best. (A group of three – you and your parents)

Role play 11

You wake up to a new bike on Christmas morning. It is exactly what you wanted. You spend the whole day riding it and admiring it. You've never felt so grateful. That night, you lock it in the garage and spend the night dreaming about riding it tomorrow. When you wake up the next morning, you discover the garage has been broken into and your bike is gone. Your mum, who is trying to help, says, "Come on, it's not the end of the world. We still have a house and each other." It does feel like the end of the world to you, but you know she's trying to help. In this role play, express your feelings to your mum and show how to deal with this devastating loss in a practical and composed way. (A pair – you and your mother)

What's the Buzz with Teenagers?

30 Disappointment: Catastrophe scale

A Catastrophe scale rates the intensity of disappointment, frustration or any emotion. Keep it in your memory or print it and use it. Catastrophe scales help us keep what's happening in perspective; "How big is this?" "How much should it matter?" "Will it matter tomorrow?" "Is it so bad that it has to wreck my whole day?" "Who can I talk to about this?" "Is there a quick way to fix this ?" It's a great way to see the light at the end of the tunnel, and get through the hurt or stress we feel in the moment.

Catastrophe Scale

A glitch

I'm a little worried, but should be able to handle this on my own.

An upset

This bothers me. It might be a good idea to chat to a friend about it.

A trouble

I'm worried! I best share this with a friend, mum, dad or a teacher because this won't go away and will still matter tomorrow.

A crisis

This is up there! This will matter for some time to come. I need to share this with those who care about me, and keep talking.

A disaster or tragedy

Oh, no. This problem is huge, even life changing. I need to connect and share with everyone in my support network. I need a plan!

What's the Buzz with Teenagers?

31 Game: Let's catastrophise! – the scenarios

Scenario
You're at home relaxing and video game controller won't work. You really wanted to play your new game.

Scenario
You have lost a valuable gold coin that is very precious to your family. You have no idea where it is.

Scenario
Without thinking, you picked up your friend's phone. You see a nasty message about you from someone.

Scenario
Everyone else has been invited to go to a birthday party, but you haven't.

Scenario
You are not with any of your friends in your new class.

Scenario
Someone ate all the chocolate that was meant to be shared, and you missed out.

Scenario
You miss out on going to the movies because you're too sick.

Scenario
Your friends are picking groups and you are the last to be picked.

Scenario
Your mother has banned pocket money because no one is doing their jobs. You need the money.

Scenario
Dad promised to bring a special treat home with him. He completely forgot.

Scenario
You are waiting for a friend to come over. Just as they should be arriving they phone and say they can't come.

Scenario
The sporting team you play for keeps on losing. The kids are great, but it's disappointing and humiliating!

Scenario
Every time you try to shoot a goal in a match you miss. You're beginning to think you're cursed!

Scenario
Your mother and father hand you your birthday present. It is not what you wanted.

Scenario
Over the last couple of days, you've been getting some texts that put you down from two friends.

Scenario
It's maths again, and you have no idea again! You need to pass this semester.

What's the Buzz with Teenagers?

32 Game: Let's catastrophise! – the numbers

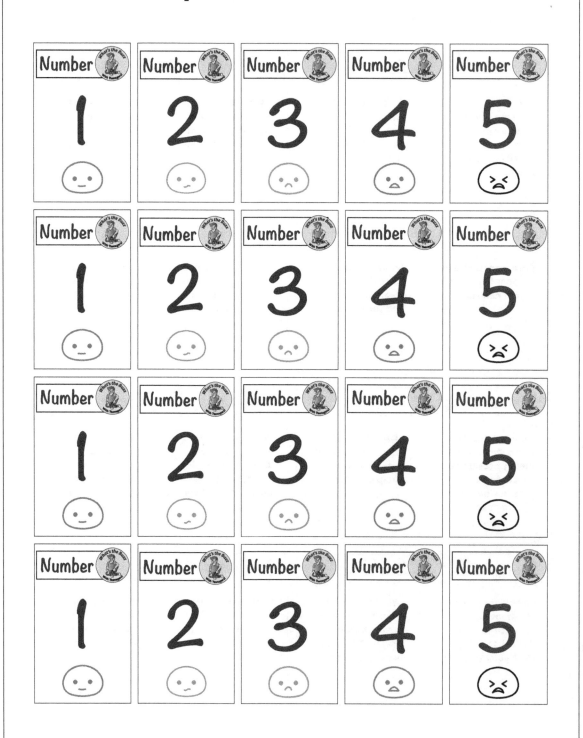

Handling anxiety

"I don't want to talk about it!"

Key social and emotional principles (learning intention)

This lesson explores what anxiety is, how our bodies identify it, and ideas to manage it more effectively. It also debunks the myth that all anxiety is bad, and that young people should never worry. Some worry serves a good purpose, but too much is debilitating. We introduce a worry scale as one idea to keep worry in a healthy perspective. To be mentally healthy, young people need a new freedom to openly share their thoughts, fears and anxieties with friends and trusted people in their lives. When equipped with quality information, everyone can participate productively, offering supportive networks loaded with sage advice.

Materials required for this lesson

- Name tags.

- Chairs in a social circle for students to sit on.

- Whiteboard/butcher's paper/screen and markers.

- Create a simple outline of the lesson on the whiteboard/butcher's paper/ screen for students to follow.

- Display the *What's the Buzz?* group values (located in the introduction or at www.whatsthebuzz.net.au/main-menu/ content-whats-the-buzz-with-teenagers).

- Organise feedback and reminder cards, or similar, to strengthen responsive behaviours (located in the introduction or at www.whatsthebuzz.net.au/ main-menu/content-whats-the-buzz-with-teenagers).

- Have Archie's story ready to read to students. This can be done directly from this lesson. Or, for a small registration fee, you can download the 16 Archie stories as you want them. Each story contains text, audio in the form of the authors reading to your students, and two large illustrations in full colour that will fill your screen. Access is available at www.whatsthebuzz.net.au/ main-menu/content-whats-the-buzz-with-teenagers

- Pencils, pens and paper for students to do Part 1 of *Show me the Buzz*.

- Print the 'Worry: Catastrophe scale' ready to play 'Rate your worry: A game show' in Part 1 of *Show me the Buzz*.

- Print the role-play cards for 'Handling worry' in Part 2 of *Show me the Buzz* (located at the end of the lesson or at www.whatsthebuzz.net.au/main-menu/ content-whats-the-buzz-with-teenagers).

- Prepare handouts for parents(s):

  One copy of this lesson for each parent to read.

  One copy of *After the Buzz: Social thinking ideas for parents and caregivers* to send home (located at the end of the lesson, ready to photocopy, or at www. whatsthebuzz.net.au/main-menu/content-whats-the-buzz-with-teenagers).

Lesson 8

Explanation

Mental illness in young people in the twenty-first century is a deepening concern. In a survey conducted by Mission Australia and the Black Dog Institute, 25 per cent of young Australians aged from 15 to 19 years were considered at risk of serious mental illness, with anxiety and depression leading the way (Bullot et al., 2017). One of the most challenging barriers to identification is that young people are not inclined to declare how they're feeling or ask for help. So, early education and intervention makes good sense. The sooner students can be reached in schools and taught how to identify the early warning signs of mental illness, which so often includes anxiety, the closer we'll get to turning current statistics around.

The starting point is to understand that all children experience some degree of worry or anxiety. Childhood is tricky because it's an early baptism into the challenges offered by life: injustice, conflict with peers, disagreements with friends, struggles with school, teachers and learning, let alone discovering how you're valued, how you see and feel about your body image, changes that family separations bring, and so much more. Fear, doubt and hesitation are natural responses to many of these situations, but without a proactive mindset and basic supportive structures these everyday worries can escalate into anxiousness, sadness and depression very quickly. We have a large and growing group of children who have become experts at making mountains out of molehills. Is this the result of parents and schools becoming risk-averse? A risk-averse style doesn't give the child – particularly a child who might be vulnerable to developing anxiety problems – an opportunity to face difficult situations and learn they can handle them. Overprotection sees kids become highly reliant on adults to fix their problems. Their resilience disappears, and their anxiety skyrockets. Is this the reason why we are in the grips of an anxiety epidemic for kids (Majdandžić et al., 2018)?

We believe that down-to-earth conversations with young people that normalise the feeling and purpose of worrying are too often absent. Children need to know and absorb that almost everyone experiences worry, and it needs to be experienced because it has a purpose. A little anxiety is a useful means to plan, prioritise, prepare and cope with life's new experiences, or to review an experience so one's performance is better next time. You see, long, long ago, our ancestors lived in dangerous times and in dangerous places. They had to go out into the wild to hunt and gather food. They knew it was treacherous to be away from the safety of their camp, and being worried helped them to be hyper-alert, hyper-fast and hyper-clever to help avoid attacks from the sabertooth tigers and other big beasts. Their worrying was productive as it aided their very survival! Today, it's different. Most of us live lives where we don't need to flee from a sabertooth tiger, but we are left with an evolutionary imprint that protects us, and it's called worry. Yes, worry is a special protection that helps us survive real and perceived danger. But sometimes our primitive system gets 'stuck' and sets off false anxiety.

In this state, young people spend more time feeling uncertain, anxious and anticipating things will turn out badly than they do giving things a go, pushing through the doubt, and building new skills and confidence. The unfortunate reality is that spending too long in a state of fear gets them 'stuck' in worry, making it hard for them to move forward. This state of being stuck, or 'stuckness', becomes their habit. Children on the autism spectrum are often slaves to this kind of crippling worry habit, and this is why they rely on expertly crafted plans to build the necessary skills to understand worry and problem-solve.

To live mentally healthy lives, young people need a new freedom to openly share their worries with friends and trusted people in their lives. When equipped with quality information, everyone can participate productively, throughout the teenage years and beyond.

1. *What's the Buzz?*

Actively greet students as they enter. Provide chairs in a social circle for them to sit on and have a brief lesson plan on the screen, whiteboard or butcher's paper for students to see. As students are settling, hand each of them a 'Thumbs up feedback card' to highlight their thoughtful behaviour and using the group values.

Let's begin

Explain that worry, or anxiety, can be a tough feeling to deal with. That's why we say, "Worry is a bully." And to prove it, do a survey with your students. Ask, "Who feels anxious sometimes?" Next, ask, "Who knows they worry a little too much?" Lastly, ask, "Who's anxious about too much too often?"

Explain that everyone feels it; for some, it's at a low level and just sometimes, but for others it's experienced most of the time and at high levels. Fourteen per cent of Australian kids and teens (close to one in five) will experience some kind of mental health issue this year. Seven per cent will experience anxiety disorder, and thousands more will feel anxiety most days, but will put up with it, never report it or get help. Sadly, we'll lose 400 precious young Australians to suicide this year because they feel too embarrassed or ashamed to talk about their worry or sadness and ask for help (www.beyondblue.com). They allow worry to bully them into not seeking help from friends, family or support networks.

Archie's story: "I don't want to talk about it!"

Archie hadn't been feeling himself since the cross-country race with Prisha. He appreciated what she did when he rolled his ankle and fell to the ground just before the finish line. Prisha caught him,

33 Archie's story: "I don't want to talk about it!" – first image

Lauren Eldridge Murray

This image can be downloaded from http://whatsthebuzz.net.au/main-menu/content-whats-the-buzz-with-teenagers and will fill your screen in colour. There is also the option to have the authors read the story to students.

but instead of taking the race for herself she pulled him up and was determined that they share the win together. In the end, they both grabbed hold of the tape across the finish line. This was the kindest thing anyone outside his family had ever done for him. It felt wonderful, weird and embarrassing all wrapped up together! Archie's feelings were still floating in this unsettled space, and to make it worse were the ridiculous comments some had made after the race. They made him feel uneasy, and the stupid comments kept going around in his head. They were:

- "Prisha, you had him! Why did you stop?"

- "Archie, you could have got up and won. Did you choke?"

- "Did you fall to get the sympathy vote, Archie?"

- "So dramatic. You and Prisha planned this, didn't you?"

While handling feelings perfectly well wasn't Archie's strength just yet, at least he knew he wasn't feeling right. He wasn't happy. He felt flat, moody and filled with anxiousness, but it made no sense. And the worst thing? He felt so alone. Was he the only person in the world with these weird feelings? Maybe. So how could he find the words to talk to Mum, Dad, Tobias, Joanna or any of his closest friends about them? They'd think he was pathetic.

Tobias' party was on this afternoon. For the first time in his life, Archie wanted nothing to do with a party and nothing to do with his friends. He needed to be home alone with Maxi, Luca, Kelvin and his Lego. Yes, his Lego. He didn't really use it anymore, but sometimes when he was feeling out of sorts his Lego comforted him because it reminded him of safer and happier times.

His mum was gardening outside and tapped on his bedroom window, pointing to her watch. He could read her lips, "Nearly time for Tobias' party. Get ready." Archie felt annoyed. Couldn't she see he wasn't excited about this? Couldn't she tell he was having a rough time? Archie didn't get ready. Instead, he hopped into bed and disappeared under his quilt. His three whippets took advantage of the opportunity and buried themselves under the quilt with him. "I want the world to disappear," he thought to himself. "I want this party to go away. I just want to be alone." Surrounded by the warmth of Maxi, Luca and Kelvin, Archie dozed in a light sleep.

Suddenly, he was woken by the ring of FaceTime on his iPad. It was Tobias. Archie wanted to ignore him, but he couldn't do that to his closest friend, so he answered. Tobias was excited, and Archie could see him moving about following his new drone as he flew it. He begged

34 Archie's story: "I don't want to talk about it!" – second image

Lauren Eldridge Murray

This image can be downloaded from http://whatsthebuzz.net.au/main-menu/content-whats-the-buzz-with-teenagers and will fill your screen in colour. There is also the option to have the authors read the story to students.

Archie to come right now and be the first person to fly it with him before his party started. Archie felt annoyed watching Tobias. "Why can't he see how miserable I feel?" he thought to himself. Archie was at such a low point. Part of him knew Tobias had done nothing wrong and he deserved to be excited about his birthday present and his party, yet another dark part of him was sure that every bit of happiness Tobias was feeling was sucking away any happiness he might find.

Then Archie was hit with a gush of panic and a feeling of hopelessness. These feelings hit hard. His heart raced, his throat felt tight and he gasped for air. And the words that followed were regrettable, and could never be taken back. Archie threw his arms into the air, clenched his fists and screamed at Tobias into his iPad, "I don't care about your drone or your party today. I can't do it." Then Archie ended the call and froze. Archie wasn't a hurtful person, and he'd never done anything like this before, especially to Tobias. Archie expelled a deep, long sigh, "Nooooooooooo!!!" His life felt like it was out of control. His mum came running in and asked, "What's all the noise about? What's wrong?"

Instantly, Archie shouted at her, "You should know! You're my mum! I don't want to talk about it! It makes me feel pathetic!"

His mum sat with him. As her hand rested on his back, she could feel is heart racing. The whippets had the right idea. They knew Archie wasn't himself, so laid glued to his side under the quilt. He wanted to fall asleep again so he wouldn't have to think about these awful feelings and what he'd done to Tobias.

Then came an unexpected knock at the door. The door swung open. It was Tobias. What was going on? He should be at his party, not here!

Discussion based on the questions and statements below will occur later in *Do you know the Buzz?* For now, simply read them to get students thinking. Encourage them to listen and respond to each question by putting their thumb up if they 'agree' or think 'yes', thumb down if they think 'no', and thumb to the side if they think 'maybe'. Move very quickly through them. No verbal responses are required.

Your thoughts on these statements and questions?

- Have you ever felt like Archie?

- Being sad from time to time is a part of life, but feeling sad most of the time isn't right. Who agrees?

- Is being anxious sometimes a normal thing?

- If you were carrying around a worry that you couldn't get out of your head, do you know what you'd do?

- Would you share your worries with someone?

- Do you know how to calm yourself, or quieten your thinking, when you're sad or worrying too much?

- Did you think it strange that Archie thought Tobias' happiness was sucking his happiness away?

- Straight away, Archie regretted what he said to Tobias. Have you ever said something to someone and regretted it?

- Is it okay to not go to a friend's party because you're feeling 'flat', 'sad' or 'troubled'?

- Is it okay to ask a friend if they're all right when you're worried about them?

- Would a good friend always check in to make sure you were feeling okay?

- Some think it's better to leave others alone and let them work out their own problems. Do you agree?

- What if you asked a friend if they're okay and they said they were, but you knew they were not? Should you do more?

- Why did Tobias leave the start of his party to visit Archie?

- What Tobias is about to do is risky and takes courage. Would you do it?

2. *Show me the Buzz*

Show me the Buzz provides students with the opportunity to discuss a variety of social and emotional ideas, absorb the thoughts of others, debate them, create role plays and receive feedback from the group. We have learned that this approach heightens understandings and the transference of skills. There is always a Part 1 and a Part 2. Choose one activity from either Part 1 or Part 2, depending on what appeals to you, the time you have and your group's likely preferences. There's plenty of content in *Show me the Buzz*, so the lesson can be revisited time and time again while continuing with this same topic.

Part 1

1. Rewrite the ending

Archie's story finishes with "Then came an unexpected knock at the door. It was Tobias. What was going on? He should be at his party, not here!" Continue the story by writing the conversation that takes place between Archie and Tobias. Tobias has bravely decided to leave his party because he wants to check on his best friend. For fun, suggest students do this in pairs. One takes on the role of

Archie and the other becomes Tobias. Then they take turns writing dialogue to each other to resolve the problem.

2. Create a role play or film

Encourage students to work in pairs or small groups to develop a role play that can be filmed and viewed by the larger group.

3. What do you worry about?

Break students into groups of three or four. Each group will need a blank A4 sheet of paper and a pen or pencil for a recorder to write with. The task is to make a list of the things that they worry about. You may wish to kick-start them by sharing a survey called *What Worries Australian Children?* The topics that proved to be most prevalent were being different, schoolwork and grades, world problems, bullying, my body and looks, friendships, health, family, and my future (Blumer, 2015). Afterwards, return to the larger group and encourage everyone to share their thoughts. You might ask them to vote on the topics that most worry them.

Alternatively, simply ask, "What are the things you worry about?" List them on the whiteboard. Let this exercise be an opportunity for students to normalise their feelings and see that there are different ways to think about issues, and that discussing them helps.

4. Brainstorm solutions for worries and sadness

As a larger group, brainstorm eight helpful ideas people do when they're feeling troubled by too much frustration, worry or sadness. Be sure to contribute organisation such as these to the discussion:

- Beyondblue – www.beyondblue.org.au/get-support/national-help-lines-and-websites

- Black Dog Institute – www.blackdoginstitute.org.au/

- Headspace – https://headspace.org.au/

- eHeadspace – www.eheadspace.org.au/

Sometimes young people won't talk to parents, friends, teachers, members of their extended family or coaches, so it's important that they are aware of these additional connections. Most offer phone and online helplines. Afterwards, arrange students into pairs and give each pair one of the helpful ideas that was brainstormed. Their task is to research this idea in greater depth, create a practical guide about how to do this, and teach it to the larger group.

5. Group discussion: When a friend needs help

On the butcher's paper, whiteboard or screen, write the heading '10 things you can SAY or DO when you sense a friend needs help'. Prompt ideas from students and record them. To finish off this discussion, throw in the provocative question, "Should you help someone who's in emotional trouble if they are not your friend?"

6. Rate your worry: A game show!

Ask four students to organise a 'Rate your worry game show'. Two students can be compères and the other two play the flamboyant assistants. In this case, they will hold up the 'Worry: Catastrophe scale' (located at the end of this lesson) using those well-known over-the-top hand, body and voice gestures. The idea is for the compères to introduce the show and explain how it's played. To play, the 'Worry: Catastrophe scale' is held by the two hosts and one of the compères reads a situation below. The audience is then invited to rate the seriousness of the worry, with one finger up indicating a slight setback, two fingers up for an upset, three fingers up for a trouble, four fingers up for a crisis, and five fingers up for a total disaster. Compères should emphasise that by rating the worry, it helps to keep it in perspective!

Here are some situations to begin with, but encourage the compères and hosts to add more of their own:

- You're at school and have forgotten your lunch and have no money.

- You might get an itch on your foot later today.

- You can't understand it, so you're worried about your maths homework.

- You must move to a new house, leave your friends and start at a new school.

- You cannot find your phone anywhere. You have no idea where it is.

- You have left your phone at a friend's house.

- You have lost your game controller somewhere in your bed.

- The cord in your game controller just fell out.

- You must go to the school camp for an entire week.

- Your dog is ill.

- Your dear granny is very sick.

- Your friends seem distant from you today.

- It's been hard to connect with your friends this week.

- Mum forgot to give you your pocket money.

- Your mum is very unhappy with your dad. You're worried they may separate.

- You didn't get invited to a close friend's birthday party.

Provide an opportunity to discuss why variations in ratings occur, as well as possible solutions.

7. Group discussion

Pose these five questions to prompt a discussion.

Question 1: Who thinks getting more sleep might beat anxiety?

Encourage discussion between students, and in the right moment introduce that without nine hours of sleep, we tend to give our inner worrier more power. Researchers at Binghamton University, New York, found that people who go to bed late and sleep for short amounts of time experience more negative thoughts than those who get to bed earlier and get nine hours of continuous sleep (Schubert et al., 2017). These worriers worried about the future and past events, and have a higher risk of anxiety, depression, post-traumatic stress disorder and obsessive-compulsive disorder. Sleep is the best tool for organisation, tolerance, continued learning, remaining at school and happiness!

Question 2: Would smelling lavender oil, or something like it, help?

Encourage discussion between students, and in the right moment add that breathing in aromas from certain essential oils can help reduce worry and stress. Increasing numbers of studies on their calming effects are now available (Brooks, 2014). The olfactory nerve gives us our sense of smell. This nerve swiftly sends signals to the brain, including the limbic system and amygdala, which are in charge of emotions, mood and memory (Wei, 2017). Lavender essential oil is one of the most well studied. It helps alleviate mild insomnia, and reduces anxiety and depression. We have also learned that the essential oils from citrus can calm anxiety and lower your heart rate in just 10 minutes, with effects continuing for almost half an hour. Essential oils are harmless, so try them to see the effect.

Question 3: Does deep breathing or controlled breathing really reduce anxiety?

Encourage discussion between students, and in the right moment acknowledge that we all get tired of hearing, "Just slow your breathing down" or "Take long, slow, deep breaths" or "Just relax." But it works! Controlled breathing is a 'super stress buster'. It leaves the body more relaxed, calmer and focused by increasing the supply of oxygen to the brain and stimulating the parasympathetic nervous system, which promotes a state of calmness.

Question 4: Will eating chocolate reduce anxiety?

Encourage discussion between students, and in the right moment state that small regular amounts of dark chocolate have been linked with health benefits, and

Lesson 8

there is some evidence that it may help people to reduce their stress responses. Apparently, it reduces cortisol, the stress hormone that causes anxiety symptoms. There are also compounds inside dark chocolate that improve mood. Also, don't forget seaweed, whole grains, almonds, blueberries and oily fish (tuna, sardines, pilchards, mackerel, herring, trout and salmon) because these foods have the capacity to improve mood, relieve stress, and are rich in nutrients to fine-tune brain chemistry. However, food is not the only answer.

Question 5: Will exercise lower worry or stress?

Encourage discussion between students, and in the right moment explain that exercise is effective for helping mild to moderate anxiety. And you don't have to get sweaty either. Simply get moving! By playing a little basketball or riding your bike just once a day, you'll quickly feel a difference. Just deciding to walk to school or walk for 20 minutes every day with your mum, dad, a friend or the dog can be a game changer. Researcher Professor Elizabeth Gould of Princeton University said that physical activity reorganises the brain so anxiety is less likely to interfere with normal function (Hills, 2013).

8. Panic or anxiety attacks

Archie experienced a 'panic attack' in the story. There was a gush of anxiety and a feeling of hopelessness. His heart raced, his throat felt tight and he gasped for air. And then he said those regrettable things to Tobias. Discuss 'panic or anxiety attacks' with a view to normalising them and promoting awareness. Key points:

- A panic attack is a feeling of sudden and intense anxiety.

- They come with physical symptoms (name them).

- They can be frightening but are not dangerous.

- They will pass after a few minutes.

- Ride it out. If you must leave the situation, then return as soon as you can.

- Share with a friend. Let them be with you. They don't have to do anything. Just understand.

- If you're breathing quickly, slow it down with some controlled breathing. It works!

- Make a panic attack plan so you handle it better in the future.

- Anticipate when and where they are most likely to happen, so you stay ahead of them.

Part 2: Role plays – handling anxiety

The role plays are in the photocopiable section at the end of this lesson. They are also available online at www.whatsthebuzz.net.au/main-menu/content-whats-the-buzz-with-teenagers. You may either read them to students, or print them and hand each group a role play. Help students to form small groups. Each role-play card states the number of students required. It does not matter if the same role play is given to several groups. Give students a few minutes to rehearse, and move between groups to provide plenty of coaching and enthusiasm.

Next, ask each group to perform their role play. If a student does not wish to perform, allow them to pass. So much can be learned through observing. Always perform role plays in the middle of the social circle. Consider capturing the action on video or photo by using your iPad, camera or smartphone. Encourage others to give constructive feedback after each role play.

3. *Do you know the Buzz?*

Do you know the Buzz? is a lively group 'discussion time' where students briefly respond to a series of questions and statements highlighted by Archie's story. The goal is for them to exchange ideas, and in the process 'mind map' their way more empathically through the complexities of social and emotional situations. This should also provide facilitators with an insight into the depth of student under-standings. To do this, have students sitting on chairs in a social circle.

Your thoughts on these statements and questions?

- Have you ever felt like Archie?

- Being sad from time to time is a part of life, but feeling sad most of the time isn't right. Who agrees?

- Is being anxious sometimes a normal thing? Explain when it is normal. When is it not normal?

- If you were carrying around a worry that you couldn't get out of your head, do you know what you'd do?

- Would you share your worries with someone? Who'd share it with a friend, a teacher, Mum, Dad, a coach or someone you trust?

- Do you know how to calm yourself, or quieten your thinking, when you're sad or worrying too much?

- Did you think it strange that Archie thought Tobias' happiness was sucking his happiness away? What does this kind of thinking suggest to you?

- Straight away, Archie regretted what he said to Tobias. Have you ever said something to someone and regretted it? Can you share? How did you fix it?

- Is it okay to not go to a friend's party because you're feeling 'flat', 'sad' or 'troubled'?

- Is it okay to ask a friend if they're all right when you're worried about them?

- Would a good friend always check in to make sure you were feeling okay?

- Some think it's better to leave others alone and let them work out their own problems. Do you agree?

- What if you asked a friend if they're okay and they said they were, but you knew they were not? Should you do more?

- Why did Tobias leave the start of his party to visit Archie?

- What Tobias is about to do is risky and takes courage. Would you do it?

- Tell me people, places or organisations you'd go to to talk about the problem.

4. *The Buzz*

The Buzz is an opportunity for the group to play games that strengthen their relationships and the skills central to the lesson.

Game: 'Too high', 'just right' or 'too low' (passive)

This game is designed to get students to think about whether a person is responding with an appropriate level of thought and concern. The idea is to read a scenario to your group. As soon as you finish, raise your eyes and look at the group. They are to call back 'too high', 'just right' or 'too low'. They call 'too low' if the person in the scenario isn't concerned enough, 'too high' if they are overanxious, and 'just right' if it's a nicely considered response.

Scenarios:

- A child has lost their precious dog. It escaped from the backyard and hasn't been gone long. They decide not to join their family to look for it because they're in the middle of a video game.

- A student doesn't understand the maths explained. They become teary, pretend to be sick and ask to go home. They don't tell anyone about it and decide they will always be bad at maths.

- Jaz and Ami are good friends. Jaz messaged Ami to call him. She tried a couple of times but he didn't answer. So she messaged him. It said, "Tried calling you a couple of times. Don't worry. Call me when you can."

- Jaz and Ami are good friends. Jaz messaged Ami to call him. She didn't get around to it.

- School begins and a student realises they have left their phone at home. All they can think about is not having their phone. How can they communicate with anyone? They feel like it's the end of the world and can't wait to be reunited with it.

- Jack's best friend shares that his father is seriously ill. Jack shrugs his shoulders and says, "Oh?"

- Jack's best friend shares that his father is seriously ill. Jack shrugs his shoulders and says, "Does he have funeral cover?"

- Dad arrives home from work with a splitting headache. As he walks in, he hears Franca playing her bass guitar. She's terrible and not getting any better. "Hi, Franca! Can you play me one song then come out for some basketball with me?"

- Dad arrives home from work with a splitting headache. As he walks in, he hears Franca playing her bass guitar. She's terrible and not getting any better. He clutches at his chest, his heart starts to race, and he's finding it hard to breathe. He's having a panic attack!

- Luca's dad is working late tonight. He hardly ever works late, and Luca is really struggling to keep calm. He's convinced himself that his dad has been in a terrible accident and keeps on playing it in his head.

- Aliya has just discovered a massive pimple on her pretty nose. She knows it's only going to get bigger and redder, and she has a class presentation to do in the morning. She decides she won't go to school and will pretend she is sick.

- Iman has lost seven library books this term. The librarian politely takes her aside and shares her concerns about the lost books. Iman's reaction is, "You have so many books, does it really matter? It's not like I tried to lose them."

- Iman has lost seven library books this term. The librarian politely takes her aside and shares her concerns about the lost books. Iman's reaction is, "You're picking on me because you've never liked me or my family. I have the same right as everyone else to borrow books. And I'll fight for my rights too!"

- Iman has lost seven library books this term. The librarian politely takes her aside and shares her concerns about the lost books. Iman's reaction is, "I'm so sorry. It's my fault. We moved to a new house and everything is everywhere. I'll search for them tonight."

Game: Calm, stressed and why? (passive)

This game is designed to help students connect that our bodies give off specific signals according to our emotional state. Let students know that when you call out a body signal, their job is to work out whether it's a sign of being calm or stressed.

If they believe the body is 'stressed', they must stand up. If they think the body is 'calm', they remain seated. They must also be prepared to say what the accompanying feeling may be.

Example: 'breathing fast' (response: students would stand up because this is a sign of a stressed body, and the accompanying feeling is likely to be anxiousness).

Example: 'an easy, open smile' (response: students would remain seated because this is a sign of a calm body, and the accompanying feeling is likely to be joy or happiness).

Body signals:

- tense eyebrows/forehead

- smiling and giggling a little too much

- relaxed, loose muscles

- feeling teary

- clenched fists

- feeling light

- blushing

- slow, steady, easy breathing

- heart pumping fast

- a 'buzzing' in your muscles – an urge to run

- soft, relaxed facial muscles

- talking too fast

- open chested, shoulders pulled back

- gentle, regular heartbeat

- sweaty hands and skin

- feeling 'bouncy'

- shallow, fast breathing

- lump in throat

- tight chest or throat

- headache

- funny tummy/'butterflies in the tummy'

Game: What's the mood? (passive)

One of the most commonly asked questions is "How are you?" Usually, a simple response such as "Okay, thanks" is enough. Here are a few expressions that describe one's feelings. Have some fun, work your way around the social circle, and see if the group can unlock these esoteric terms:

Expression: 'bent out of shape' / Meaning: feeling very annoyed or angry

Expression: 'on cloud nine' / Meaning: feeling extremely happy

Expression: 'spaced out' / Meaning: not concentrating on what is going on around you, a bit like daydreaming

Expression: 'shaken up' / Meaning: feeling shocked or very surprised

Expression: 'on pins and needles' / Meaning: feeling anxious or nervous

Expression: 'over you' / Meaning: had enough, sick of you

Expression: 'on tenterhooks' / Meaning: feeling edgy or nervous

Expression: 'beat' or 'bushed' / Meaning: feeling exhausted

Expression: 'head over heels' / Meaning: the feeling of being completely in love with someone

Expression: 'fed up' / Meaning: feeling really frustrated

Expression: 'chilled out' / Meaning: feeling relaxed

Expression: 'under the weather' / Meaning: being slightly sick rather than seriously ill

Expression: 'Why the long face?' / Meaning: feeling gloomy or sad

Expression: 'a dirty look' / Meaning: a way of showing anger or disapproval by staring hard at someone

Expression: 'if looks could kill' / Meaning: someone looking angrily or aggressively

Expression: 'on cloud nine' / Meaning: feeling extremely pleased or happy

Expression: 'walking on air' / Meaning: feeling joyful, thrilled

Expression: 'keep your chin up' / Meaning: be happy despite bad things

Expression: 'down in the dumps' / Meaning: a depressed or sad look

Expression: 'you're not yourself' / Meaning: feeling slightly ill or upset

Expression: 'on top of the world' / Meaning: to feel extremely happy

After the Buzz: Social thinking ideas for parents and caregivers

Lesson 8: Handling anxiety

Key social and emotional principles (learning intention)

This lesson explores what anxiety is, how our bodies identify it, and ideas to manage it more effectively. It also debunks the myth that all anxiety is bad, and that young people should never worry. Some worry serves a good purpose, but too much is debilitating. We introduce a worry scale as one idea to keep worry in a healthy perspective. To be mentally healthy, young people need a new freedom to openly share their thoughts, fears and anxieties with friends and trusted people in their lives. When equipped with quality information, everyone can participate productively, offering supportive networks loaded with sage advice.

After the Buzz presents further ideas for parents, guardians and educators to encourage the social and emotional thinking students have touched on during the lesson. In this lesson, your child learned that worrying, in the main, is normal because it helps us to make sense of our world. Your child also discovered that most of us do much better when we try to understand our worry patterns and work with them to fix the problems driving them.

What's happening at home?

A few children are predisposed to worry. They are our 'natural-born worriers'. Beyond this, a sensible beginning point is to assess the influences occurring within your family: a separation, a divorce, arguments, financial difficulties, racial taunts, recovery following a car accident, a sick family member – even a story aired on the evening news can trigger feelings of distress, dread and helplessness. From time to time, stop and take stock about what's happening at home.

Become familiar with their worries

Do you know what your child worries about? Is there a recurring theme? Do their worries concern self-esteem, perfectionism, separation, fear, death or are they

After the Buzz ... Lesson 8

related to social encounters? Once you know, it is possible to teach specific strategies to work with.

Be the best role model

Let your children see you logically deal with worries and problems. Whenever you can, allow them to witness you using positive self-talk and positive thinking to find solutions. As we 'talk it out loud', the logical order of what can be done enhances our motivation and chances of success. Show your children how they can also rely on this. Let them hear you say, "I know I can do this. First, I'll . . ."

Make time to talk about the highs and lows of the day

Many parents deliberately build this time into evening meal conversations. It's a perfect forum to share successes and problem-solve troubles that may have arisen during the day.

Always deal with worries in the daytime!

Why? In the gloominess of the dark at bedtime, everything seems at its worst and positive thoughts are hard to gather. A useful way to help your child deal with worry is to get them to draw it, along with ideas to deal with it. Then get them to place it into their worry tin. It's just a matter of buying a small tin with a slot in the lid. For extra security, so the worries can't possibly escape, you might buy a tin with a tiny padlock on the lid. Once the worry has been discussed, drawn, written and folded up into the slotted tin, it doesn't need any further energy spent on it. The fascinating part is that when the worries are looked at weeks later, most children will say, "Those worries are pathetic now!" This delivers a healthy message about how much value we should give to worrying. As most of us have learned over the years, so few of our worries come to fruition. Using a worry tin in this way is a powerful teacher of this for children.

Get a worry doll

OXFAM (www.oxfam.org.au) has long sold 'Guatemalan worry dolls' in many cities around the world. These dolls are crafted around the image of Guatemalan children wearing traditional costume. The idea is the worry doll can take care of a child's worries so they can sleep peacefully. So, before climbing into bed, ask your child to share a worry with you and the worry doll. Then by placing it under their pillow, the doll can take care of it while they sleep.

What is 'holey thinking'?

Remind your child that worries are simply thoughts, and they have the power to choose their thoughts. Also, their thinking may be distorted or 'filled with holes', and the problem is that 'thought holes' paint a very inaccurate picture. To illustrate this, your child might think:

- "I didn't get invited to the movies with them . . . why don't they like me?"

- "My computer's frozen . . . everything goes wrong for me!"

- "My home group teacher wants to see me . . . what am I in trouble for?"

Show them how to beat this impulsive and distorted thinking. It starts by having an awareness about it. Without this awareness, it's too easy to arrive at a skewed perception of reality. These holes cause real emotional distress (Jain, 2016).

A three-step plan to quash worry

Step 1: Work out how serious it is

Use the worry scale from this lesson and ask your child to rate their worry anywhere between 1 and 5, with 1 being a slight setback and 5 being an irreversible disaster. So often, worriers catastrophise and think the worry is so much worse than it really is. Rating the worry helps to keep it in a healthy perspective.

Step 2: Challenge their thinking

Gently ask logical questions such as: "Well, what usually happens?" "What is most likely to happen?" "What do we usually do?" "How likely is that?" "What plans can be made to deal with it?" Your resolve will slowly help to replace frightened thinking with realistic thinking.

Step 3: Teach your child to switch

Train them to switch the anxious thought with a happy thought. To start, ask everyone in the family for their three happiest or most comforting thought patterns. Once they've shared them, you can coach them to either switch this happy thought on, or to get up, walk away and do something that makes them feel happy.

The problem of too much reassurance

It's vital to reassure children that they are safe, and you understand their worries. However, when we talk too intensely about a child's worries, and dissect and rehash them, this can unintentionally leave the child with the impression that

After the Buzz . . . Lesson 8

there must be something very serious to be anxious about. Be mindful to strike a healthy balance! There's a world of difference between being supportive and building helplessness.

Never forget – humour, playfulness and light-heartedness

Well-placed humour inspires a lightness that reaches a long way towards disarming worry. Never be shy about telling your child a funny or disarming story to help put things in perspective.

A few children need a worry specialist

Growing up is hard for some children. Sometimes they go through phases where they seem to have a bigger worry each day. This may well be the time to seek expert professional support – a school counsellor, a psychologist, a paediatrician, a psychiatrist, a social worker or someone linked to a local community health centre. The influence of a skilled professional can have your child experimenting with interventions and ideas that will amaze you and leave them feeling far more in control.

References

Blumer, C. (2015) *What Worries Australian Children?* Available at: www.abc.net.au/news/2015-10-05/btn-happiness-survey-australian-children-mental-health/6820652 (accessed July 2018).

Bullot A., Cave, L., Fildes, J., Hall, S. and Plummer, J. (2017) *Mission Australia Youth Survey Report.* Available at: www.missionaustralia.com.au/what-we-do/research-evaluation/youth-survey (accessed July 2018).

Brooks, M. (2014) *Aromatherapy May Ease Work Stress.* Available at: www.medscape.com/viewarticle/824880 (accessed July 2018).

Hills, S. (2013) *You Can Walk Away Stress: Scientists Discover How a Stroll Can Soothe the Brain.* Available at: www.dailymail.co.uk/health/article-2356004/You-CAN-walk-away-stress-Scientists-discover-stroll-soothe-brain.html (accessed July 2018).

Jain, R. (2016) *How to Stop Automatic Negative Thoughts.* Available at: www.huffingtonpost.com/entry/how-to-stop-automatic-negative-thoughts_us_58330f18e4b0eaa5f14d4833 (accessed July 2018).

Majdandžić, M., Lazarus, R., Oort, F., van der Sluis, C., Dodd, H., Morris, T., et al. (2018) The structure of challenging parenting behavior and associations with anxiety in Dutch and Australian children. *Journal of Child and Adolescent Psychology*, 47(2): 282–295. Available at: www.ncbi.nlm.nih.gov/pubmed/29053375 (accessed July 2018).

Schubert, J., Coles, M. and Arnedt, J. (2017) Later bedtime is associated with decrements in perceived control of obsessions and compulsions. *Sleep*, 40(1): A420–A421. Available at: https://doi.org/10.1093/sleepj/zsx050.1127 (accessed July 2018).

Wei, M. (2017) *6 Aromatherapy Essential Oils for Stress Relief and Sleep.* Available at: www.huffingtonpost.com/marlynn-wei-md-jd/6-aromatherapy-essential-_b_9805630.html (accessed July 2018).

What's the Buzz with Teenagers?

35 Worry:
Catastrophe scale

A Catastrophe scale rates the intensity of worry, frustration or any emotion. Keep it in your memory or print it and use it. Catastrophe scales help us keep what's happening in perspective; "How big is this?" "How much should it matter?" "Will it matter tomorrow?" "Is it so bad that it has to wreck my whole day?" "Who can I talk to about this?" "Is there a quick way to fix this?" It's a great way to see the light at the end of the tunnel, and get through the hurt or stress we feel in the moment.

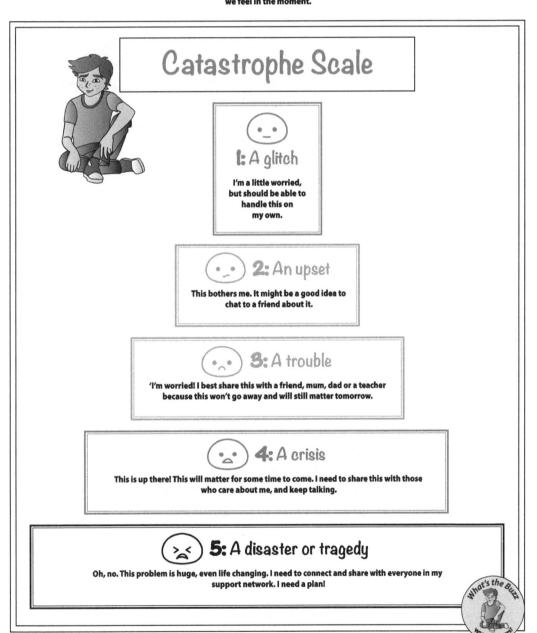

What's the Buzz with Teenagers?

36 Role-play cards: Handling anxiety

Role play 1

You've noticed your friend has been distant lately. They don't smile as much, they're quieter and they don't laugh when everyone else is sharing a joke. Somehow they have placed themselves on the outside of the group. This role play picks up the moment you sit with them and quietly ask, "Are you okay?" They answer, "Yes." You can tell they're not okay. Show how you could sensitively persist. (A pair – you and your friend)

Role play 2

You're feeling flat and you're not interested in doing the things you usually love to do. You're not excited to go places or see your friends. You feel full of dread about going to school. Show one way you could get some help. If time persists, do a 'take two' and show another way to take care of yourself. (Just yourself, or include one or two others)

Role play 3

You've just arrived at school and your class is getting ready for an assembly. You are leading it and you're feeling anxious. To make things worse, you've just spilled the smoothie you were eating on your way to school over the front of your shirt, and that's not going to disappear before you get up on stage. How embarrassing. Show a clever and creative way to handle this. (Just yourself, but you can include others if you need them)

36 Role-play cards: Handling anxiety *continued . . .*

Role play 4

You are the only person in your group of friends who didn't get invited to a party. Naturally, you're feeling hurt. You thought the person having the party was your friend, so this is genuinely an unpleasant surprise. The role play begins with you explaining what has happened and how you feel to a close friend. Show how you'd work through your feelings as you discuss this with them. The focus for this role play is also on the friend who is listening. We want to see them as a good listener offering support and help. (A pair – you and your friend)

Role play 5

Your backpack is falling apart. It's old, and has a lot of history and a smell to it. But the truth is your mother and father do not see this as important. Your friends don't understand why you just don't get a new one. Every time you bring it up with your parents, they say, "Hey, it's only a school bag! It's a First World problem! Get a grip!" To you, it's not that simple. You want a new bag desperately. In this role play, show your best effort to have one last go at problem-solving your way through this you're your mum and dad. (A group of three – you and your mum and dad)

Role play 6

You're not keeping up with maths. You get quickly and easily confused in class, and as for the homework you feel totally lost. Your parents are great, but they work a lot and maths isn't their thing anyway. There's only so many times you can ask your teacher for help. It's already embarrassing and causing you to worry. In this role play, you're speaking with two friends. Together, show how you could problem-solve and arrive at a helpful solution. (A group of three – you and two friends)

---

36 Role-play cards:
Handling anxiety *continued . . .*

Role play 7

Your friend took their mother's precious antique gold ring to school without permission, and now they've lost it. Apparently it has been in the family for 200 years. They are incredibly stressed. Suddenly, you see they are struggling to breathe, teary and rocking. You know enough about them to know that this is a panic attack. In this role play, show what you will *say* and *do* to reassure and calm them. (A pair – you and your friend)

Role play 8

It feels as though you're the only person in your class that isn't allowed to use social media. It's getting awkward and you're feeling left out socially. You understand why your parents are worried about it, but your friends' parents are okay with them using it. The problem races around in your head each night while trying to go to sleep. You know this isn't right. You must deal with it. This role play begins as you approach your parents to talk to them about this. Let's see you in action with wise words and a mature approach because this is the only way to show your parents you're ready for something that they believe you're not. (A group of three – yourself and your mum and dad)

Role play 9

Your teacher's new iPad disappeared. The principal calls for an on-the-spot bag check. The iPad is found in your school bag, much to your disbelief and horror. You did not take it, and now find yourself in the principal's office about to answer some tough questions from your teacher and the principal. You feel sick with worry. In this role play, we want to see you feeling very anxious, but show us how you regain your composure, stay calm and handle the situation in the best possible way. (A group of three – yourself, the teacher and the principal)

---

36 Role-play cards: Handling anxiety *continued . . .*

Role play 10

You're having a rough time with your best friend. Lately, they seem cold towards you. Sensibly, you decide to talk about it privately with a close friend. After school, your best friend approaches you and says you've betrayed the friendship because you shared private things that you should not have shared. They are very annoyed. You are completely shocked because you did not share anything except about how you were feeling. In this role play, show us a great way to handle this challenging situation with your best friend. (A pair – you and your best friend)

Responding to dominating behaviours

"Put your hand up if you don't want Rafi to be in our group"

Key social and emotional principles (learning intention)

The first goal of this lesson is to teach the concept of social dominance. We all use social dominance to help us fit into social groups. Some become outspoken, argumentative, hurtful, bossy, even aggressive. This is an extreme way of social dominance, and these behaviours are often referred to as bullying. Others develop leading behaviours that are more submissive. These are friendly, inclusive and generous patterns of behaviour. The second goal highlights how to respond to dominating behaviours – how to bring it to a close, move away, share concerns with friends or safe adults, and resist a fixation on someone who isn't yet their best self.

Materials required for this lesson

- Name tags.

- Chairs in a social circle for students to sit on.

- Whiteboard/butcher's paper/screen and markers.

- Create a simple outline of the lesson on the whiteboard/butcher's paper/ screen for students to follow.

- Display the *What's the Buzz?* group values (located in the introduction or at www.whatsthebuzz.net.au/main-menu/content-whats-the-buzz-with-teenagers).

- Organise feedback and reminder cards, or similar, to strengthen responsive behaviours (located in the introduction or at www.whatsthebuzz.net.au/main-menu/content-whats-the-buzz-with-teenagers, ready to print).

- Have Archie's story ready to read to students. This can be done directly from this lesson. Or, for a small registration fee, you can download the 16 Archie stories as you want them. Each story contains text, audio in the form of the authors reading to your students, and two large illustrations in full colour that will fill your screen. Access is available at www.whatsthebuzz.net.au/main-menu/content-whats-the-buzz-with-teenagers

- Pencils, pens and paper for students to do Part 1 of *Show me the Buzz*.

- Print the 'Responding to dominating behaviours cards' in Part 1 of *Show me the Buzz* (located at the end of the lesson or at www.whatsthebuzz.net.au/main-menu/content-whats-the-buzz-with-teenagers, ready to print). You will also need Blu-Tack or tape to attach the cards to a whiteboard surface or similar.

- A few sheets of A4 paper and pencils to play the game 'Draw me if you can?' in *The Buzz*.

- A cucumber and a knife to play the game 'Cucumber-face challenge' in *The Buzz*.

- Prepare handouts for parents(s):

    One copy of this lesson for each parent to read.

    One copy of *After the Buzz: Social thinking ideas for parents and caregivers* to send home (located at the end of the lesson, ready to photocopy, or at www.whatsthebuzz.net.au/main-menu/content-whats-the-buzz-with-teenagers).

Lesson 9

Explanation

Until recently, social power imbalances, highlighted by repetitive insults and spiteful attacks between young people, was addressed through an anti-bullying paradigm. The act of bullying is defined as repeated physical harm, intimidation, purposeful isolation, name-calling, systematic put-downs, spreading of hurtful lies and teasing, frightening text messages, or attacks via instant messaging services (Rigby, 2002a). The problem with the anti-bully paradigm is that it is too constrained, and consequently not real world. The general profile of a bully is impossible to describe. A few bullies are obvious manipulative brutes, but most swing between being an occasional victim to using bully behaviours themselves to deal with problematic social situations. These include the need for social recognition among peers, fear of competition, the anxiety of being at the bottom of the social pecking order, or angry revenge behaviours because of poor treatment.

Tackling bullying through an anti-bullying paradigm has been largely unsuccessful over the years, even though we have copious amounts of data about bullying. We know that about 17 per cent of students are bullied in most primary schools each week, and typically this takes place outside of the classroom. The incidence of bullying rises to 23 per cent by Year Nine, and recipients and perpetrators are evenly split (Rigby, 2002b; Slee et al., 2008; Cross et al., 2009). Cyberbullying is on the rise and is hard to track, but would you be surprised to hear that many adolescents refuse to tell their parents as they worry they'll have their phones taken away or may be barred from using their tablet or computer? They say that telling about any kind of bullying has the potential to make things worse. Once they tell, they face the unpredictable reaction from the bully, risk others becoming involved, watch adults mishandle delicate matters, and feel as though their powerlessness has been further increased. Students repeatedly say that most teachers and parents don't understand the complexity of bullying, and even when they do, they haven't the time to counsel, support and maintain appropriate repair for those involved. In saying this, our kids offer us a real challenge. Without the development of a culture focused on improving ways to communicate and reconcile differences, school anti-bullying programs will continue to deliver very ordinary levels of success.

A better paradigm is to teach the concept of social dominance. By doing so, students can understand that social dominance is a behaviour style inspired by a natural need to get the resources we need: food, love, recognition, friendship, power, belongings, money and much more. We show social dominance by behaving in ways we think will help us to fit into our social groups. To get a higher ranking, some become opinionated, argumentative, bossy, even aggressive. They think that this pattern of domination will give them more control and more choice over the group. This is an extreme way of showing social dominance, and is bullying. Conversely, others develop a dominant behaviour pattern that is more submissive. They are easier-going and show friendly behaviours to find a social status that works for them.

We should be explaining to students that friendships are never perfect, even though we'd love to think they are; that there are always varying degrees of power between friends – and that's normal! In theory, a perfectly balanced friendship would see friends always take turns and always decide what to do based on utter fairness. There would always be complete reciprocated respect, a joint dependence and shared influence. In a perfectly balanced friendship, there would be no selfishness, no bigger ego and no anxiety that often spurs one to shine more brightly at the expense of another.

Let's openly teach young people that each of us express socially dominant behaviours. And as we evolve, we learn the difference between a pattern of behaviour that is friendly and generous compared to patterns that are argumentative, bossy or nasty. We must also teach how to recognise the bullying pattern of behaviours, and how best to respond: to say no, to stop engaging, to bring a conversation to a swift close, to resist competing for power, to walk away, to share concerns early on with friends and safe adults, to go for a run, to do things that bring relief and happiness, and to resist a fixation on someone who isn't yet their best self. This takes practice. Our mission as educators and parents is to ensure this kind of firewall – or protective understanding – is consistently discussed, modelled and maintained.

1. *What's the Buzz?*

Always greet students as they enter. Provide chairs in a social circle for students to sit on and have a brief lesson plan on the whiteboard or butcher's paper for students to see. As students are settling, hand each of them a 'Thumbs up feedback card' to highlight their thoughtful behaviour and using the group values.

Let's begin

Introduce the key learning intentions by quickly working through the three questions below.

1. Ask, "What is social dominance?"

Social dominance is a behaviour. We see it in social animals, and it's a big part of human interaction. It happens as we compete with each another to make sure we fit in and feel valued by others.

2. Ask, "What is dominating behaviour?"

To get a high ranking in front of others, some people become outspoken, argumentative, bossy, rude, threatening or aggressive. They think these behaviours will

Lesson 9

give them more control over the group. Others develop a dominant style that is more submissive or cooperative. They are easier-going, kinder and show friendly behaviours to find social status.

3. Ask, "How does bullying fit into this?"

A bullying pattern of behaviour is an extreme way of dominating another. It usually includes the following:

- The spreading of lies, name-calling, hurtful comments, either face-to-face or on social media.

- Excludes and isolates the victim.

- Persists despite intervention.

- The bully enjoys what they're doing.

- Concerned with being popular.

- Shows contempt for others who may be different in some way.

- Openly teases and taunts.

- Uses hand gestures, facial expressions and body language that deliberately hurt others.

Archie's story: "Put your hand up if you don't want Rafi to be in our group"

It was second semester and chemistry had given way to biology, but Mr Shay, with his dancing eyebrows, darting eyes and best style ever, remained the group's teacher. Archie could see he was just as keen on biology as he was on chemistry. Archie loved biology because it helped him make sense of the world, life and behaviours of all kinds of things.

Today, Mr Shay was discussing social dominance behaviours in mice. It was fascinating because Archie could see the same dominating behaviours in the world of people too. Just like mice, some people behave to get power, to be a boss and to rule over others. Just like mice, some people are more relaxed and easier-going. Archie laughed out loud when Mr Shay pointed out people don't go around weeing in different places to plant dominance smells like mice do!

Then something unexpected happened. Archie suddenly became aware of Tamara's raised voice coming from the other side of the classroom. She was arguing with Rafi, who, along with Jasmine, Arabella, Olive and Izzy, were usually quiet under her nasty spell.

37 Archie's story: "Put your hand up if you don't want Rafi to be in our group" – first image

Lauren Eldridge Murray

This image can be downloaded from http://whatsthebuzz.net.au/main-menu/content-whats-the-buzz-with-teenagers and will fill your screen in colour. There is also the option to have the authors read the story to students.

Tamara had history when it came to bossing and hurting people, and everyone knew it. Some called her 'Queen Bee', some called her 'Mean Girl' and a few called her a lot worse.

You might remember what Tamara did to Archie, back in Year Three, when Jack brought his puppy to school for the class to hold. As she finished her turn, she deliberately looked and smiled at Archie, moved closer to him, extended her hands with the puppy in them, and as he reached out to take the puppy she quickly pulled it away and handed it to Tommy sitting on the other side. At the time, Archie thought, "Why does Tamara do things like that?" Who knows why, but Tamara still behaved in the same dominating way.

Tamara was well known in the middle school for leading a group of girls who did whatever she wanted. She endlessly reminded them that by being in 'her group', they were cool. She would also remind them that if they didn't do as she said, she'd make them pay and it would hurt.

Archie carefully tuned into what they were saying. "I don't care how you feel. I did what I did because you've crossed the line," screeched Tamara.

"But you were mean to me," answered Rafi.

"It is what it is. The more you go on and on, the more pathetic you sound. Everyone knows you're pathetic," boiled Tamara.

Feeling crushed, Rafi pulled her eye contact away and dropped her head.

"Wow! You look like a baby. Why don't you cry like one?" taunted Tamara.

"You're just a jealous, lonely person. You don't matter," sighed Rafi.

"Your crybaby face sure looks like I matter. Lonely? Just remember, I'm the one who friended you, and now I'm unfriending you. You can't win, Rafi, and no one wants you," hissed Tamara scornfully.

"How am I trying to win?" argued Rafi.

Mr Shay stopped teaching. He launched into action by getting to their desk – fast. He knelt down between them and firmly said, "It's the wrong place for this. We're leaving together, now." Instantly, he helped the girls up and began walking with them. He shot a glance with his big brown darting eyes to everyone and said, "The exercises on page 57 is homework. Start them now and remember to help each other out. Thanks." Mr Shay, Rafi and Tamara walked away.

38 Archie's story: "Put your hand up if you don't want Rafi to be in our group" – second image

Lauren Eldridge Murray

This image can be downloaded from http://whatsthebuzz.net.au/main-menu/content-whats-the-buzz-with-teenagers and will fill your screen in colour. There is also the option to have the authors read the story to students.

Archie shot a look at Joanna who was sitting next to him. "What was that all about?" he asked.

"It started last weekend. Rafi had her birthday party and took the group horse riding, but since then Rafi has started to look too popular for Tamara's liking," explained Joanna.

"Did Tamara go horse riding too?" queried Archie.

"Yes! But too many girls in the group liked it too much, and Tamara is feeling threatened. She's not happy unless she's got total power over her little copycats. She owns them," explained Joanna.

"Seriously? Talk about dominance behaviour in mice – this is real life, people dominance behaviour!" joked Archie.

"So, at lunchtime," Joanna continued, "Rafi went to sit with the group and Tamara said as loudly as she could, 'Hey, put your hand up if you don't want Rafi to be in our group.' Everyone did because Tamara dominates the girls and they're scared of her. No one wanted to be the next target. The worst thing was how Rafi played into Tamara's trap. She was so used to keeping Tamara happy that she kept asking what was wrong and kept defending herself. This opened the door for Tamara to go on and on and embarrass her in front of the group. Now she's been humiliated again in front of the whole class."

Archie was lost for words. All he could think is maybe some people, like Tamara, do go around weeing all over the place to dominate!

Discussion based on the questions and statements below will occur later in *Do you know the Buzz?* For now, simply read them to get students thinking. Encourage them to listen and respond to each question by putting their thumb up if they 'agree' or think 'yes', thumb down if they think 'no', and thumb to the side if they think 'maybe'. Move very quickly through them. No verbal responses are required.

Your thoughts on these statements and questions?

- Do you think you understand what a dominating behaviour looks like?

- Do you agree with the following statement? "Only girls show dominating behaviours to each other."

- Have you experienced someone trying to dominate you?

- Can you remember how you felt?

- Can you remember what you did about it?

- Have you ever tried to dominate someone by using a bullying or hurtful pattern of behaviours?

- Do you understand why some choose to bully or use hurtful patterns of behaviours?

- Do you know why Tamara decided to push Rafi away from the group?

- Did Rafi handle it well, in your opinion?

- Do you agree with the following statement? "When someone decides to have a go at you, it's always best to argue back and defend yourself."

- Rafi kept defending herself and played into Tamara's dominating style. Can you think of an idea that would have been more effective for Rafi?

- Would you describe the girls in Tamara's group as weak characters?

- If you were in a similar group, would you just do what the leader told you to do?

- Was it a good idea for Rafi to bring it into the classroom and defend herself again?

- Did Mr Shay handle it well?

- Is Archie right? Are some people dominant over others so they feel as though they have greater value?

2. *Show me the Buzz*

Show me the Buzz provides students with the opportunity to discuss a variety of social and emotional ideas, absorb the thoughts of others, debate them, create role plays and receive feedback from the group. We have learned that this approach heightens understandings and the transference of skills. There is always a Part 1 and a Part 2. Choose one activity from either Part 1 or Part 2, depending on what appeals to you, the time you have and your group's likely preferences. There's plenty of content in *Show me the Buzz*, so the lesson can be revisited time and time again while continuing with this same topic.

Part 1

1. "Where did Rafi go wrong?" – rewrite, retell or perform a play

When Rafi joined the group at lunchtime, Tamara said, "Hey, put your hand up if you don't want Rafi to be in our group." Everyone did because Tamara had years of practice at dominating people and the girls were intimidated by her. No one wanted to be her next target. Ask the group, "Where did Rafi go wrong?"

The answer here is that Rafi tried to argue the point with Tamara. She failed to see that Tamara was an expert at having the last say and winning verbal battles. Discuss what would have been a better approach. Next, arrange students into groups of two or three to rewrite, retell or perform a play showing how Rafi could have dealt with Tamara's dominating behaviour more effectively. Remind students that it's not about having the last word or the most cutting words; it's all about bringing the power play to a dignified close – and fast.

2. Group discussion – 'real life'

Lead the group to brainstorm eight assertive ideas they could *say* or *do* when confronted by someone like Tamara in real life – someone who shows a pattern of behaviours that intend to harass or hurt. What can be *said* and *done* to bring this to a quick, dignified close? To do this, create a two-column list on the whiteboard or screen. At the top of the left column, write 'Useful ideas to SAY', and at the top of the right column 'Useful ideas to DO'. Generate four ideas in each column.

3. Group discussion – 'social media'

Lead the group to brainstorm six assertive ideas they could use when confronted by someone like Tamara on social media – someone who shows a pattern of behaviours that intend to harass, hurt or belittle. What can be done to protect yourself and deal with the problem? Create a list of ideas generated by student discussion on the whiteboard or screen.

4. Watch this film clip and discuss

Arrange for students to watch the film clip 'How to stop a bully' (www.youtube.com/watch?v=G8l3dMjdmzc). After 52 seconds, pause the clip and ask, "What did Brooks do that made the bully's power grow stronger?" Discuss and record comments. Restart the clip and pause again at 1 minute 57 seconds. This time ask, "What did Brooks do that was different, and neutralised or defused the bully's power?" Discuss and record comments.

Remember, this demonstration was also to entertain an audience. Brooks kept the bully engaged for too long, showed too much investment and used too many words. He also made a big mistake by trying to make fun of her by singing at her – not wise. Highlight what he did well.

Restart the clip and run to the end. Then ask students:

- What are the most important messages to take away?

- What do you think a bystander witnessing someone being bullied should and should not do?

5. Sledging

This is a form of verbal abuse, and we often see it in competitive sports such as boxing, cricket, tennis, hockey, basketball and so on. The aim is to use hurtful comments to break the concentration of a player and upset their performance. An example of sledging was when test cricketers Mark Waugh and Adam Parore traded insults: "I remember you from a couple of years ago. You were sh!# then and you're useless now," said Waugh. Parore replied, "Yeah, that's me. And I remember you were dating that old, ugly woman. I see you've married her now. You dumb idiot!" Ask students:

Lesson 9

- Is sledging, or trash talk, a dominating behaviour?

- Was the exchange between Waugh and Parore just sporting banter or is it abuse?

- What's the difference between banter and abuse?

- When verbal abuse such as this is used at school or in the workplace, the consequences are serious. So, do you think sledging should be banned from sport?

- Is there a difference between a bully and someone who sledges, or trash-talks? Explain.

6. Quiz: Do you show bullying patterns of behaviour?

You can present the quiz to students yourself or organise several students to run the quiz with your group. This quiz will help everyone to discover just how much they rely on dominating patterns of behaviour. To find out, answer either 'yes' or 'no' in your head.

Question 1: Have you ever kept on upsetting someone because you thought they were younger, weaker, smaller, different or less than you?

Question 2: Do you make mean faces or bad hand gestures about others when they're not looking?

Question 3: Do you spread untrue stories or say mean things about others in life or on social media?

Question 4: Do you make fun of or tease others, or make sure that you don't include them?

Question 5: Have you whispered to a friend in front of another person because you wanted to upset this person?

Question 6: Have you deliberately not invited someone to your party so they would find out and feel hurt?

Question 7: Have you ever been in a group that sees itself as 'popular' and will not include most people?

Question 8: Have you made fun of others because they are different?

Question 9: Have you hurt or threatened to hurt someone?

Question 10: Have you punched, pushed or hit someone because you could?

7. Helpful and unhelpful possibilities

Arrange students in a large social circle. Place all the 'Responding to dominating behaviours cards' on the floor face up in the middle. These are in the photocopiable section at the end of this lesson or can be downloaded at www.whatsthebuzz.

net.au/main-menu/content-whats-the-buzz-with-teenagers. Explain that the cards show *helpful* and *unhelpful* possibilities to solve bully-styled or dominating behaviours. One by one, students pick up a card and fasten it to the whiteboard or butcher's paper in the column headed 'HELPFUL POSSIBILITIES' if they think the statement is helpful, and in the column headed 'UNHELPFUL POSSIBILITIES' if they believe the solution is unhelpful. Once fastened, the group will give strong applause if they agree and faint applause if they disagree. Be ready for some discussion because there will be plenty!

Part 2: Role play – responding to dominating behaviours

Here's the scenario to set up the role play.

As the facilitator of the group, you are to take on the role of a young teen who shows dominance behaviours, represented by aggressive and argumentative language with a superior attitude. In this role, you are an accomplished basketball player who plays district basketball at a high level. It's early in the season, and last night was the night for new people to try out at the club. You saw the new kid in your class trying out last night, but because you're so exclusive you didn't bother to acknowledge them. It's the next day at school and the new kid sees you.

> Immediately, they walk up to you and say, "Hey, I saw you at the try-outs last night. Gee, you're a great player."
>
> You reply sarcastically, "Oh yeah, I saw you 'trying' out."
>
> They respond, "I'm hoping to join your team."
>
> You reply, "I don't think so. Not in this life." Continue a little longer in this vein . . .

Explain this scenario to the group. Then ask if anyone wants the role of the new kid. Their job will be to listen and respond by assertively bringing the conversation to a close. Remind them that bringing the conversation to a close does not mean defending, arguing, having the last word or being nasty to gain power back. What it does mean is staying composed and keeping their dignity. A big part of defusing any horrible situation is to look and sound confident, even if you're not. Urge them not to look flustered or get upset.

Choose one student at a time. If a student does not wish to perform, allow them to pass. So much can be learned through observing. Always perform role plays in the middle of the social circle. Consider capturing the action on video or photo by using your iPad, camera or smartphone. Encourage others to give constructive feedback after each role play.

3. *Do you know the Buzz?*

Do you know the Buzz? is a lively group 'discussion time' where students briefly respond to a series of questions and statements highlighted by Archie's story.

The goal is for them to exchange ideas, and in the process 'mind map' their way more empathically through the complexities of social and emotional situations. This should also provide facilitators with an insight into the depth of student understandings. To do this, have students sitting on chairs in a social circle.

Your thoughts on these statements and questions?

- Do you think you understand what a dominating behaviour looks like?

- Only girls show dominating behaviours to each other.

- Have you experienced someone trying to dominate you? When? What happened?

- Can you remember how you felt? Give me some adjectives to describe the feeling at the time.

- Can you remember what you did about it?

- Have you ever tried to dominate someone by using a bullying or hurtful pattern of behaviours? Why did you do it?

- Do you understand why some choose to bully or use hurtful patterns of behaviours? Tell me the reasons.

- Do you know why Tamara decided to push Rafi away from the group? Can you explain?

- Did Rafi handle it well, in your opinion?

- When someone decides to have a go at you, is it always best to argue back and defend yourself? Why or why not?

- Rafi kept defending herself and played into Tamara's dominating style. Can you think of an idea that would have been more effective for Rafi?

- Would you describe the girls in Tamara's group as weak characters?

- If you were in a similar group, would you just do what the leader told you to do?

- Was it a good idea for Rafi to bring it into the classroom and defend herself again?

- Did Mr Shay handle it well?

- Is Archie right? Are some people dominant over others so they feel as though they have greater value?

4. The Buzz

The Buzz is an opportunity for the group to play games that strengthen their relationships and the skills central to the lesson.

Game: Saying only 'yes' or 'no' (moderately exciting)

The aim of the 'yes' or 'no' game is to honestly and creatively answer questions from the group without saying the words 'yes' or 'no'. And there are a few additional rules too! First, students may not nod or shake their head to indicate a 'yes' or 'no'. Second, every response must be new and inventive. Sit the person answering the questions in front of the group, facing them. The first member of the group might ask, "Are you a boy?" A clever answer could be, "I'm sure I am!" or "Of course not!" Each group member takes turns asking questions. As soon as the person facing the group says 'yes' or 'no' or nods or shakes their head, they are out and replaced by the person who asked the question.

Game: Two truths, one lie (passive)

This is an ideal forum for students to offer a little information about themselves and to learn more about others. Explain that each of them will be given a chance to state two things that are true about themselves and one thing that is a lie. Each of the three statements should be confidently delivered. The group will try to guess which statement is the lie. Guessing the lie is the aim of the game! The best idea is for an adult to begin so they can model how it is done.

Game: Draw me if you can (moderately exciting)

Divide the group into pairs. If you need to, a group of three will work just as well. One player becomes the 'communicator' (for groups of three, have two 'communicators') and the other the 'drawer'. Provide the 'drawer' with a white A4 sheet of paper and a pencil. Arrange for each pair to move to a space in the room that offers a little privacy.

Huddle the 'communicators' in close to you and show them a simple line drawing you have drawn on your own sheet of A3 paper. It may be as basic as a square with a diagonal line running through it, or a circle divided into quarters with one quarter shaded in, or the Olympic rings with several overlaps shaded in. Start simply as you can always build the complexity of drawings in subsequent attempts. Once the 'communicators' have seen your drawing, they return to their partner.

The task of the 'communicators' is to sit with the 'drawer' and use their words to help them create the drawing they have just seen. 'Communicators' must keep their fingers folded and hands in their laps – that's right, no pointing! If things go very badly in the drawing process, 'communicators' can suggest discarding the drawing and begin a new one. Once everyone is finished, hold up your original drawing so they can compare. Next, get 'communicators' and 'drawers' to swap roles and try a new drawing together.

Game: Have you ever had . . . ? (exciting)

For this game, you'll need everyone in the group sitting on a chair in a social circle, except for one student. This student stands in the middle. Once everyone is settled, the student standing in the middle begins by asking a "Have you ever had . . .?" question. Here are some starters to tune you in. "Have you ever had . . .

- . . . a broken bone?"

- . . . to run to save your life?"

- . . . the chance to make another person feel good?"

- . . . a car accident?"

- . . . takeaway?"

- . . . a bad day?"

- . . . a visit to a friend's house?"

- . . . a trip to the zoo?"

- . . . a snake in your arms?"

- . . . horse-riding lessons?"

- . . . a big vomit?"

- . . . diarrhoea?"

- . . . diarrhoea and vomit at the same time?"

- . . . a perfect test score?"

- . . . a goldfish as a pet?"

Once they make a statement, everyone sitting on the chairs must stand up and find a new chair to sit in if their answer is 'yes'. Otherwise, they stay seated. In this moment, the person in the middle attempts to sneak on to a chair. Whoever misses out on a chair is the next one in the middle to ask a question. And so this game continues!

Game: Cucumber-face challenge (moderately exciting)

This game is great fun, and can be played with two or three, or with a much larger group. You'll need one slice of cucumber for every person in your group. Invite one player at a time to sit on a chair and place a slice of cucumber on their cheek or forehead. On go, their task is to move the slice of cucumber down their face, without using hands, and into their mouth. If the cucumber falls off their face, they're out, and the next person takes the seat ready to try what is tricky but far from impossible. Have a camera at the ready for some wonderful facial shots!

After the Buzz: Social thinking ideas for parents and caregivers

Lesson 9: Responding to dominating behaviours

Key social and emotional principles (learning intention)

The first goal of this lesson is to teach the concept of social dominance. We all use social dominance to help us fit into social groups. Some become outspoken, argumentative, hurtful, bossy, even aggressive. This is an extreme way of social dominance, and these behaviours are often referred to as bullying. Others develop leading behaviours that are more submissive. These are friendly, inclusive and generous patterns of behaviour. The second goal highlights how to respond to dominating behaviours – how to bring it to a close, move away, share concerns with friends or safe adults, and resist a fixation on someone who isn't yet their best self.

After the Buzz presents further ideas for parents, guardians and educators to encourage the social and emotional thinking students have touched on during the lesson. Our children rely on us to consolidate these skills by positively modelling them, and emphasising the language and ideas contained within the lesson. This lesson alerted students to the concept of socially dominating behaviours, why they happen and how to respond to them more effectively.

Teach what socially dominating behaviours are

Socially dominating behaviour is usually inspired by a natural desire to gain essential resources: food, love, recognition, friendship, power, belongings, money and much more. We all show social dominance by behaving in ways we think will give us a higher ranking. To do this, some become outspoken, argumentative, bossy, even aggressive. They think that this pattern of bullying-styled behaviours gives them more control and more choice. Meanwhile, others develop dominant behaviours that are submissive. They are easier-going and show friendly and generous behaviours to find a social status that works for them.

Teach what bullying is and isn't

Bullying is repeated verbal, physical, social or psychological destructive behaviour by a person or group directed towards a less powerful person or group that is intended to cause harm, distress or fear. Types of bullying include:

- verbal or written abuse – targeted name-calling or 'jokes', or displaying offensive signs or posters;

- violence – including threats;

- sexual harassment – unwelcome or unreciprocated conduct of a sexual nature, which could reasonably be expected to cause offence, humiliation or intimidation;

- homophobia and other hostile behaviour towards students relating to gender and sexuality;

- discrimination, including racial discrimination – treating people differently because of their identity; and

- cyberbullying – either online or via phones.

Bullying is not when an unpleasant or distressing incident occurs. A single episode of nastiness or aggression, while upsetting, is not bullying. Similarly, rejection or dislike is not bullying unless it involves thoughtful and repeated attempts to cause distress, exclude, or create dislike by others (www.education.vic.gov.au/about/programs/bullystoppers/Pages/what.aspx).

Teach the imperfection of being human

We all agree that someone who shows a dominating/bullying pattern of behaviours needs intervention and active support to change. So, let's not demonise them. It's more constructive to talk about the bigger picture around relationships and friendships. They are rarely perfect. In a perfect world, a perfectly balanced friendship would see each person take turns and decide what to do based on utter fairness. There would always be complete mutual respect, a joint dependence and shared influence. In a perfectly balanced friendship, there would be no selfishness, no big egos and no anxiety that often spurs one to shine more brightly at the expense of another. Human beings are not perfect, and children are not yet fully evolved to be the best they can be. We need to be kind to each other and stick to the golden rule: "Do unto others as you would have them do unto you."

Teach children how to respond to a bullying pattern of behaviour

When confronted by someone using a pattern of behaviour that is argumentative, bossy and nasty, what's the best response? Teach that it's best to say fewer words, to make one assertive statement, to say no, to stop engaging, to bring the conversation to a swift close, to walk away, to share concerns early on with friends and safe adults, to go for a run, to do things that bring relief and happiness, and to resist a fixation on someone who isn't yet their best self. This takes practice. Our mission as educators and parents is to ensure this resilient understanding is consistently discussed, modelled and maintained. Watch this film clip with your son or daughter: 'How to stop a bully' – www.youtube.com/watch?v=G8l3dMjdmzc.

After 52 seconds, pause the clip and ask, "What did Brooks do that made the bully's power grow stronger?" Discuss and record comments. Restart the clip and pause again at 1 minute 57 seconds. This time, ask, "What did Brooks do that was different, and neutralised or defused the bully's power?" Discuss and record comments.

Remember, this demonstration was also to entertain an audience. Brooks kept the bully engaged for too long, showed too much investment and used too many words. He also made a big mistake by trying to make fun of her by singing at her – not recommended. Highlight what he did well.

Restart the clip and run to the end. Ask, "What are the important messages to take away? What do you think a bystander witnessing someone being bullied should and should not do?" A new understanding about responses to bullying styled behaviours has emerged. It is no longer acceptable for anyone to stand by and witness someone being bullied without doing something about it. Everyone in a school and within local communities has an obligation to intervene in a way that keeps everyone safe.

Talk openly about socially dominating behaviours

Conversations about dominating behaviours send a strong signal to everyone that this mindset is well understood, and being a solitary victim is never the answer. Let your children know they can always talk to you, teachers, friends at school, friends outside school, other trusted parents, a relative or a caregiver. Talking about it is healthy, and is not the same as 'telling tales' or 'dobbing'.

Movies and shows to watch and discuss:

- *A Girl Like Her* – www.youtube.com/watch?v=-G8qLskQJbg

- *13 Reasons Why* – www.youtube.com/watch?v=JebwYGn5Z3E

- *Cyberbully* – www.youtube.com/watch?v=fk_YSO0py7s

- *Spijt!* – www.youtube.com/watch?v=q3sOlOMTcNs

- *Mean Girls* – www.youtube.com/watch?v=pKU430xlxqA

- *Odd Girl Out* –www.youtube.com/watch?v=rORqs6tEVkU

Books to read and discuss:

- *Dear Bully* by Dawn Metcalf

- *Tease* by Amanda Maciel

- *Real Friends* by Shannon Hale

- *The Boy in the Dress* by David Walliams

After the Buzz … Lesson 9

- *Lord of the Flies* by William Golding
- *The Loser List* by Holly N. Kowitt

Visit anti-bullying websites together

All of us have a right to feel safe at school and at home. Let your child know this. There are many excellent websites for adults and children to learn how to cope with bullying:

- https://bullyingnoway.gov.au/
- www.headspace.org.au/young-people/understanding-bullying-for-young-people/
- www.sacbc.com/PMA_page.htm
- https://antibullying.nsw.gov.au/
- www.stopbullying.gov/
- www.cybersafetysolutions.com.au/

What next?

Children, adolescents and adults must never ignore a serious threat. When threatened with intimidation, harm and violence, either as gestures, verbally or physically, share it immediately with parents, teachers, friends and trusted adults. The same applies to a bystander. Urge bystanders to bullying-styled behaviours to keep themselves safe but find a way to reveal what's happening to others who can help. Given the awful potentials, it is far safer to overreact than underreact. It may be that the person who is voicing these violent threats, thoughts or plans needs compassionate – but very specialised – help by a mental health professional.

References

Cross, D., Shaw, T., Hearn, L., Epstein, M., Monks, H., Lester, L., et al. (2009) *Australian Covert Bullying Prevalence Study.* Available at: www.education.gov.au/search/site/NationalSafeSchools (accessed August 2018).

Rigby, K. (2002a) *New Perspectives on Bullying.* London: Jessica Kingsley.

Rigby, K. (2002b) *A Meta-Evaluation of Methods and Approaches to Reducing Bullying in Pre-Schools and in Early Primary School in Australia.* Canberra: Commonwealth Attorney-General's Department.

Slee, P., Spears, B., Owens, L. and Johnson, B. (2008) *Behind the Scenes: Insight into the Human Dimension of Covert Bullying.* Available at: https://docs.education.gov.au/system/files/doc/other/behind_the_scenes_-_insights_into_the_human_dimension_of_covert_bullying_-_final_short_report.pdf (accessed August 2018).

After the Buzz . . . Lesson 9

What's the Buzz with Teenagers?

39 Responding to dominating behaviours cards

What's the Buzz?   **Responding to dominating behaviours**   **card 1**

If you think someone is mistreating and dominating you . . .

Look them in the eye and calmly say, "I understand that's what you think. It doesn't make you right."

What's the Buzz?   **Responding to dominating behaviours**   **card 2**

If you think someone is mistreating and dominating you . . .

Roll your eyes, shrug your shoulders and walk away.

What's the Buzz?   **Responding to dominating behaviours**   **card 3**

If you think someone is mistreating and dominating you . . .

Totally ignore them by just getting on doing what you need to do.

What's the Buzz?   **Responding to dominating behaviours**   **card 4**

If you think someone is mistreating and dominating you . . .

Say, "You've no idea, you lowlife!"

What's the Buzz?   **Responding to dominating behaviours**   **card 5**

If you think someone is mistreating and dominating you . . .

Smile and say, "You might have a point, but it doesn't matter to me."

What's the Buzz?   **Responding to dominating behaviours**   **card 6**

If you think someone is mistreating and dominating you . . .

Yawn and say, "Sorry, everything you say is so boring."

What's the Buzz with Teenagers?

39 Responding to dominating behaviours cards *continued . . .*

What's the Buzz? Responding to dominating behaviours card 7

If you think someone is mistreating and dominating you . . .

Scream in their face.

What's the Buzz? Responding to dominating behaviours card 8

If you think someone is mistreating and dominating someone nearby . . .

Jump right in and threaten the bully yourself.

What's the Buzz? Responding to dominating behaviours card 9

If you think someone is mistreating and dominating you . . .

Run, tell a teacher and insist they fix the problem for you.

What's the Buzz? Responding to dominating behaviours card 10

If you think someone is mistreating and dominating you . . .

Spread mean lies about them.

What's the Buzz? Responding to dominating behaviours card 11

If you think someone is mistreating and dominating you . . .

Quietly and hesitantly say, "Please stop it. I don't like it when you say that. It hurts my feelings!"

What's the Buzz with Teenagers?

39 Responding to dominating behaviours cards *continued . . .*

What's the Buzz?   Responding to dominating behaviours   card 12

If you think someone is mistreating and dominating you . . .

Look them in the eye and say, "We should agree to disagree."
Then walk away.

What's the Buzz?   Responding to dominating behaviours   card 13

If you think someone is mistreating and dominating you . . .

Say, "I'm not sure what you've got against me because I think you're okay."

What's the Buzz?   Responding to dominating behaviours   card 14

If you think someone is mistreating and dominating you . . .

Say, "I'd like to talk about this later when we're alone." Then walk away.

What's the Buzz?   Responding to dominating behaviours   card 15

If you think someone is mistreating and dominating you . . .

Wiggle your hips and do a little dance. Then stick your face into their face and say, "You're nothing!"

What's the Buzz?   Responding to dominating behaviours   card 16

If you think someone is mistreating and dominating you . . .

Send them a mean text message or post something nasty on social media to pay them back.

What's the Buzz with Teenagers?

39 Responding to dominating behaviours cards *continued . . .*

What's the Buzz?   Responding to dominating behaviours   card 17

If you think someone is mistreating and dominating you . . .

Do your best to ignore it, but talk to Mum, Dad, a teacher or close friends about it.

What's the Buzz?   Responding to dominating behaviours   card 18

If you think someone is mistreating and dominating you . . .

Go home and make Mum and Dad fix it for you.

What's the Buzz?   Responding to dominating behaviours   card 19

If you think someone is mistreating and dominating someone nearby . . .

Move closer, look at them and say, "Hey, is everything okay?"

What's the Buzz?   Responding to dominating behaviours   card 20

If you think someone is mistreating and dominating you . . .

Twirl around three times, make a wild squawking sound and run away flapping your arms.

What's the Buzz?   Responding to dominating behaviours   card 21

If you think someone is mistreating and dominating someone nearby . . .

Quietly move away and get help from a teacher, a parent or a trustworthy adult.

Being hurt, trolled or abused online

"Tick tock, we're waiting for your head to rock"

Key social and emotional principles (learning intention)

Becoming the target of online hurt or hate can happen easily as young people enter the online world. In this lesson, we view online antagonism as an extension of bullying. We suggest responding using much the same style discussed in Lesson 9, 'Responding to dominating behaviours' – a practical and disarming response to actions designed to hurt. This lesson aims to understand why some choose to bully online and what young people can do to protect themselves and others. Beyond responding wisely, we must empower young adolescents to use this technology sensibly, safely and with kindness.

Materials required for this lesson

- Name tags.

- Chairs arranged in a social circle for students to sit on.

- Whiteboard/butcher's paper/screen and markers.

- Create a simple outline of the lesson on the whiteboard/butcher's paper/ screen for students to follow.

- Display the *What's the Buzz?* group values (located in the introduction or at www. whatsthebuzz.net.au/main-menu/content-whats-the-buzz-with-teenagers).

- Organise feedback and reminder cards, or similar, to strengthen responsive behaviours (located in the introduction or at www.whatsthebuzz.net.au/main-menu/content-whats-the-buzz-with-teenagers, ready to print.

- Have Archie's story ready to read to students. This can be done directly from this lesson. Or, for a small registration fee, you can download the 16 Archie stories as you want them. Each story contains text, audio in the form of the authors reading to your students, and two large illustrations in full colour that will fill your screen. Access is available at www.whatsthebuzz.net.au/ main-menu/content-whats-the-buzz-with-teenagers

- Pencils, pens, coloured pencils, textas, Cray-Pas oil pastels and paper for students to do Part 1 of *Show me the Buzz*.

- Provide tablets or laptops for groups of students as they explore the activity 'What is netiquette?' in Part 1 of *Show me the Buzz*. Prior to the lesson, be sure to check out the recommended websites.

- Provide pencils or pens and slips of paper to do the 'Social media safety quiz' in Part 1 of *Show me the Buzz*.

- Provide tablets or laptops for each student to complete either of the 'Cybersmart safety quizzes' in Part 1 of *Show me the Buzz*. Prior to the lesson, be sure to complete each of the quizzes yourself.

- Prepare 14 to 20 small items, such as a pencil, paper clip, watch, book, shoe, apple, stapler, toy car and so on, on a tray to play 'Kim's game' in *The Buzz*. You'll also need a large towel, pencils or pens, and slips of paper to record on.

- Organise a basketball or a soccer ball and one pin from a 10-pin bowling set to play, 'Take the troll's device away!' in *The Buzz*.

- Prepare handouts for parents(s):

  One copy of this lesson for each parent to read.

  One copy of *After the Buzz: Social thinking ideas for parents and caregivers* to send home (located at the end of the lesson, ready to photocopy, or at www. whatsthebuzz.net.au/main-menu/content-whats-the-buzz-with-teenagers).

Lesson 10

Explanation

Going online is like opening the legendary Pandora's box! It heralds the possibilities of horrors and delights. Today, the online world starts very early for children. A common scenario sees a child entering it at just 5 or 6 years of age as they play a new video game that quietly links them to others in the world through audio or text. Yet many parents have little knowledge of this bonus chat function. While it can heighten the fun, it also permits others to verbally attack, humiliate or write offensive remarks to unsuspecting children without a parent available to guide and protect. Then, just a few years later, young adolescents begin a wild exchange of texts and images, sometimes lewd and offensive, with a secrecy and sophistication that outperforms their parents' capabilities.

First, let's define what being trolled online means for us in this lesson. A troll is someone who decides to post annoying, hurtful or hateful messages and images in a forum, a chat room, a blog, or on social networking sites such as Facebook, Twitter, Reddit, Instagram, Tumblr and others. Their intention is to irritate, antagonise, bully, humiliate and provoke a response. The *Online Cambridge Dictionary* describes an online troll as 'someone who leaves an intentionally annoying message on the internet, in order to get attention or cause trouble' (https://dictionary.cambridge.org/dictionary/english/troll).

Where does this term come from and what motivates people to do this? The backstory is that there is a mythical creature from Scandinavian folklore actually called a troll. Apparently it's an ugly, dirty, angry creature that lives in damp, dark places, such as caves and underneath bridges. It's an opportunist, and lays in wait ready to attack and snatch up anything that passes by for a quick bite to eat. The troll has no morals or conscience, and will do what it takes to get what it wants. To get a good visual of the Scandinavian troll, see 'The three billy goats gruff' – www.youtube.com/watch?v=f4kdZTnizG4. The internet troll is a contemporary version of this creature. The modern internet troll hides behind their device, possibly in a dark and messy bedroom, and wants to disrupt the lives of others with words and images that are disturbing, threatening or hateful.

Sadly, what makes trolling so easy is that anyone can do it and remain anonymous behind a false user account while presenting themselves with an imaginary avatar. Sometimes so-called friends deliver the worst of attacks. Every internet troll has their own reasons to troll someone or a community. Usually, it's because they are experiencing bleak things in their own life that trigger the darkest of feelings. Perhaps the drive to hurt someone else brings them temporary relief.

In a survey of 1,500 adolescents, 25 per cent reported suffering from occasional online abuse, usually as offensive or threatening remarks (Gani, 2016). It appears people are more likely to be targeted due to sexual orientation, race, religion, disability or transgender identity. Four per cent said they had been singled out for abuse for a sustained period of time. The survey also found 80 per cent of respondents had witnessed online hate towards others during the past 12 months, but 93 per cent said victims had received some support online, mostly from friends.

Here are a few sensible ideas to deal with the emotional fallout online trolls cause. And remember, how deeply children are affected will depend on their age, maturity, experience, sensitivity and the quality of social networks they've built:

1 *Establish what it is.* Trolling is bullying, or more to the point it is cyberbullying. This behaviour is unacceptable.

2 *Explain why it happens.* In brief, it's to get attention or may be inspired by jealousy or revenge – perhaps the perpetrator has a need for power and perceives this as fun. It also happens because it's easy to get away with.

3 *Discuss the concept of dominating behaviours and how best to deal with them.* Refer to Lesson 9, 'Responding to dominating behaviours', because these same principles can be adapted when confronted by trolling. Try not to perceive the experience as catastrophic; instead, use it as an opportunity to learn and grow. After all, the ability to aptly handle criticism is a precious life skill.

4 *Be realistic.* Once anyone enters the online world, these criticisms and attacks – low-level or high-level – are inevitable. They range from awkward misunderstandings to attacks that are vile and calculated.

5 *Always ask for help or advice.* Encourage your students to share the problem with their wisest friend, a parent or a teacher. As an adult, please be aware why young adolescents are reticent to seek advice and support from you. First, they worry that we will overreact and make the situation worse. Second, they are frightened that we won't see things as they do, and because of this we'll stop their access to social media, which is their lifeline to friends. Third, many teens feel as though they should be able to handle this themselves. Then when they realise they've made some mistakes along the way as they've tried to handle it, it's too embarrassing to share everything with those who should matter.

6 *Ignore, block and unfollow.* Teach students to use the site, game or app's privacy settings to do this. Do not engage with the troll, or trolls, or take this too personally.

7 *Flag and report the behaviour.* As quickly as you can, use the community reporting tools to let the company or organisation know someone is abusing their guidelines. They usually take it seriously and will often help.

8 *Take screenshots.* If the trolling is persistent, personal, threatening, nasty and hateful, save the evidence in case things worsen. Be sure to teach young teens how to take screenshots and save evidence.

The final word here is that the internet can be a fabulous medium, offering boundless benefits, supports and interactions, but we need to work together to make the web a safer place for everyone. We have a vital role to play in educating every young person about the pitfalls and what to do to manage them.

1. *What's the Buzz?*

Actively greet students as they enter. Provide chairs in a social circle for them to sit on and have a brief lesson plan on the whiteboard/butcher's paper/screen for students to see. As students are settling, hand each of them a 'Thumbs up feedback card' to highlight their thoughtful behaviour and using the group values.

Let's begin

Welcome to the last lesson in *What's the Buzz with Teenagers?* in this book. However, there are another six lessons available online at www.whatsthebuzz. net.au/main-menu/content-whats-the-buzz-with-teenagers if you wish to build the program out to 16 lessons. They include:

Lesson 11: Maintaining relationships: Feedback and compliments

Lesson 12: Effective listening

Lesson 13: Competition, winning and losing

Lesson 14: Charity: Acts of kindness

Lesson 15: Perseverance

Lesson 16: Self-identity

Gain the attention of the group and ask the questions below. State that for the moment, you want them to think about the answers rather than replying:

- Who regularly uses social media?

- Which platforms do you use?

- Who's ever received naked, pornographic or harassing images?

- Who's ever received mean messages meant to upset you?

- If you have, what did you do?

- If you haven't yet, what do you plan to do?

- Would you ask for help?

- Who would you ask and who would you not ask?

Start Archie's story straight away.

40 Archie's story: "Tick tock, we're waiting for your head to rock" – first image

Lauren Eldridge Murray

This image can be downloaded from http://whatsthebuzz.net.au/main-menu/content-whats-the-buzz-with-teenagers and will fill your screen in colour. There is also the option to have the authors read the story to students.

Archie's story: "Tick tock, we're waiting for your head to rock"

Raif was Daisy's older brother by two years. Everyone knew him, mainly because he was different. Raif had Tourette's syndrome, and because of this his shoulders jerked, his head rocked and he stuttered sometimes. He couldn't help it and there was no cure. Raif dealt with it the best he could but hated it. He was intelligent, did advanced maths, and was a techno whizz as well as a funny and a decent person.

At Castle Rock Primary School, kids had teased Raif for years about his Tourette's. They would follow him around and quietly chant, "Tick tock, when's your head gonna rock, tick tock when's your head gonna rock, tick tock when's your head gonna rock." Teachers worked hard to stop the torment, but there were always kids who'd find a way to get at him when teachers weren't around. Raif's one failing was his pride. When he was being bullied, he wouldn't say a word to anyone – not even to Daisy, who loved him to the moon and back. Raif thought it was a sign of weakness to ask for help, or that sharing would make it worse. This made Daisy feel even more responsible for keeping an eye on him. She knew that no one could deal with this stuff alone!

Archie and his friends liked Raif and happily included him, but Raif never really grabbed hold of their friendship. Beginning middle school had offered a new start and new hope for Raif, but it wasn't long before the torments started again. He couldn't bear their shifty looks, nasty gestures and belittling jokes. It cut so deeply. So, for the last term, he'd been doing homeschool.

Raif, Daisy and his parents thought he'd be safe at home, but the bullies were relentless. They switched their attention to social media and continued to stalk and taunt him. The hate messages came thick and fast every day: "Go hang yourself." "You're retarded." "We're so happy you're not around anymore." "We know where you live, tick tock." "Don't leave your house or we'll get you." "Why are you even alive?" As usual, Raif said nothing. However, he got quieter and quieter, stopped doing schoolwork, wouldn't come out of his room, slept a lot, and lost interest in his beloved maths and technology.

Then it happened. As Daisy and Archie were walking out of school to go home, Daisy received a text from her mum. It read, "Wait at the front gate. It's urgent. I'm in the car on the way. Be there in five." Daisy showed Archie the message and in an instant they both had Raif on their minds. Within moments, Daisy's mum pulled up and ran from the car to Daisy. She held Daisy close and told her that Raif was safe with the police, and Dad was with him too.

41 Archie's story: "Tick tock, we're waiting for your head to rock" – second image

Lauren Eldridge Murray

This image can be downloaded from http://whatsthebuzz.net.au/main-menu/content-whats-the-buzz-with-teenagers and will fill your screen in colour. There is also the option to have the authors read the story to students.

"Why is he with the police?" asked Daisy.

"The police found him sitting on the ledge of the bridge near home. He wanted to jump into the river and drown himself. He said it was the only way to stop the hate he was getting sent," answered Mum.

"I didn't know they were doing that. Did you know it was happening?" asked Daisy.

"No," sighed Mum, rolling her eyes and shrugging. "You know Raif – he bottles everything up."

With that said, Daisy and her mum got into the car and anxiously drove to the police station. Later in the afternoon, Archie received a group message from Daisy that included Ayman, Tobias, Prisha and Joanna. Daisy was hoping they might come over and visit Raif because he was asking for them. She mentioned that it was weird because he'd never asked for anyone before!

Once everyone arrived, Raif explained what happened and offered each of them an apology. All five insisted that he didn't need to apologise, but he said he did because he'd become so caught up in feeling bad that he turned his back on them.

Archie asked, "So, Raif, why the change?"

Discussion based on the questions and statements below will occur later in *Do you know the Buzz?* For now, simply read them to get students thinking. Encourage them to listen and respond to each question by putting their thumb up if they 'agree' or think 'yes', thumb down if they think 'no', and thumb to the side if they think 'maybe'. Move very quickly through them. No verbal responses are required.

Your thoughts on these statements and questions?

- Have you ever been bullied face-to-face by someone or by a group?

- Do you know someone who has?

- Have you ever been intimidated, threatened or trolled online?

- Do you know someone who has?

- Who agrees? "Social media can be both good and bad."

- To those of you who have been bullied or harassed, did you ask for help?

- Did it get sorted in the end?

- Did you collect evidence?

- Do you understand why people post hurtful things and troll others?

- Who did not or would not ask for help?

- Whose parents are likely to overreact and take your devices away or take you offline?

- Who would always ask for help?

- Do you have one or two people who you'd share your feelings with and ask for help?

- Who agrees? "No matter how proud you are, there are times when asking for help is smart."

- Is there one helpful idea you can take from Archie's story about Raif?

- In the story, Raif showed signs of depression. Do you know what these are?

- At the end of the story, Archie asked Raif why he'd changed his thinking. Do you know why Raif changed?

2. *Show me the Buzz*

Show me the Buzz provides students with the opportunity to discuss a variety of social and emotional ideas, absorb the thoughts of others, debate them, create role plays and receive feedback from the group. We have learned that this approach heightens understandings and the transference of skills. There is always a Part 1 and a Part 2. Choose one activity from either Part 1 or Part 2, depending on what appeals to you, the time you have and your group's likely preferences. There's plenty of content in *Show me the Buzz*, so the lesson can be revisited time and time again while continuing with this same topic.

Part 1

1. Group discussion

Ask, "What is an internet troll? What do they do? Why use the word troll? Where does it come from?" Play 'The three billy goats gruff' – www.youtube.com/watch?v=f4kdZTnizG4.

Do you see the connection between an internet troll and the mythical Scandinavian troll? Explain. Why do trolls decide to troll people? Is a troll likely to be someone you do or don't know? In addition, provide students with paper, coloured pencils, textas or Cray-Pas oil pastels, and ask them to draw their imaginary idea of an internet troll. Suggest they make it a hybrid of the traditional Scandinavian troll – who is dirty and angry, and lives in damp, dark places – and the modern internet troll – who hides behind their device in a dark, messy bedroom, aiming to upset others with hurtful and hateful words and images.

2. Screenshots

If you are being trolled, you should – among other things – collect evidence. Take screenshots of the texts and images you receive so you have proof of the abuse. How do you take a screenshot? And once you take it, where is it kept so it's safe and you can access it when needed? Encourage students to grab their phones and teach each other how to take a screenshot, and know where it's stored and how to retrieve it.

3. Pose this question to your group

"Think about Raif's online trolls from the story. Do you think his trolls were people he knew from school or random others he'd never met before? Give reasons for your suggestions." As students feed back their ideas to this question, mention that a lot of trolling comes from people we know, who are jealous, can't cope with differences or disability, may be having a bad time themselves, or are being influenced to do bad by others they have let have power over them.

4. Sexting

The task for each group is to develop two safe ideas to deal with each of the following situations.

First, organise your group to watch 'Teen sexting: the legal consequences – www.youtube.com/watch?v=JZ5mW4qQuuM. A clinical psychologist discusses the consequences for engaging in teen sexting. Next, divide students into groups of two, three or four. Choose someone to record for each group. Hand the recorder a blank A4 sheet and felt-tip pen to write with.

> Situation 1: You receive one inappropriate text or naked image from someone you know. What should you do?
>
> Situation 2: You receive a series of threatening texts that scare you. What should you do?
>
> Situation 3: Your friends keep sending you pornographic images of girls you know. What should you do?

Once done, reform into a larger group and share the ideas.

5. Group discussion

Work through the following questions and encourage students to discuss their thoughts with each other. Write the questions on the whiteboard or screen before beginning and leave space to record their answers.

- What are your favourite online activities?

- Which social media platforms do you use mostly?

- Who do you stay in touch with through your phone and the internet?

- What is positive online communication? Give an example.

- What is negative online communication? Give an example.

- Have you ever received any negative online communication?

- What's your best advice to deal with negative online communication?

6. "What is netiquette?"

Break the group into small research teams, perhaps pairs or groups of three. Each team will need a device and create a file to record ideas on. Their task is to explore the question "What is netiquette?" Afterwards, they are to report back to the larger group with what it means, and two good ideas they've discovered about it. Give the teams 10 minutes to work on the task. Provide each team one of the following websites to work from:

- www.education.vic.gov.au/Documents/about/programs/bullystoppers/ afnetiquette.pdf

- www.bbc.co.uk/webwise/guides/about-netiquette

- www.education.com/reference/article/netiquette-rules-behavior-internet/

- www.flinders.edu.au/teaching/ict-in-education/university-guidelines/netiquette.cfm

- http://edtech2.boisestate.edu/weltys/502/netiquette.html

- www.psychologytoday.com/us/blog/teen-angst/201012/cyber-etiquette-teens

- www.parentcircle.com/article/ten-tips-for-your-teen-on-netiquette/

- www.teenlit.com/netiquette.php

- https://securingtomorrow.mcafee.com/consumer/family-safety/ netiquette-teaching-kids-online-manners/

- https://medium.com/digital-parent-central/parenting-in-the-digital-age-netiquette-how-to-teach-our-kids-and-ourselves-to-behave-online-995118a3f983

7. Social media safety quiz

Let's see how much you know about social media safety in just 24 questions. Thumbs up if you believe the statement is true, and thumbs down if you think it's false. You might want to keep score.

1 When you keep getting pestered and receive hateful messages or hostile images on social media from someone, we say they are a troll and are trolling you. (true – thumbs up)

2 If you're being pestered or receiving hate texts or images on social media, keep it to yourself. (false – thumbs down)

3 Never ask your mum or dad for help with anything on social media because they can't help. (false – thumbs down)

4 Sent or received images or texts can always be retrieved later, even if deleted. (true – thumbs up)

5 You have no control over how many times a post is shared and where it will end up. (true – thumbs up)

6 Always accept friend requests because it's polite. (false – thumbs down)

7 A photo of you having fun with friends or family is an appropriate image to post. (true – thumbs up)

8 It is okay to upload pictures of anyone without getting their consent. (false – thumbs down)

9 A photo of you or a friend doing something embarrassing is an appropriate post. (false – thumbs down)

10 It's okay to post or send nudes, or sexually explicit pictures, to others. (false – thumbs down)

11 If someone irritates you, it's okay to send them a threatening message. (false – thumbs down)

12 Bosses and managers may check your social media accounts when you apply for a job. (true – thumbs up)

13 A good rule online is never post or say anything that your parents or grandparents would feel uncomfortable about. (true – thumbs up)

14 If you're in trouble or worried about something on social media, share the trouble with a friend, parent, teacher, relative, coach or even the police. (true – thumbs up)

15 An unprotected or open profile makes you an easier target for cyberbullying/ trolling. (true – thumbs up)

16 It's okay to fill out online questionnaires with your personal details, school and home address. (false – thumbs down)

17 Keep your passwords secret. (true – thumbs up)

18 Be very careful, and be sure to talk to trusted adults, before meeting someone you have only talked with online. (true – thumbs up)

19 Profile pictures should always be of you, so people know it's your account. (false – thumbs down)

20 Posting images, comments or updates three or more times a day is a good idea. (false – thumbs down)

21 Always post pictures when you are away on holidays. (false – thumbs down)

22 Never accept a friend request from a person that you don't know. (true – thumbs up)

23 The 'recommended friends' list is a list of people you should add because they are safe and friends. (false – thumbs down)

24 When you set up an Instagram account, always make sure you write a bio. (false - thumbs down)

8. Arrange for students to try the online cybersmart safety quiz created by the Australian government (www.esafety.gov.au/kids-quiz/)

Sam is a cartoon girl and talks users through the quiz using both text and voice. It will take about 15 minutes to complete, has 11 questions, and covers emails, passwords, the dangers of online advertisements and disturbing videos. It's perfect for young teens. Another option is to use 'Meet the Creeps quiz – are u safe online' – http://creepquiz.eq.edu.au/. The 'Creep quiz' is another excellent way to highlight what we can do to protect ourselves while online. We advise you do each of the quizzes before introducing them to students. There are several ways you could work with these; organise for each student to have their own device and work through the quiz, or pair students up so they can share ideas as they answer the questions, or you may complete the quiz on a screen and elicit responses from the whole group.

Part 2: Role plays – being hurt, trolled or abused online

The role plays are in the photocopiable section at the end of this lesson. They are also available online at www.whatsthebuzz.net.au/main-menu/content-whats-the-buzz-with-teenagers. You may either read them to students, or print them and hand each group a role-play. Help students to form small groups. Each role-play card states the number of students required. It does not matter if the same role play is given to several groups. Give students a few minutes to rehearse, and move between groups to provide plenty of coaching and enthusiasm.

Next, ask each group to perform their role play. If a student does not wish to perform, allow them to pass. So much can be learned through observing. Always perform role plays in the middle of the social circle. Consider capturing the action on video or photo by using your iPad, camera or smartphone. Encourage others to give constructive feedback after each role play.

3. *Do you know the Buzz?*

Do you know the Buzz? is a lively group 'discussion time' where students briefly respond to a series of questions and statements highlighted by Archie's story. The goal is for them to exchange ideas, and in the process 'mind map' their way more empathically through the complexities of social and emotional situations. This should also provide facilitators with an insight into the depth of student understandings. To do this, have students sitting on chairs in a social circle.

Your thoughts on these statements and questions?

- Have you ever been bullied face-to-face by someone or by a group? What happened?

- Do you know someone who has?

- Have you ever been intimidated, threatened or trolled online? What happened?

- Do you know someone who has?

- Who agrees? "Social media can be both good and bad."

- To those of you who have been bullied or harassed, did you ask for help? Who did you ask?

- Did it get sorted in the end? What did you learn?

- Did you collect evidence? How did you do this?

- Do you understand why people post hurtful things and troll others? Tell me.

- Who did not or would not ask for help? Why not?

- Whose parents are likely to overreact and take your devices away or take you offline?

- Do you have one or two people who you'd share your feelings with and ask for help? Who are they? How would you expect to be supported?

- Who agrees? "No matter how proud you are, there are times when asking for help is smart."

- Is there one helpful idea you can take from Archie's story about Raif? What is it?

- In the story, Raif showed signs of depression. Do you know what these are? Name them.

- At the end of the story, Archie asked Raif why he'd changed his thinking. Do you know why Raif changed?

4. The Buzz

The Buzz is an opportunity for the group to play games that strengthen their relationships and the skills central to the lesson.

Game: Find the troll (exciting)

Sit everyone in a social circle. Select one person as an online investigator and ask them to leave the room for a few moments. While they are away, choose one person who will play the troll. The troll's job is to lead the group, and in this game the others must follow the troll's lead.

As the online investigator returns to the room, the troll may, for example, have everyone clapping in rhythm. Then, after 20 to 30 seconds, the troll changes their action to finger waving, and the group must quickly follow. New actions might include raising and lowering eyebrows, clapping fingers, winking, poking out tongues, head rolling, pulling at one or both ears, leg slapping, and on and off smiling.

The online detective's goal is to discover who the troll is! This requires sharp observational skills.

Game: Kim's memory game (passive)

Place between 14 and 20 small items, such as a pencil, paper clip, watch, book, shoe, apple, stapler, toy car, and so on, on a tray. For older and more capable students, use the upper number of items. Cover with a large towel. Next, sit everyone in the social circle. Place the tray in the middle of the circle and remove the towel for everyone to see. You may wish to touch and name each item, so students have the advantage of both seeing and hearing. Once done, cover the items on the tray with the large towel. Next, help students to form pairs or groups of three. Hand each group a pen or pencil and a piece of paper so they can record every item they can remember. The objective is for each group to work quietly together and record every item on the tray. Give them five minutes.

A novel variation is to add four or five different styled and coloured trolls to the mix of items. Students adore these little critters!

Game: Take the troll's device away! (exciting)

This game requires one basketball or soccer ball, and one pin from a 10-pin bowling set. The ball represents the group's will to use netiquette and disarm the troll. The pin represents the troll's device, and the person standing in the centre of the circle is the troll.

To begin, arrange players to stand in a large circle facing towards the centre. A pin is placed in the centre of the circle and a troll is chosen to protect it. The troll stands in the centre of the circle next to the pin. The aim of the game is for players in the circle to knock the pin down with the ball by bowling it over. All throws are underarm, and the ball must travel along the floor. The troll may use their hands, arms, legs and feet to protect the pin, but may not kick it at others. The person who knocks the pin down and disables the troll becomes the new troll. Players quickly learn that unless they cooperate by talking, sharing and rapidly rolling the ball to one another, it is very difficult to get the troll out.

Game: Trolls versus the law (exciting)

This game will get players moving and puffing! First, split the group into halves, although exact numbers are not essential. Name one half 'trolls' and the other half 'the law'. Arrange groups so they stand on opposite sides of the room.

To begin, ask them to swing around and turn their backs towards one another. When you call 'go', each team walks ever so cautiously backwards, slowly getting closer and closer to each other. When the players hear you call 'trolls', the trolls turn and chase the law, who run back home as fast as they can. The trolls try to tag them before they reach home. Similarly, when the players hear you call 'the law', the law chases the trolls, attempting to tag them before they reach home.

If a player is tagged, they must join the team that tagged them. Continue the game for as long as you like, or until one side is caught out.

After the Buzz: Social thinking ideas for parents and caregivers

Lesson 10: Being hurt, trolled or abused online

Key social and emotional principles (learning intention)

Becoming the target of online hurt or hate can happen easily as young people enter the online world. In this lesson, we view online antagonism as an extension of bullying. We suggest responding using much the same style discussed in Lesson 9, 'Responding to dominating behaviours' – a practical and disarming response to actions designed to hurt. This lesson aims to understand why some choose to bully online and what young people can do to protect themselves and others. Beyond responding wisely, we must empower young adolescents to use this technology sensibly, safely and with kindness.

After the Buzz presents further ideas for parents, guardians and educators to encourage the social and emotional thinking students have touched on during the lesson. Our children rely on us to consolidate these skills by positively modelling them, and emphasising the language and ideas contained within the lesson. As always, here are a few practical ideas to build out at home.

How safe is your child online?

The website www.pandasecurity.com/mediacenter/family-safety/10-questions-to-test-how-safe-your-teen-is-online/ presents a quick 10-question quiz for parents to gauge how safe their young adolescent is online.

Do the quiz together and you'll quickly discover whether they are safe and informed, or whether they need more information. The reason why most teens don't take appropriate precautions is because they are either misinformed or uninformed.

Haters and trolls are people who go online, usually anonymously, and write nasty or hateful comments with the intention of upsetting someone. At some stage, this is likely to happen, so it's best to be prepared. Make a start by sharing this clip with your child: '5 tips for dealing with haters and trolls' – www.youtube.com/watch?v=jQMc8HIc2eY.

We think there is a sixth tip you might want to add, and that's never deal with haters or trolls alone. Encourage your child to come to you for help. However, be aware that young adolescents are reticent to seek support from parents because they worry we'll overreact, we won't see things as they do, and will stop their access to social media, which is their lifeline to friends. Do your best to calm these fears.

Sexting

Sexting, which is the sending of sexually explicit photographs or messages between teens, is more common than most parents choose to think. In most countries, it is an offence that can amount to a criminal charge, potential prison time and registration as a sex offender. In the following clip, clinical psychologist Dr Lisa Strohman discusses the consequences for engaging in this risky behaviour. It's worth watching with your child: 'Teen sexting: the legal consequences' – www.youtube.com/watch?v=JZ5mW4qQuuM.

Here are a few facts about sexting and the impact it has on young people. Yes, talking about sexting with your kids can feel uncomfortable, but they must know. It's a great starting point to see if they can fill in the gaps missing in these statements:

1 Sexting is creating, sharing, forwarding or posting sexually explicit .... or .... using the internet or a mobile phone. (texts or images / pictures)

2 Sexting is very ...., but this doesn't make it .... (common / right)

3 Sending, receiving or forwarding a naked or .... is the most common form of sexting. (semi-naked / photo)

4 Sexting might seem like a bit of fun, but it is .... (illegal)

5 If you're sexting, you can be .... and potentially registered as a .... (charged / sex offender)

6 When you send a sexy image, you have .... control over where it goes after that. (no)

7 A sexy image of yourself, or the one you have forwarded, could end up being seen by ...., ..., ..., ..., ..., ..., strangers and your peers. (your principal / the police / your boyfriend's/girlfriend's parents / your parents / your teachers / your grandparents)

8 Being caught sexting may damage your .... and possible career .... in the future. (reputation / choices)

After the Buzz ... Lesson 10

271

9 Even though sexting may make you feel .... or popular, it is .... and .... (good / thoughtless / wrong)

10 Just because someone sexts you .... mean you must respond in the same way. (does / not)

Your kids need your help to find a balance

The powerful appeal of video games is clear – they're fun, the action is fast, contests are inviting, and screens feed the brain with rich visual and auditory incentives. While engaged, our brains set up an enticing positive feedback loop that's hard to break away from. And this comes at a time when the on and off switches in young people's brains are not yet fully developed. In truth, they will not be fully developed until they reach their mid to late twenties. This is why most teens find it so hard to self-regulate screens. Even the most basic act of receiving a text message triggers the brain's reward centre! Researchers talk about the impact of sending and receiving messages being like a hit from a drug, and the more you get and send, the better you feel, and the more you want to get and send! In addition, don't forget the luring trend to capture everything in pictures and share them with everyone to prove we matter. Watch this clip with your teen: 'Addiction to technology is ruining lives – Simon Sinek on Inside Quest' – www. youtube.com/watch?v=sL8AsaEJDdo.

We'd like to encourage you to use your poise, leadership and connection to create an approach to help your children find balance between screens for gaming and other aspects of living a real life. It's just plain common sense – 'moderation in all things' or you risk living with dysfunction. Working towards a balance is a much healthier approach than coming down heavily on kids by banning, hiding and blatantly limiting screens and devices. Heavy-handedness is more likely to push kids into becoming oppositional, defiant and deceitful.

Are you striking the right balance?

Too many parents falsely believe that technology, apps and gadgets are essential for their child's development, but this belief is often inspired by a secret need to use screens to babysit their children. So, how much time should a child spend in front of a screen? A study of 4,899 British kids by the University of Oxford found that children who play console or PC games for an hour or less per day tend to be more social and satisfied than kids who don't play any video games at all. If, however, children and teens spend three hours or more in front of video games per day, they are more likely to be less happy than non-gamers, as well as more likely to have problems with hyperactivity, attention, academic learning and relating to their peers (Przybylski, 2014).

After the Buzz ... Lesson 10

There is a social benefit for teens online

The fact is that most adolescents have friends and acquaintances both at school and online, so if you're considering stopping or pulling back your child's online time, you'll need to consider the impact this will have on their relationships. Accept the very real possibility that your child may be criticised when those from their online community notice their absence. There aren't easy answers. One thing we do know is that your child will appreciate you understanding that screens are an important part of their social world.

A mistaken few argue that young people can blossom socially in the freedom and concealment of online games and in chat rooms. Our response is that kids need to have real lives independent of their cyber ones in order to develop cognitively, socially, emotionally and physically. They need a complete set of interpersonal skills that an exclusive online life cannot provide.

The Facebook, Instagram and Snapchat platforms

These are popular social media apps for many young teens, and while they state users must be at least 13 years old, this does not stop younger children from joining by simply clicking the button that says they are old enough. Many kids use them without the knowledge of their parents. Each claim to have controls that monitor friends added, manage privacy settings and limit the applications kids use, but these are insufficient and provide nowhere near the safety a helpful parent can. Providing there are mechanisms in place by parents to protect kids, these are reasonable platforms for young people to keep in touch with friends. However, to keep your kids safe, here's what we suggest.

The password

By knowing your child's password, you have full access to their profile. Passwords need to be changed every now and then, but always ensure you have the new one. This permits parents to check the newsfeed, conversations, friends added, and what's being posted. To us, this must be an enduring rule.

You must be your child's 'friend'

Parents must be 'friends' with their child on all social media apps. On Facebook and Instagram, this is easy, but Snapchat isn't as simple. By being 'friends', a parent must be able to view *all* pictures, videos, posts, updates, tags . . . everything! This helps to keep kids safe, keeps their reputations intact, and minimises unwanted surprises. At the risk of worrying parents, it is not unusual for teens to keep one account for their parents' eyes and use a second secret account for friends, peers and everyone else.

After the Buzz . . . Lesson 10

Responsibility

While users can't be completely responsible for silly or offensive things their friends post on their wall, they are responsible for anything posted from their own account. If they allow a friend access to their page, and comments are made or posts uploaded, your child will be held morally and legally responsible. Although these can be deleted, they are never permanently erased from the system, and can be used as evidence in disputes.

Others watch

What your child posts may eventually be seen by everyone – brothers, sisters, friends, grandparents, relatives, principals, youth leaders, teachers, family friends, neighbours, bosses and the police. Whenever your kids post something, teach them to ask themselves, "Would I be happy for my principal, teacher or grandmother to see this?"

Friends

Social media is all about connecting people. Work with your kids to avoid 'friending' people just because they want more friends or popularity, and never 'friend' people they don't know. It's best to restrict it to people they know personally. The key questions when considering friend requests are: Do I trust this person to see my posts and pictures? Am I sure this person won't use what I post in the wrong way? Are they adding me because they're my friend, or do they just want to spy?

Conflicts

If your child is struggling over angry or thoughtless words someone has posted online, encourage them to keep calm and sort it out face-to-face. If things are spinning out of control, be proactive and call your child's school or the other parents to give them the best chance to work it through with support. Our brains are better wired for face-to-face social exchange, and things can go seriously wrong when we must make guesses about the emotional state of others based on text only. The hardest part of social media is that the context of comments can be easily misinterpreted. While Snapchat has the ability to send videos, they are often staged and can confuse the message.

Personal information can become public

Sadly, there are devious people in the world who want to do harm to others. They hack accounts to gain access to people's private information and their friend lists. To remain safe, never post personal information – physical address, full birth date, school and so on. Never write updates such as "Parents are gone," "Away on holiday," "Home alone" or "Bored" because such statements invite untrustworthy people to do malicious things.

When worried, ask for help

Participating in social networks opens all kinds of new situations for parents and teens to deal with. Even experienced adults run into trouble from time to time. So, expect your kids to run into tricky scenarios too. Give them a safe place to turn when a rough time emerges without fear of punishment or embarrassment. Don't expect complete honesty all the time, but if you're open with them and provide support, then you have a better chance of helping them work through an issue when it comes up.

References

Gani, A. (2016) *Internet Trolling: Quarter of Teenagers Suffered Online Abuse Last Year.* Available at: www.theguardian.com/uk-news/2016/feb/09/internet-trolling-teenagers-online-abuse-hate-cyberbullying (accessed August 2018).

Przybylski (2014) *Electronic Gaming and Psychosocial Adjustment.* Available at: http://pediatrics.aappublications.org/content/pediatrics/early/2014/07/29/peds.2013-4021.full.pdf (accessed August 2018).

After the Buzz ... Lesson 10

42 Role-play cards: Being hurt, trolled or abused online

Role play 1

You and your good friend are having a great Saturday afternoon together relaxing by the pool. During the afternoon, you both check your Facebook. You can't believe what you see. On your Facebook wall is "No one likes you – not even the person you are sitting with right now, and we know who it is and where you are." Use this situation to create two role plays. First, show an open, optimistic and confident response to this unfortunate post. Next, show a negative, dramatic and emotional response. (A pair – you and your friend)

Role play 2

Your two best friends tell you that they've discovered something you should know. They've found there's an Instagram account that a lot of people in your year level are adding. It's dedicated to posting rude and hurtful memes and pictures about you. This is completely unexpected, and you're feeling embarrassed and angry. You and your friends think you know who started the account. Show how you could best handle this upsetting news and effectively deal with it. (A group of three – you and your two friends)

Role play 3

You're at home scrolling through Facebook. You see a picture of your sister and her boyfriend they have posted while at the beach. Some of the comments coming in are mean: "You could do better than her." "Dump her and I'll be your girlfriend." "As if you're dating her!" "What's she wearing? Didn't she look in a mirror?" "Why date her?" While some people have defended her, others have liked the nasty comments. You feel like getting on to Facebook straight away and giving the haters a piece of your mind, but that wouldn't be the wisest of moves. Show the wisest thing to do. (A group of three – you, your sister and her boyfriend)

---

42 Role-play cards: Being hurt, trolled or abused online *continued . . .*

Role play 4

Patrick had been hiding the terrible time he was having on Instagram. He didn't want anyone to know that he was being seriously trolled. The horrible texts and images were getting worse, and there were more and more of them. He also had an idea who they were coming from. Show two different ways he can think about this and try to deal with it. Make one of the approaches calm and constructive, and include the help of sensible others. Make the other one a reactive approach with a poor outcome. (A group of three – Patrick and two others – the others act like a thinking bubble and talk through each of Patrick's ideas)

Role play 5

You're surprised to find out that a so-called popular group of kids at school have created a Snapchat account called 'Find a hook-up for Amy'. You know Amy and she's nice. The idea is to get someone to hook up with Amy at a party on Saturday night. You feel awkward for Amy because you know she wouldn't want this. What should you do? You decide to talk it over with a friend who is also a friend of Amy's. The role play begins with you and this friend meeting to discuss the problem. Together, come up with a helpful idea. Remember, a helpful idea might not solve the problem, but it doesn't reward the poor behaviour of others. (A group of three – you, your friend and Amy)

Role play 6

Felix and his older brother Jayden have nothing to do and are home alone. So, they decide to have some fun on social media. They share a photo of Jayden's girlfriend just after she tripped over at their place yesterday. The photo captured one of the silliest

---

42 Role-play cards: Being hurt, trolled or abused online *continued . . .*

faces ever because she was in pain. But their comments are too harsh. Within minutes of posting it, there's loud banging on the front door, and it's Jayden's girlfriend's mother and father. They are both annoyed and let the boys have it! They demand the boys make this right. Show what her parents say and how the brothers repair this very embarrassing misjudgement. (A group of four – the two brothers and the parents)

Role play 7

You're working on your laptop and a notification pops up to say you've been added to a group chat. You check it out and find it includes two of your closest friends from school and a few others you don't know so well. As you read through the chat, you realise that everyone is talking about you! The conversation is unkind. You're confused as to why they've added you and why they're saying these things about you. Role-play what you do next. Be wise, go slowly and enlist the help of sensible others. (A group of three – you and two friends, or you and your parents)

Role play 8

As Jacob packed his bags for camp, he felt sick. He knew he would be harassed by the usual group of girls. For a long time, they'd sent texts to tease him about the birthmark on his face. He hated his birthmark and they knew it. They were so sneaky because the texts made it sound like they were friendly, but it was the opposite. What they'd say to him in real life, so no one else could hear, was awful. Show a role play where he receives another of these texts while at camp. As usual, it looks okay, but it had a hidden meaning that hurt. Show Jacob calmly confronting the girls, knowing there's a teacher nearby who will overhear them. In this role play, the girls are exposed for their true, mean intentions. (A group of four – Jacob, the teacher and the two girls)